Law Mart

MW00440381

Anthropology of Policy

Cris Shore and Susan Wright, editors

Law Mart

Justice, Access, and For-Profit Law Schools

Riaz Tejani

Stanford University Press
Stanford, California

Stanford University Press
Stanford, California

Printed in the United States of America on acid-free, archival-quality paper

Library of Congress Cataloging-in-Publication Data

Names: Tejani, Riaz, 1977– author.
Title: Law mart : justice, access, and for-profit law schools / Riaz Tejani.
Other titles: Anthropology of policy (Stanford, Calif.)
Description: Stanford, California : Stanford University Press, 2017. | Series: Anthropology of policy
Identifiers: LCCN 2016049765 | ISBN 9780804796477 (cloth : alk. paper) | ISBN 9781503603011
    (pbk. : alk. paper) | ISBN 9781503603028 (e-book)
Subjects: LCSH: Law schools—United States. | For-profit universities and colleges—United States. |
    Law—Study and teaching—Economic aspects.
Classification: LCC KF274 .T45 2017 | DDC 340.071/173—dc23
LC record available at https://lccn.loc.gov/2016049765

Typeset by Thompson Type in 10.25/15 Brill

For Elina

Contents

Acknowledgments ix

Preface xi

Introduction: Marketing Justice 1

1 Enrollment: Precarity, Casualization, and
Alternative Admissions 27

2 "Charter Review": Policy as Culture and Ideology 57

3 The Legal Education Moral Economy Bubble 85

4 Law School 2.0: Marketing Integration, Educating Investors 111

5 Shared Governance in the Proprietary Legal Academy 135

6 "They Want the Rebels Gone": Contract Relations
in a Fiscal State of Exception 157

7 The Policy Cascade: Deregulation and Moral Hazard 177

Conclusion: The Trouble with Differentiation 205

Appendix: List of Abbreviations 221

Notes 223

References 251

Index 265

Acknowledgments

AS a work of ethnography this book is the result of numerous conversations—most friendly, some adversarial, all beneficial. I cannot individually thank the many confidential research participants cited throughout, so I thank them collectively. In sharing their personal impressions and opinions, they shined available light on a relatively obscure, fast-changing social field and did so with courage and integrity. This text is built primarily on their generosity.

I also benefited immensely from conversations with several key legal education commentators. Erwin Chemerinsky shared his thoughts generously amid a very busy national speaking schedule. Bryant Garth helped me understand the debates early in the development of the project. Bill Henderson found time to offer guidance amid his own numerous appearances and deadlines. Brian Tamanaha spoke with me at length about a wide array of topics reflected here. And Elizabeth Mertz, who has long advised and inspired me, shared valuable feedback in conversations about this work in particular and legal ethnography more generally.

Meanwhile, senior colleagues in anthropology were also directly influential. Carol Greenhouse encouraged me to reflect deeper on the questions raised by a "native" ethnography of an American for-profit law school. And Don Brenneis offered invaluable, critical guidance on early versions of the manuscript.

The text later benefited from close readings by several key colleagues. Kara Hatfield read a draft of the full manuscript pushing me to clarify ideas, sharpen observations, and, when possible, simplify the writing. McKay Cunningham lucidly read early chapters and shared deep reflections on legal education, recruitment, and true diversity. Richard Gilman-Opalsky reviewed several chapters and reminded me to stay sharp in thinking about neoliberalism and its philosophical antecedents.

Others offered broader guidance on subtopics central and adjacent to the main discussion here. T. Price Dooley and Jason Pierceson lent interdisciplinary perspective on the politics of public policy. And Kyle McEntee advised me several times about the potential for qualitative research in legal education transparency and regulation.

Others influenced the project in more general ways. My colleagues in the Department of Legal Studies at UIS were a great support as I drafted the manuscript and completed revisions. Former teachers, in particular George Lipsitz, Ariela Gross, and João Biehl, remained with me in spirit throughout the writing. I also thank Francine Banner and Marren Sanders for conversations about legal education over the years, and John DiMoia for valuable exchanges about higher education. And Michael O'Connor and Celia Rumann warmly shared their own experiences with forces similar to those described at the center of this book.

Group audiences at various academic presentations offered considerable feedback reflected in these pages. Participants in the AALS Qualitative and Mixed Methods workshops in 2017 and 2016 raised several of the methodological concerns addressed here. I also thank members of the American Bar Foundation for comments during a 2016 Research Seminar, members of the Department of Anthropology at UC San Diego for comments in early 2016, and members of the Department of Criminology, Law and Society at UC Irvine for feedback in late 2015. I likewise thank the organizers and participants in the Race, Law and Education Panel at the 2015 Present and Future of Civil Rights conference at Duke Law School and the Anthropology of Regulation panel at the 2014 Annual Meeting of the American Anthropological Association.

Last but not least I salute the key individuals who shepherded this project through publication. Cris Shore and Sue Wright lent sharp guidance as series editors since the inception of this book. And Michelle Lipinski at Stanford University Press provided invaluable editorial discipline and support throughout.

Without these people this book could not have been produced. Now that it has, as they say, residual errors or omissions remain my own.

Preface

C AN deregulated markets solve complex social problems? That may be the underlying question of the text you are reading. The problems in this story relate in particular to the pursuit of justice. One is the problem of "access to justice" defined by many as the inability of millions of poor and middle-income people in America—for reasons of cost and geography—to obtain adequate legal representation.

Another is the "crisis" of the legal profession—a predicament associated paradoxically with a glut of new lawyers relative to legal job openings, and the reportedly high demand for affordable legal services among many communities. This problem is nowadays explained by a theory of "structural change" wherein corporate fiscal austerity, high-tech services like LegalZoom, and the birth of new career niches such as Washington State's Limited License Legal Technician have combined to reduce demand for traditional legal work. Although there has long been talk of a lawyer overabundance, the structural change thesis describes an irreversible exacerbation of that.

And finally, the "crisis" of legal education forms a third key problem to which the market has been a proposed solution. Law schools are now soul searching about the moral, economic, and pedagogical values they have long espoused. Although professional readiness is one object of that introspection, a more important one may be the moral hazard law schools have generated over the years by raising tuition while focusing less and less on students. Charging students exorbitant fees to learn many things other than legal practice might have been a palatable approach if information about this had been readily available and if the buyer could indeed beware. The problem was that, until recently, this was not the case. That lack of information has since been lessened by the courageous and principled works of writers like Elizabeth Mertz and Brian Tamanaha. Mertz's study of moral distanciation in law school language and learning opened our eyes to the social costs of reproducing "thinking like a lawyer," whereas Tamanaha's insider account of law school governance, accreditation, and faculty incentives spotlighted causation behind the explosive growth in tuition and, in turn, career-limiting student debt loads.

If these have been the problems, a more open market has lately been posited as the best solution. More importantly, this approach has been endorsed or accepted by many of the sharpest minds in American legal education and legal profession today. Like the antiseptic qualities of sunlight, they seem to say, the competitive context of an open market should winnow out weak, underperforming players. Good law schools, in other words, will simply push out bad ones. For this to occur, several have said, a true market needs free rein. Regulation, in this case most proximately by the ABA Council of the Section of Legal Education and Admissions to the Bar, needs to roll back or step aside. Freed from the Council's strict Standards for accreditation, some say, law schools will be better able to compete, innovate, specialize, and above all, *differentiate*.

Given the regulatory opening to cut costs, schools will offer cheaper services, charge less, and attract students interested not in the prestige and high tuition of high-ranking established research schools, but rather in the simple, practical skills needed to "hang up a shingle." Such students, many hope, will include those from groups historically marginalized within the legal profession— ethnoracial and socioeconomic minorities.

Differentiation of this kind, reformers say, will solve the three problems just mentioned. Originating from diverse communities, graduates will "return home" to offer the kinds of legal services—wills, divorces, criminal defense— that their communities "need." Servicing those needs, new graduates will then ameliorate the access problem. Applying their skills in dispersed areas of high demand albeit lesser pay, graduates will evade the structural change dilemma. And by patronizing new, innovatively streamlined curricula, students will support the renewal of legal education.

But, according to available evidence, the impact of this model is more complicated. Differentiation by deregulation has partially occurred among American for-profit law schools. Once allowed accreditation for the first time in the ABA's century-long history, for-profit law schools studied and adopted many of the legal education reform proposals offered by key studies like the McCrate and Carnegie Reports and advocated by legal education reformers, suggesting what students needed was more skills and less "knowledge" of the law. Taking these seriously, law schools like New Delta School of Law (NDSL), described here, promised to offer students a more practical skills-based curriculum while spending less on faculty and hiring many off the tenure track. Support for research was minimized, and, rather than working paper symposia, professors were offered bimonthly teaching workshops. The whole thing sounded more student friendly.

But when their bills arrived, most students were paying more to attend NDSL and its sister schools than the neighboring ranked public law school programs. Students noted periodic dress code warning emails from administration announcing the presence of mysterious "visitors" on campus. These visitors, I would learn through this research, included representatives of venture capital firms, including Warren Buffet's famous Berkshire Hathaway, ostensibly on the market to acquire a law school franchise. For many, the school was up for sale and tuitions would remain high to reflect well on auditor balance sheets.

As this book explains, NDSL is one of the more advanced cases of law school "differentiation" available. The institution combines the ideals of social inclusion with simplified pedagogy and reduced fixed costs. Yet under the for-profit model, savings from austerity are not to be passed on to students in reduced tuition. Financed by private equity capital in exchange for promises of high rates of return on investment, savings created by differentiated law teaching go to offsite investors.

And, according to the ethnographic evidence here, students, faculty, and staff are aware of all this. On one level or another, they understand that a greater chunk of the surplus value they created is being taken "out" of the school to benefit others elsewhere. The question—one that journalists writing about for-profit education and for-profit law schools in particular are unequipped to answer—is how and why these people stay. What motivates them to teach or matriculate in these environments even in the face of public criticism and skepticism? What keeps them coming in each day despite recurring announcements about declining enrollments, program austerity, and falling student outcomes such as bar passage and employment rates? What does prospective failure mean to people so preoccupied with professional success? Describing my three fraught years embedded in this environment and imbricated with the lives of these flesh-and-blood people, these are the questions this book hopes to answer.

R. T.

Introduction

Marketing Justice

"Good intention" is a hall pass through history, a sleeping pill that ensures the Dream.

—Ta-Nehisi Coates

EVER since she was eight years old, Melanie had wanted to go to law school. But life after college, as she puts it, "took a little detour." Married to an injured veteran with a child on the way, she took a health-care job to secure benefits for her family. Years later she herself was diagnosed with a tumor and, faced with her own mortality, recommitted to her professional dream. "I applied to Big State University and was rejected," she says. "[I] then applied to New Delta because it was the only other law school I could geographically manage with two kids and a disabled husband."[1]

Keshia received an unsolicited email from New Delta School of Law (NDSL) after taking the Law School Admissions Test (LSAT) in 2008. "They kept pestering me for a long time," she says. "I got into a law school in Mississippi and on a couple of wait lists. Then, due to my extremely dysfunctional family and my parents' divorce, I ended up living with friends in Chicago and then my brother, who is a lawyer, in Dallas. . . . My brother and I were at odds, and *I picked law school over living in my car.*"[2]

In legal education, students like Melanie and Keshia might be considered "nontraditional." Enrollment was a last resort or an afterthought to other life events. But for New Delta they were typical; the institution caters to working students by maintaining flexible admission standards and degree completion schedules. Melanie and Keshia are also Asian American and African American, respectively, and therefore ethnoracially "diverse." NDSL embraces student and faculty diversity as a distinguishing feature in a crowded legal admissions field.[3] More importantly, it markets this as part of a concerted effort to increase "access to justice" by affording racial minority and low-income students—groups historically known for nontraditional paths and lower academic indicators— the unique opportunity to become attorneys. School executives suggest these students will "return" to marginal communities to set up small firms in needed practice areas such as family law or wills and trusts. But this suggestion is not strictly charitable. New Delta School of Law is a "for-profit" institution whose ability to gain access to untapped markets of prospective students serves a vital business function.

In this book I ask what marketing justice in this fashion says about contemporary ties between law and economics. Does the grafting of a social justice mission onto finance capitalism materialized through professional higher education make *justice* itself another commodity? And do failures of policy to adequately protect the vulnerable in this sector say something new about the ordering of economics, law, and morality? These questions are addressed in an ethnographic narrative assembled from nearly three years of participant observation at one for-profit law school and from dozens of interviews among its participants: students, staff, and faculty. It describes the business model in global context, recruitment of students and employees, idiosyncratic organizational culture, and a series of governance shifts occasioned by wider transformations in the legal services industry and law school regulatory establishment. Above all, it offers the reader a glimpse beyond numerical inputs and outcomes into the hearts and minds of people who attach their fortunes to these complicated institutions.

New Delta School of Law is one of six for-profit law programs stamped with American Bar Association (ABA) accreditation[4] and one of three owned by a corporate entity I will call Law Corp. Law Corp, in turn, is owned by a $5 billion private equity firm whose thirty-one other holdings include medication monitoring, senior care, and mortgage-lending firms, among other things. As a private equity property, Law Corp is designed to draw in "capital commitments" from large and institutional investors—including among them Ivy League university endowments—in exchange for high rates of return in the range of 20 percent. But the equity market is a competitive one, and investors can place their money in any number of different funds and industries. Therefore, Law Corp goes to great lengths to publicize its especially liberal mission. "[Our] mission," its website reads, "is to 'establish the benchmark of inclusive excellence in professional education for the 21st Century.' This mission is supported by three key pillars (1) ... 'serving the underserved,' (2) providing an education that is 'student-outcome centered,' and (3) graduating students who are 'practice-ready.'" Law Corp might best be described as having two missions—one socially just and public; the other capitalist and occluded. As in other recent examples of "financial morality," these operate in concert, not in conflict. Writing about Wall Street culture prior to the economic collapse, anthropologist Karen Ho emphasizes that "moral imbrication with larger American understandings of what constitutes economic righteousness . . . has enabled the financial sector to fight back challenges to its power."[5]

In its early years of operation, New Delta, along with its fellow Law Corp consortium schools, appeared to offer a win-win opportunity for students, faculty, staff, administration, corporate officers, and off-site private equity investors. As higher learning became a safe pathway to upward mobility, for-profit education catering to marginalized communities grew in popularity. In the early 2000s, the private equity market was booming, and capital flowed rapidly into education companies aimed at this audience. Officers and administrators worked under conditions of financial fluidity uncharacteristic of the nonprofit higher education sector. In a post–New Age context emphasizing increased work–life balance, staff were hired from other rigid corporate work environments to join the seemingly laid-back and intellectual milieu of a freestanding graduate school. Law faculty were recruited to join the well-compensated, respected, and "elite" world of legal academia.[6] And students were granted the opportunity of professional upward mobility after virtually no other school had accepted them or had done so with comparable financial aid incentives.

But, in the Great Recession of 2009, the U.S. financial sector nearly collapsed, bringing down with it much of the legal services industry (see Figure I.1). As lucrative law jobs evaporated, so did student employment outcomes and, in turn, a significant portion of law school enrollments. In this climate, law schools near the bottom of the national rankings felt the greatest pressure.[7] After growing explosively from 2005 to 2012, NDSL saw its admissions projections cut in half; by 2014, it had laid off roughly one-third of its faculty.[8] As bar passage rates fell rapidly in this period, the decline was experienced disproportionately among minority students—themselves overrepresented in this unique institution. Yet, the school continued to bill students at premium tuition rates. And on the advice of outside consultants attempting to help the company maintain financial sustainability, NDSL rearranged its academic calendar, core curriculum, and faculty contracts to squeeze greater value out of dwindling resources. Throughout all of this, equity investors promised high returns at the height of the private equity boom still had to be paid their contractual share of revenues, and those

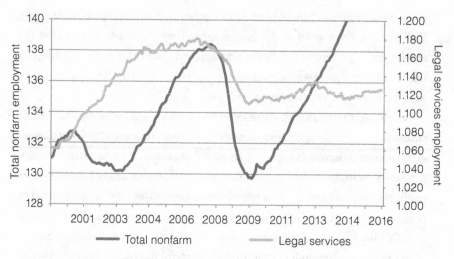

Figure I.1. Rise and fall of legal services employment and total nonfarm employment in millions.

SOURCE: U.S. Bureau of Labor Statistics, Current Employment Statistics survey.

revenues continually flowed from federal public financing under Title IV of the Higher Education Act (HEA).

How had this situation come about? In 1995, the ABA, sole national regulator and accreditor of U.S. law schools, was faced with a dilemma.[9] Prior to this, the modern U.S. legal education establishment had dismissed the idea of for-profit ownership. As Bryant Garth, then-president of the American Bar Foundation, told me,

I remember it well, because I remember that everybody in legal education pretty much, including me . . . did not want the for-profits to come. We all thought it would undermine some of the values that we think are fundamental to legal education, but as I recall . . . they sued as an antitrust violation and forced the ABA to capitulate.

The ABA Council of the Section of Legal Education and Admissions to the Bar (Council) accredited its first proprietary law program in 1999, followed by five more over the next twelve years. Since that period, the Council has in its regulatory capacity appeared to treat these six schools no differently than the other 200-some nonprofit programs operating under its purview.[10] Further still, as this book illustrates, the regulatory body has until very recently leaned toward "letting the market decide." Rather than applying stricter or differential standards to law programs using Title IV student loan moneys as the nearly sole basis for *private* profit, the ABA has taken marketization one step further.[11] What, then, are the implications of this growing faith in market rationality in the crucible of legal expertise and lawyer socialization?

Moral Hazard in the Production of Legal Expertise

For-profit law schools heighten and draw attention to wider problems of moral hazard in legal education. Moral hazard, as it is generally understood, is the separation of risk-generating behavior from its harmful consequences.[12] In the context of New Delta and other private equity and corporate controlled institutions of higher education, moral hazard describes the condition in which schools are paid up front (thanks to Title IV funding) but the high risk of attrition or failure to find sustainable employment is borne by students well into the future. This separation gets its moral dimension from a long-held belief in Western philosophy that actors should be held responsible for injuries resulting from risks they produce.[13] With rising tuition costs and falling student outcomes, the legal education sector has witnessed an increasing separation of this kind. This has been cogently observed by others who suggest that over-regulation by legal educators acting in their own self-interest may be greatly to blame.[14] Partial or complete deregulation of the law school accreditation process, they say, would permit greater *differentiation*. This would allow schools to *innovate* and diverge from the one strict model traditionally expected by the ABA. That model, which typically required faculty research, security of position (such as tenure), prescribed credit hours for legal doctrine and skills courses, a maximum student–faculty ratio, and specific bar outcomes, has prevented schools from specializing in niche areas and catering to practitioner-only training.[15] To some scholars, this has precluded the rise of lower-cost trade school law programs.

But for-profit programs like New Delta effectively are trade schools. They make significant choices about student programming, faculty scholarship, and security of position to save on fixed costs. Problematically, these savings are not passed on to students or taxpayers. On the contrary, with the benefit of Title IV student loans and a hands-off regulatory approach, these schools and their shareholders have remained relatively shielded while passing the risk of market fluctuations to students and their creditors. The primary argument of this book, then, is that for-profit law schools reveal key problems of allowing unfettered marketization to resolve today's complex problems in legal education.[16]

Proprietary law schools are a proverbial "canary in the coal mine"—not just for legal education but for higher education more broadly.[17] They focalize the key issues we should be concerned about today: subjection of student learning to global market forces, opening of academic governance to moneyed influence, and conversion of security of position and social protectionism into (unequally) bargained-for casual contractual relations. All of these may be grouped under the broader heading of neoliberalism.

Meanings

Neoliberalism, here as in much ethnographic work today, forms the contextual backdrop for the story told about New Delta.[18] For purposes of this text, more properly an ethnography about the policy *workings* of neoliberalism, I employ a simple definition: It is a form of market fundamentalism that determines judgments over governance.[19] Under its guidance, policy actors seem to believe that the rationality of the marketplace—a fictional web of interconnected free economic exchange—exerts normative authority strong enough to displace the need for substantial state regulation. For some, the market fundamentalism of neoliberalism is not normative at all but merely a condition of possibility for the dominant normative value of "wealth maximization." In my view, however, informed by the policy landscape surrounding the for-profit law school subindustry, neoliberalism *is* normative. As an overarching philosophy holding that less regulation is always better, it exerts normative weight from higher to lower levels of authority. This approach most closely resembles that taken by Wendy Brown, who writes that "neoliberalism transmogrifies every human domain and endeavor, along with humans themselves, according to a specific image of the economic."[20] In this story, a hands-off approach at the Department of Education influences policy actors at the ABA Council of the Section of Legal Education, which in turn influences the approach of accreditation site visit teams, and so forth. Once state regulation becomes viewed as an *enemy* of efficient socioeconomic activity, subsidiary authorities may also be deterred from acting in their full regulatory capacity.

In this book, *marketization* will be understood as the exposure of a good, service, organization, or process to market forces. *Corporatization* is an evolution into a hierarchical workplace organization with separations among labor, management, and executive officers.[21] *Financialization* refers to the conversion of an institution or organization into an apparatus for financial investment. This generally introduces a new set of stakeholders—the shareholders—and the restructuring of the corporatized entity for value maximization in their name. If corporatization describes internal organization, financialization describes submission of that to off-site investor demands. And *neoliberalization*, although it may include each of the preceding developments, refers to a rearrangement in values such that these same economic mutations become disembedded from social and moral constraints.[22]

Consonant with these mutations is *neoliberal access*—a concept borrowed here from researchers who have examined Australia's variable approach to incorporating marginal groups into higher education.[23] As they have said, neoliberal access is

Social inclusion viewed in terms of increased opportunities to access education and employment . . . based on neoliberal theories of economic growth through investment in human capital to address skills shortages. These theories propose that social inclusion is facilitated by access to the social capital of the dominant culture.[24]

For these writers the term seems to carry descriptive weight only. Here, I develop it as a more critical notion that describes social inclusion devoid of social protectionism.

Early last century, the economic anthropologist Karl Polanyi saw the future of capital as a battle between free marketeers and social protectionism.[25] The former could be envisioned as the "robber barons" of the American Gilded Age and the latter as the trade unionists of the New Deal era. This opposition, Polanyi said, resulted in a kind of "double movement" or oscillation in the evolution of capital.[26] But although he was accurate in predicting the ongoing battle this would result in, Polanyi was ultimately wrong in suggesting it would result in an eventual reconciliation for capital.

Present-day neoliberalism sidesteps this tension. As the philosopher Nancy Fraser explains, capital's ingenuity was to co-opt the social movements that emerged in the wake of the 1930s.[27] Whereas trade unions and Marxists had once sought social protection, identity-based social movements of the 1960s sought "emancipation." Emancipation, meanwhile, could be construed variably from revolutionary fragmented subjectivity to free market "full" participation—entrepreneurial citizenship, to put it more crudely. More conclusively, she writes, the ingenuity of neoliberalism has been to resignify emancipation as entrepreneurial citizenship and suggest that this requires free markets to enfranchise all. Emancipation, in other words, is to come not from protection but from "access."

Access

Through its self-framing and public marketing—both to students and private equity investors—New Delta cohered much of its existence from financial model to pedagogical practice around the neoliberal approach to open *access*. Access was multivalent at this site. For officers of the parent company Law Corp, it included *access to public moneys*—Title IV federal financial aid dollars sanctioned by repeated ABA accreditation stamps. According to Rose, a former professor, leaders felt entitled to this income stream. "Law Corp's approach to regulation of their 'right' to federal money," she said, "is to fight it with money and lobbying and to creatively come up with the numbers to satisfy it."

For faculty and administration, it meant *access to justice*—the provision of legal services to new "underserved" communities by admitting low-performing student members of these communities to the study of law. And to students, it meant *access to legal education* or *legal profession* through a nearly open admissions process. For most of these students, some very bright and talented, New Delta was the only school that would accept them. For agents of the parent company, each student, irrespective of ability, represented a public income stream. For faculty, the challenge of bringing these students up to bar passage or law practice levels was made honorable by the mission of "serving the underserved," as described in Chapter 2. Here, open access offered a reconciling narrative for the moral dilemma that employees found themselves in. Narratives of this kind, Jarrett Zigon has written, "are better understood as the articulation of the ethical process of attempting to regain moral comfort in the world by charitably negotiating moral breakdowns."[28] This constellation, clustered around the ideological power of neoliberal *access*, was like fuel powering the institution's operational engines. But it was by no means unique to this environment or educational subsector. As Joel and Eric Best explain, the ideology of "access" has driven global increases in educational demand, employer expectations of uniform higher educational attainment, and, perhaps most importantly, "crushing" student loan debt.[29]

Access, in other words, has deep costs that are both political economic and moral. The political economic costs of open access are the more obvious. Most apparent is an immense public finance structure and bureaucracy that must ensure the availability of monetary resources to maintain access. Education, health care, and housing all require money up front, even if the expectation is that this is simply a mortgage against future value. Despite the stated policy that student loans are "nondischargeable," students do seek restructuring or simply default on payments, leaving the original source of their tuition money—taxpayers—on the hook and without the marginal social benefits initially expected.[30] These costs become truly political economic when legislators and policy makers fail to appreciate or fail to manage the growing problem. Public faith in educational regulation is shaken, and institutional legitimacy of bodies like the U.S. Department of Education (ED)[31]—heretofore tolerant of for-profit colleges—is undermined.

The moral costs of open access are related. By relying on a public finance system that offers easy credit to students on the promise of future earning increases—once a reliable wager but certainly no longer—regulators seem to allow mortgaging of the future. By doing so without substantial inquiry into educational quality, particularly at for-profit colleges and universities marketed especially to ethnoracial minority and nontraditional students, policy makers have effectively transferred public moneys over to private entities for conversion into and extraction as investor returns. Under what now amounts to a "preponderance of the evidence" that such institutions are of questionable value to graduates, lawmakers may actually be complicit in burdening especially vulnerable student populations. All of these contribute to the growing moral costs of neoliberal access embraced for decades in the higher education regulatory environment. Similar costs have been well documented in other areas of deregulated modern life, from home mortgage lending to health insurance coverage.

But New Delta is particularly important for training students for the legal profession and for its claim to improve public access to justice. Formal legal expertise carries exceptional weight in our modern world. And although often lambasted in Western popular culture, lawyers are also quite memorably depicted as heroic, morally searching figures.[32] The lay public places a high premium on lawyer morality, and law schools training attorneys under conditions of heightened moral hazard run the collateral risk of teaching questionable ethics by example.

Lawyers are also gatekeepers of state sovereign authority. Licensed attorneys in the United States are viewed as agents of the state or, more properly, as "officers of the court."[33] The precise technical meaning of this phrase is subject to debate, but an ethnographic meaning holds that lawyers in any formal dispute, embodying the adversarial nature of both our civil and criminal justice systems, are representatives of those systems and not simply free agents within them. This translates into a duty to uphold the sanctity of the court in the face of temptation for tactical lawyering that might promote a client but undermine the judicial forum or waste its resources. But attorney duties go beyond obligations to observe legal and institutional norms. In some jurisdictions they appear formally as duties to exercise moral judgment against "corrupt motives" and in favor of helping "the oppressed."[34] These moral obligations resemble those of other learned professions, notably medicine, and are heightened by the high selectivity rate of the bar in most states. Lawyers are in a privileged position and are at least formally expected to honor this.

But if neoliberalism is characterized by the displacement of the political by the economic, lawyers may play perhaps one of the most important intermediary roles in this process.[35] Trained today through intensive reading and writing that evacuates emotional response and moral judgment from norm creation and dispute settlement, students leave law school transformed in their political subjectivity but armed with expertise and credentials to make direct high-level impact on the world around them. The rise of Law and Economics thinking, in the law of torts, for example, has taught a generation of attorneys to evaluate "reasonable care" through the lens of an economic calculus that purports to capture the underlying reasoning of most modern social behavior. What does it mean that our most potent policy guild comes to view and act on the world in this way? It means at least that attorneys may be an underappreciated link in the chain between economic essentialism and political displacement.

A second quality that makes New Delta so illuminating is its unique combination of business model and ideology. The study of this combination calls for ethnographic inquiry because a focus on law school policy alone misses its constructed rationality. As Cris Shore and Susan Wright have said, "Policy can serve to cloak subjective, ideological and arguably highly 'irrational' goals in the guise of rational, collective, universalized objectives."[36] On the business side, it may be true that all law schools secure Title IV income streams and retain any surplus they result in. Many also circulate a portion of this surplus to the university campus or system in which they reside—all the while keeping at least a portion in the program. But distinguishing for-profit from non-profit law schools is the presence of outside investors—in New Delta's case a private equity fund grouping together institutions and large net worth individuals. Private equity is a unique investment format characterized by higher risk, higher returns on investment, relatively short capital commitments, and relatively high involvement of investors in local business operations.[37] At New Delta, in times of market downturn, investors still had priority to be paid, so students and faculty had to stand ready for cutbacks to programming and support. Company officers had to maintain a relatively high degree of influence over local operating decisions even in areas such as academic calendaring, faculty retention, and curriculum design. If nothing else, this ethnographic account, built on participant observation and direct informant interviews, offers an unprecedented empirical glimpse into how these involvements played out in daily organizational life.

The involvement of investors was only one facet of a larger structural embrace of capital. To make this sensible, other components had to be secured in place. One of these was the embrace of market rationality as such. Although not unique to private equity businesses, this was—at the time the school was founded, at least—somewhat unusual in legal education.[38] Officers talked about "student-centered learning" in a way that mirrored "customer service" orientations in retail enterprises. And they spoke of their unique "value proposition"—a phrase pulled straight from marketing textbooks of American business schools.[39] If New Delta were to succeed, they collectively seemed to say, it would have to be by offering a more competitive "product" in the crowded law school marketplace. If it *did* succeed, the logic continued, it must have been because the business edged out its competition. Notably muted, however, was a recognition that competitiveness might be secondary, and that NDSL had tapped into a demographic niche where students unable to enroll elsewhere (but eligible to receive Title IV money on credit) remained in supply for law schools willing to accept them.[40]

It is useful to think of neoliberal access in this case as inverse to what anthropologist João Biehl has called "social abandonment."[41] Embracing the discourse and policy of access, for-profit educators animated by a mission to "serve the underserved" reached into a socially abandoned (for professional purposes) class, as if to resuscitate members for a higher-cost "second chance," premised in part on eligibility for public finance streams. Whereas education had already been federally financed widely as a "public good," the for-profit higher education environment recaptures this stream for private gain.

Although this model—with the free flow of public money and seemingly endless supply of lower-end law school candidates—appears to be recession proof, it subjected vulnerable students to fluctuations in the wider global economy. As New Delta learned in the early 2010s, law schools had to fight to maintain incoming class profiles at existing LSAT and grade-point average (GPA) levels. Although NDSL—already at the bottom and thus unrestrained by rankings—could drop admissions standards to maintain class size and revenue volumes, and indeed did so, this practice was ultimately limited by graduate bar passage rates, so important for marketing and reaccreditation. Shrinkage of the first-year (1L) class size in consecutive years after 2011 did mean immediate budget shortfalls, and, with investor capital agreements still to honor, this led to palpable cuts in support for faculty and student activities and organizations.

So the key distinguishing feature of for-profit law schools is not the business model alone nor its basis in the production of expert legal actors, but the unique distribution of risks and consequences created and the pervasive ideological work conducted to try to reconcile this.

Why the Law School "Fourth Tier" Matters

Some may still wonder why an ethnography of a nonelite fourth-tier law school matters in the study of legal education or in the anthropology of law and policy. The present case is important in part because the current state of American legal education may be the result of an ongoing intellectual and social marginalization of so-called nonelite law programs—effectively the *majority* of schools training the *majority* of American lawyers (!). On-line blogs such as *Third Tier Reality* post stories about these schools alongside pictures of soiled toilets and alarmist headlines such as "Grab the Bleach."[42] The website *Outside the Law School Scam*, meanwhile, claims that all 200 ABA programs in the United States can be categorized simply into "(1) The T-13 (2) The Traps (3) The No-Names (4) Joke Schools."[43] Accordingly, the vast majority of lawyers produced in the United States come from schools not even worth mentioning for these bloggers. A similar omission of nonelite law schools from serious discussion, though perhaps expected in the popular culture and on-line trade tabloids, would be intellectually negligent among legal academics and sociolegal scholars today. It belies the politics underlying academic hierarchy and professional advancement.

Reputational superlatives are not sound criteria by which to justify social science inquiry. In the tradition of our key social theorists, law scholars should acknowledge to the contrary that our most valuable lessons have often emerged from the social, political, and economic margins.[44] For-profit law schools *are* indeed marginal. And yet, in their embrace of market rationality and increasing subjection of students and faculty to market vicissitudes, they are a bellwether. Their study offers a prescient glimpse of potential changes to come under held assumptions in legal education specifically and higher education more broadly. And the moral dilemmas they reveal have potential to reach far and wide in their impacts.

So this story is paradoxically exceptional and generalizable. Emergent fiscal and pedagogical practices in this subsector have actually become more widespread across legal education as schools borrow the profit-generating model to survive the crisis. Meanwhile, as one will see in the following chapters, the private equity model underpinning New Delta also means that this law school must appear to remain on the leading edge of fiscal-pedagogical innovation. The pressure posed by capital agreements with large investors introduces a second layer of marketization; the school must perform well vis-à-vis not only the legal education admissions market but also amid a tightening capital investment market. So many of our commercial institutions now fall into this position.

Conversations

This ethnography of New Delta, then, joins three parallel conversations. The first is among prospective law students. For roughly half a century, the choice to attend law school had been considered a safe one in the United States. For parents of graduating college students, it offered the comforting sense that their children would have a profession, an income, and cultural capital for the rest of their days. To the extent that parenting may be about ensuring survival of the next generation, they could sleep better at night knowing their child had entered law school. For the student, this decision could be an easy way to "cleanse" him- or herself of any nonvocational undergraduate education. But the rising cost of law school tuition coupled with the decline in highly paid legal services jobs—"structural change," as discussed in Chapter 3—have changed the calculations that once led to comfort among these groups. As some have said, any cost–benefit analysis that once made law school a "sure thing" for financial sustainability has shifted away from supporting the choice to attend for most students.[45] And yet, the argument of these writers rests largely on "rational-choice theory," an approach popular among legal educators lately that presupposes the cost–benefit thinking of "rational" individual actors in a society. Latent in this theory are the assumptions that individual values plugged into the equation are uniform and that the calculation takes place among individuals acting as atoms rather than members of broader social communities.

The very fact that many students continued to enroll in schools like New Delta, or that so many faculty were comfortable teaching in them, is strong evidence that "rational choice" may fail to explain this industry. To better understand why students and their families continued to participate, we must ask the more complicated question of what law school in general, and this one in particular, means to the people who choose to learn and teach within it. This study of meaning is essential to understanding the value judgments made by so-called rational actors. Without it, we are left to impute our own valuations of things like a "JD degree" in immigrant communities, or the "first business suit" owned by a first-generation college-graduate-turned-lawyer. The meaning of such symbols may drastically influence local applications of the cost–benefit thinking some writers have presupposed as uniform. Some may feel a "positivist" approach—one more interested in the rules of play for this social field—has more to offer the study of legal education and legal profession. My own contention is that interpretivism (the study of meaning) is more important than ever and has something unique to offer in this domain of hegemonic professionalization.

The book joins a second conversation among experts of legal education and legal profession intervening on several issues pertinent to this group. The first is rapid change in legal services and student preparation for the profession. Law has become increasingly subject to the kind of global flows first identified by Arjun Appadurai in his seminal piece, "Disjuncture and Difference in the Global Cultural Economy."[46] There, Appadurai suggested that globalization comprises the complex emergence of "scapes" or fields through which symbols, capital, bodies, technologies, and violence flowed. Legal services have been dramatically affected by these global connections. One example of this has been the outsourcing of expertise itself. As writers like Mihaela Papa and David Wilkins have pointed out, increased literacy and legal skills training in the Global South, particularly in Anglophone India, has allowed the outsourcing of key lawyering tasks such as document review.[47] At the same time, technology-based legal service providers like LegalZoom have further channeled demand away from traditional American law practices.[48] And, finally, these transnational and technological changes have supported an expectation among large corporate clients that lower-level tasks are no longer to be completed by highly paid first-year associates.[49] Demand for new graduates to occupy six-figure salaried positions—the ones that had justified uniformly high law school tuition—has dwindled. After the disappearance of thousands of high-salaried law jobs during the collapse of the late 2000s, these global pressures combined to impose what many have called a "structural change" in legal services away from a well-compensated unitary legal profession.

Whether to call this a "crisis" has itself been a second issue of debate. In one camp, authors like Brian Tamanaha, William Henderson and Paul Campos have argued vigorously that what we have seen amounts to a "crisis" for the legal academy.[50] JD programs, they point out, have raised tuitions exorbitantly over the past two decades, thanks in part to the artificial price insulation allowed by an erstwhile "no questions asked" federal student loan policy. Because the creditor in this case largely does not inquire into outcomes, reputational variations make little difference in the price of attendance. Prices have increased because true informational transparency—where applicants would know clearly about their future options in advance based on accurate reporting—has been lacking.

On the other side are influential legal educators like Bryant Garth and Erwin Chemerinsky. Garth has said emphatically that there is no distinct crisis in legal education because difficulties experienced are actually a subset of wider economic turbulence affecting other sectors.[51] Current "crisis talk," he elaborates, can actually be historicized as part of a recurring and sometimes racialized battle in the legal profession between the establishment and newcomers.[52] The important points, he continues, are that lawyers still control this debate and that social perceptions of "insider" and "outsider" institutions have changed or widened.[53] Chemerinsky, meanwhile, rejects the label of *crisis* altogether.[54] His thinking may reflect an almost ethnographic impulse that says, "Elitism may or may not be good, but it is what we are stuck with" in promoting *true* access to justice, as his law school at UC Irvine claims to do.

Regardless of the label used to describe the academic impacts of structural change, what the crisis debate reveals on review is something more serious: the now widespread acceptance of "market" as the dominant metaphor for describing the social landscape of legal education. "Market talk" has somehow become the lingua franca of legal education reform dialogues. Information, in this way of speaking, becomes important not in its own right but as a variable in "rational" decision making. JD degrees become not the concluding symbol of a three-year education and socialization process but a "product" to be compared between offerors who may or may not be similarly situated. And law schools, no longer socially transcendent institutions, become vendors—service providers in a crowded guild. The legal educators cited with respect previously and throughout this book seem to reflect in their writings, my conversations with them, or both, acceptance of this thinking. Even where that acceptance appears reluctant or "ethnographic," it remains prominent and recursive. "The market" in their imaginings of present and future has tended to become naturalized as the sole context in which the solution to crisis talk—either its vindication or its vanquishing—can be found.

That acceptance is itself a symptom of the larger problem underlying the New Delta story and the wider dilemma of legal education today. The tacit acceptance of market rationality even among legal education reformers results from a difficulty in imagining social realities outside of contemporary market fundamentalism. So entrenched is the idea of the free market as governing principle that its hegemony remains largely unchallenged by some of the more respected professional educators of our time.[55] Taking this one step further, one might even wonder whether law itself as an academic discipline is well equipped to grasp the role hegemony plays in the teaching and administration of justice in our society. Rather than using the breakdown of the economy and its alarmingly immediate impact on legal studies and services to comment critically on the very pervasiveness of market ideology, law's sharpest thinkers seem to accept, even if reluctantly, neoliberal thought in search of a redeeming metaphor to resolve social dilemmas the latter has itself created. This "neoliberal capture" of elite legal educators illustrates at high level the way in which, as Wendy Brown writes, "Neoliberal rationality . . . configures human beings exhaustively as market actors, always, only, and everywhere as *homo oeconomicus*."[56]

Thirdly, the proprietary ownership model has been posited by some as a solution to current problems. "Sometimes it takes a for-profit entity," one dean has recently written, "to right a wrong—in this case the lack of diversity in law schools."[57] For New Delta, this belief prompted admissions officers to push the student body diversity rate from roughly 30 percent before the "crisis" to roughly 42 percent just after. Private enterprise, the sentiment goes, has usually operated more efficiently and more deftly in fast-changing economic conditions. If the legal services industry requires greater differentiation, or faster adjustment to globalization, who better to meet this need than a global private equity firm? As some feel, nonprofit, and especially public, university systems remain entrenched in bureaucratic decision making and inflated civil service protections, and they depend lazily on annual state budget allocations. For-profit companies, they imply, have the right entrepreneurial and innovative esprit de corps necessary to survive and even leverage the present structural changes.

These claims might be convincing if the educational world were simpler. But, as one of my informants says, "Students are not widgets." This simple phrase captures much of what the story here illustrates. What forces prevent school proprietors from growing fast to earn more revenue? What corporate authority will ensure that faculty governance is respected and academic freedom secured? What company department will develop cultural capital when tradition is cast off as the enemy of innovation? As this story suggests, faith in the virtues of proprietary models to solve the crisis in legal education should be checked against these questions. Some may feel that all "low-end" law schools have had to engage in similar tactics to preserve enrollment. But the key point here is to connect recruitment and marketing measures with assured investor returns. Differentiation, innovation, and skill-based learning may be valid reforms, but placing them in the service of investors ahead of students can lead to the dramatic events described in the chapters that follow.

These debates tap into classic studies of professionalism and law. There, scholars across the disciplines have long been in conversation about the roles of culture, hegemony, and professional socialization. Early writings include C. Wright Mills's *White Collar*, as well as Talcott Parsons's "Law as an Intellectual Stepchild."[58] More recent studies have included work on the role of charismatic individuals in making up the global dispute resolution profession,[59] on public trust and access in the legal profession,[60] and on the future of legal services in an information economy.[61]

Finally, this book enters a third conversation among anthropologists of global law and economics grappling with the production and deployment of expertise itself. Annelise Riles offers a comprehensive glimpse at the role of legal reasoning in the formation of global financial exchanges.[62] She writes that law "is in fact doing far more work than [lawyers] could possibly imagine, and that legal expertise is an ensemble of far more nuanced and fine-grained pattern of theories and practices than they acknowledge to themselves."[63] Building on this, I suggest that financialization of the production of legal expertise itself accelerates the process by which legal knowledge comes to serve the global market. Similar interest in the relation among knowledge, finance, and "the global" has been well developed in the writings of Bill Maurer and Karen Ho. Maurer describes the ways in which money and its self-reflexive avoidance, manipulation, and accumulation contribute to global systems of exchange and market making.[64] Ho shows us how "the global" becomes a trope for international financial institutions to recruit and draw in capital, sometimes with no commitment to overseas communities other than an empty office held for legitimacy.[65] Although similar to Ho's work on Wall Street, this book may be somewhat more moralizing: law, legal reasoning, and the incubators of legal thought and practice carry elevated *fiduciary* duties and deserve higher scrutiny in a way that the abstract money making of Wall Street so far does not (quite). I take with some caution any suggestion that the legal services "bubble" might be a mere *variant* of the larger financial bubble and crisis. As similar as these are, the production and distribution of legal expertise in a society has direct implications on "justice," the concept by which we come to assess all other forms of misfeasance: financial, violent, reputational, and otherwise. The legal bubble and the financial bubble are related but separate symptoms of a larger problem: the breakdown of "the social" scholars like Carol Greenhouse associate with neoliberalism.[66] Therefore, the suggestion that even indebted graduates from bottom-tier law schools (much like many subprime borrowers) may be still "happy they attended" due to personal gains in prestige should recognize that this is not the sign of hegemony's absence but likely a symptom of a more *complete* hegemony indexed by individual gratitude for social or communal harm.

This book builds perhaps most directly on Elizabeth Mertz's work showing that transmission of legal expertise occurs through a key *sociolinguistic* process.[67] In her seminal account of law school language, Mertz describes how learning to "think like a lawyer" requires first-year law students to reorient themselves toward language and, in turn, morality.[68] In addition to tapping into procedural and doctrinal history and tradition, word choice serves to distance the student from the litigants or parties to any dispute. Contractual "unfairness" must be couched as "unconscionability," for example, or "responsibility" for tort harms must be phrased as either "liability or no liability." The "language of law school" socialized into the professional experience of incipient students, Mertz teaches us, is a major predicate to the moral separation of legal experts from their social environments.

In the context described here, moral separation becomes evident in the very fiscal model on which the law school is founded and the policy choices made to support this. Using a regulatory aporia created in the 1990s antitrust suit previously mentioned, the firm that owns New Delta enjoys substantial distance between the revenue it creates for equity investors and the debt it creates for students. That many of these students come from racial minority and socioeconomically marginal communities is of little concern; under the corporate mission drilled into employee practices these students represent communities "underserved" by the mainstream legal academy, to be "served" by the charitable staff, teachers, and administrators of these fledgling for-profit law schools. Above all else, Mertz's demonstration of the socialization process offers credence for the suggestion raised near the end of this book that the moral hazard cultivated under this arrangement may flow toward students through similar channels of intramural interaction.

Contemporary moral anthropology offers a broad theoretical frame in which to evaluate this production and distribution of moral hazard. As Didier Fassin has written, there are important reasons to consider works such as this one under the heading of moral anthropology because:

> It explores the moral categories via which we apprehend the world and identifies the moral communities we construe, examines the moral signification of action and the moral labor of agents, analyzes moral issues and moral debates at an individual or collective level . . . Moral anthropology [also] encompasses the delicate topic of the moral implication of the social scientist: it is reflexive as much as descriptive.[69]

This project is a moral anthropology in both senses. It seeks immanently to understand how financiers, administrators, and my informants—largely former law faculty and students—made moral sense of the rare worlds of legal education, proprietary higher education, and proprietary legal education. Potential value from studying their efforts is heightened here precisely by the high stakes moral environment of law, lawyer training, and the legal profession. This is, in other words, a study of moral world making.[70]

At the same time, the story offers me, the writer and researcher, opportunity to reflect on my position and that of academic colleagues not only in proprietary law schools but in all of U.S. legal education. As debates about "crisis" play out in law journals, trade publications, and news media, the moral positioning of law professors remains relatively obscured. In some cases, law professors have been published in news outlets as legal "journalists" with little reflection on their own positionings in the larger law school economic structure. I do not bemoan these writers for encouraging all of us, especially future law students, to think more critically. But I note the absence of reflexive moral stability in their positions and draw connections to my own as a one-time participant observer. I view my proximity to this industry as a unique opportunity to shed light on the interpretive, moral, and policy sides of this reality. But, unlike them, I do this with the formal theoretical and ethical formation of an urban ethnographic researcher.

Given this unique position, my work joins the rich and growing contemporary anthropology of policy. Policy forms a linkage between the separate spheres of morality and law. As Shore and Wright have written:

Looked at anthropologically, the relationship between policy and morality sheds interesting light on the art of government. Both policy and morality attempt to objectify and universalize ideas. . . . However, whereas morality is explicitly concerned with ethics, policy purports to be more pragmatic, functional and geared to efficiency.[71]

Legitimating normative authority on the basis of moral distance, policy in this fashion sits alongside law as an expert discourse and institutional field. But, unlike law, policy operates beyond the traditional organs of state functioning at sites such as universities, think tanks, nonprofit organizations, and activist networks. Policy, in short, is the less-formalized normative field in which social, political, and economic decisions affecting people and communities are made. Less exclusive than law, it is also more pervasive, more susceptible to change, and less concerned with rote application.[72]

This book considers questions of linkage, directionality, and space in the ethnographic understanding of policy. In trying to understand *linkages*, it describes the *policy cascade*—the flow of policy innovation and implementation from one center of normative authority outward to affected industries and populations through concentric circles or levels of authority. This flow, it must be noted, has *directionality*. Policy made at the Department of Education, in this case, begets more policy at the ABA Council of the Section of Legal Education and Admissions to the Bar and then still more at the local law school level. Students and faculty, experiencing the impact of these norms, may be able to shape or change them through collective action, but they lack the institutional power to generate their own policy. Seemingly obvious at a glance, this observation has deeper implications, one of which is that the policy cascade flows in one direction "down" a power gradient and rarely backward. These observations point to the more general *spatial* dimension of policy speaking of it as "flowing," as "moving," or as "located" in the space between morality and law.

The Approach

Unlike journalistic or popular critiques of proprietary legal education, the idea for this book emerged inductively from deep experience with the narrow and arcane worlds of private equity and legal education. On completion of my law training and while on leave from graduate study in anthropology, I joined the legal team for a private equity fund manager ensnared in the nationwide public pension "pay-to-play" scandal of the mid-2000s. Through experience in this litigation, I noted the idiosyncrasies of private equity fund management, including in particular its widespread practice of broaching public–private financial and ethical divides in pursuit of vast capital commitments from sensitive institutions such as state public pension systems.

Then, on completion of the PhD at Princeton University, I obtained a tenure-track position at one for-profit law school through the Association of American Law Schools (AALS) national job market requiring the standard two courses per semester teaching load compensated at roughly the standard rate for entry-level law faculty. I entered the position with a conviction that if conditions proved idiosyncratically illuminating, the experience should form the basis of a new ethnographic project on marketization in higher education and legal expertise. Roughly one year into the position, following some of the dramatic events described in the chapters that follow, I came to fully embrace the potential of this conviction. By that time, working conditions in this environment had evolved considerably. Whereas it started out as an environment with a slightly unusual institutional culture, it quickly became one capable, intentionally or otherwise, of ruining lives in the name of financial sustainability.

To explain why and how, this book relies on three categories of ethnographic evidence to describe the single field site of New Delta School of Law, a pseudonym given to the actual American law school objectivized in my study. Readers, particularly academic lawyers, may feel that use of a pseudonym is capricious given the narrow field of for-profit law schools and relative identifiability of each. To this I offer two responses. First, my aim is not perfect confidentiality but a modicum of reputational insulation. This book is an academic one aimed at educating policy experts and scholars and not strictly a polemical one intended to harm the commercial standing or brand name of these institutions. Perhaps more importantly, thousands of school alumni are now in the job market seeking positions that would help pay down their current student debt loads; in producing an expository text of this nature, I prefer to minimize the difficulties recent graduates may face in seeking professional stability and financial solvency. Second, the use of a pseudonym is a writing device I employ to generate distance between myself and the field site and its actors. After spending three years at this site with these people, I remain invested in their well-being. As with any ethnographic research, this was one in which the distinction between Self and Other faded and remains murky. Partly in an effort to regain and reflect on that distinction, therefore, this book uses pseudonyms for all local institutional, geographic, and personal referents. The one exception to this throughout will be references to well-known legal educators unaffiliated with NDSL and consulted as "secondary" informants.

The first type of ethnographic evidence relied on includes notes and timelines derived from participant observation. During my three years on the faculty at NDSL, I taught hundreds of individual class sessions with first-year law students; attended dozens of general and faculty meetings; carried on countless private conversations with students, faculty, and staff; and generally observed policy debates, changes, and implementations. In this case, I chose not to compile a synchronic field diary and rather compiled extensive notes after leaving the "field" heavily cross-referencing these for accuracy in consultation with many of the key informants quoted here.

Second, I rely here on publicly available legal documents resulting from a number of civil suits involving U.S. law schools. These cases include contract claims by former employees, as well as fraud claims by current and former students. When possible, I have made efforts to "read" these documents ethnographically—through the eyes of my informants—and, where necessary, I have omitted citations to them where they would identify informants meant to remain anonymous here.

A third evidentiary source was a rich body of informant interviews I gathered after initial participant observation and therefore after I left my position. These interviews, approximately fifty in total, amounted to roughly 650 pages of double-spaced transcripts. They include accounts from former[73] students, faculty, staff, and administrators and deliberately represent a nearly equal number of men and women, traditional and nontraditional, and white and nonwhite research participants. All formal interviews were semistructured, guided by a series of general questions with follow-ups. Out of caution for these generous informants, I limit my details about the sample to these.

Additionally, if one seeks to understand policy "from below," one must embrace intimacy with subject populations even if doing so renders us less intimate with "official" voices. The primary voices captured in the story are those of students and faculty rather than administrators or investors. The reasons for this are above all practical; if the virtue of ethnography is intimate interpretive insight from members of circumscribable communities, this virtue becomes attenuated when the researcher seeks omniscience or loyalty to no one. In this case, students and faculty confided in me (with informed consent) because I had been "one of them." I capture their side of the story here because, in institutional perspective, theirs mattered least—though they made up a demographic majority of their community. For this reason, this book does not attempt to be an "objective" account of life at New Delta—if such a thing is even possible. From it, one cannot necessarily impute malice to individual administrator, executive, or investor decisions. To seek to is to downplay the institutional capture neoliberalism is known for.

Structure of the Book

This account takes a narrative form meant to capture the dramatic events at New Delta following my arrival and preceding my departure three years later. Although the story forms a complete expository whole, its chapters also stand alone as discrete sections with subsidiary claims.

Chapter 1 presents the recruitment and training practices that fill the new institution with flesh and blood people. Here, I discuss New Delta's practices for recruitment of faculty and enrollment of students—its techniques for finding the human resources making up its organization. Through the use of various techniques the school and its parent company generated and maintained *managed precarity*—a condition in which teachers and students remain as employees and clients out of felt necessity more than elective choice.[74] Chapter 1 suggests that the operationalization of professional diversity through increased access to legal education permitted NDSL to forestall market discipline at a time when many expressed faith in the winnowing function of a legal education free market.

Chapter 2 gives readers a window onto the corporate culture of the proprietary law school. There, I propose that the unique, curated culture of NDSL served to hold back community reflection on the moral hazard of for-profit legal education. Through structured repetition and reflection, faculty and staff were taught to embrace the ideology of access rather than dwell on their underlying business model—one that generated millions of dollars annually in subprime student debt and transformed them into off-site investor returns.

Chapter 3 describes the feverish growth of the school in the years following the onset of the Great Recession. This sudden growth, leading to logistical problems inadequately prepared for, had immediate effects on the 450 new students brought in as first years in 2011. Nevertheless, as I claim in this chapter, difficulty meeting investor obligations—rather than any great concern for logistical or pedagogical limitations—would quickly impose a limit to this large burst of entrepreneurial expansion.

Chapter 4 describes the resulting pressure for comprehensive curricular reform. It suggests that Legal Ed 2.0, as the plan came to be known, had less to do with substantive improvements for law student learning than pacifying investor fears about the new "crisis" in legal education. Under new professional realities, fourth-tier law schools had to reinvent themselves or risk dissolution. Law Corp, fearful of the investor "call" on its capital, ordered each of its three schools to develop a new curriculum. So they did.

Chapter 5 moves from reinvention to survival. Here, I describe in detail how school administration conducted and mediated faculty deliberation and democratic ratification of the revised curriculum proposal. This includes a retelling of the unique manner in which the reforms were ultimately passed and the direct impact this had on governance, academic freedom, and basic feelings of respect and dignity among students and educators in this unique environment. Above all, I suggest, Law Corp officers succeeded in confirming a marketable reform agenda by framing the debate as one between tradition and innovation.

Chapter 6 describes the manner in which a fiscal "state of exception" changed the structure of school governance by altering the terms by which employees were retained in the organization. That shift, I maintain, from *customary* to *contractual* security of position, situates this story within the larger context of neoliberal governance and legal culture pervading this period. On one hand, academic employees were asked to expand their duties into business development. In one notable episode, NDSL sent several of its professors to the southern African nation of Botswana to establish ties with the national bar to train judges and attorneys in common-law jurisprudence and develop this as a new income stream. On the other hand, with threats of a reduction in force in the air, NDSL revised its employment terms with faculty, resulting in a conflict with and ultimate termination of tenured senior professors. Amid the rapid spread of this information on social media, students flew into a panic and began requesting letters of recommendation to transfer out in greater numbers.

In Chapter 7, I argue the regulatory frameworks governing schools like New Delta have been greatly shaped by the rhetoric of student access. Accepting school officials' narrative that the main hurdle to professional diversity is simply *becoming* a lawyer, the scrutiny of key regulatory actors—here the ED and the ABA—was, for most of the period described here, unable to properly grasp the harm for-profit law schools may be liable to generate. In other words, such schools may not only produce substantial moral hazard, they may also distribute it to a new generation of would-be legal advocates.

The Conclusion recaps the book's main themes to reassert two core claims. The first, directed at law and policy audiences, says that differentiation by marketization—by exposure of law schools to the disciplinary power of free markets—may likely exacerbate professional inequalities. No longer just a proposal, market differentiation has already appeared at New Delta and its sister schools. Under it, thousands of students have been trained and graduated to practice law among the public. As my informants describe in the following chapters, these students enter a local profession that stigmatizes them for this pedigree.

The second claim, directed at social researchers such as anthropologists, underscores how "market" thinking has influenced so many, reformers included, in American academic law. That influence seems to have crowded out other, more complex understandings of law school training as a public service, a civic duty, or a process of expert socialization and acculturation. It may in turn be symptomatic of a larger epistemic vulnerability in academic law—one that social researchers, perhaps more familiar with the lived realities produced by economic fundamentalism—may be able to help remedy.

Chapter 1

Enrollment

Precarity, Casualization, and Alternative Admissions

"**H**E'S an anthropologist. He's going to study *us*."

I cringed when I heard this, as I had not yet turned to academic lawyers as an object of study. That would soon change. In the meantime, I was having dinner with future colleagues from New Delta School of Law. There, in a midpriced Mexican restaurant near the center of the city, just miles from the then-campus, I got my first experience of the people I would work alongside for three years. As part of the obligatory faculty recruitment ritual, they were there to learn my skills and etiquette as a conversationalist, debater, and evening diner. Those attending included a former state supreme court clerk, a former state trial court judge, a former corporate in-house counsel, and one alumnus of Yale Law School. We spoke about state immigration politics, international terrorism, and law teaching failures described in the Carnegie Report released a few years earlier.[1]

The morning after, I gave a "job talk" about my long-term fieldwork on the European Constitution and its defeat in France. After I finished, one faculty member approached me—an older gentleman whom I later learned had sat on the local bench for many years. "Interesting talk," he said, "but I'm not sure how it would benefit our students at all." A second professor approached: "Nice work. I did PhD fieldwork in Russia, but nothing as extensive," she said kindly. A third faculty member then chimed in: "That was the most interesting talk we've had here." One month later, I was invited to join the tenure-track faculty the following fall. The offer came just in time—I accepted the position from a laptop in a postpartum recovery room a day after the birth of my first child.

Precarity is a powerful force in today's world. It inspires young families to accept work in new places and move across state lines. It permits employers to maintain a docile labor force. And it promotes students to seek out further education and remain loyal to "predatory formations" in higher learning.[2] In this chapter, I discuss New Delta's practices of enrollment and recruitment for both faculty and students—quite literally its techniques for finding the human resources making up its organization. Through the use of various techniques, I will suggest, the school and its parent company generated and maintained *managed precarity*—a condition whereby teachers and students come to remain loyal employees and clients out of feelings of insecurity more than elective choice. This builds on recent theoretical writings on precarity as an immanent condition of contemporary global capitalism as it migrates further away from the values of Western social protectionist movements.[3]

As philosopher Richard Gilman-Opalsky points out, discussions of precarity that fail to specify its precise conditions can undermine the critical efficacy of this concept. What is needed, he says, "is to distinguish different forms and causes of precarity."[4] Therefore *managed* precarity, it should be said, is a milder version of the conditions experienced by the global dispossessed and displaced, but it captures the local instrumentalization of similar forces among late modern business enterprises aimed at maximizing "shareholder value."[5] It is a tool for creating organizational coherence in institutions or businesses of moral instability. This, in turn, serves what Emile Durkheim famously called "organic solidarity," a "modern" form of cohesion that binds separate actors through a division of labor to succeed or survive.[6] Like organs in a body, the disparate actors work in increasingly specialized ways to assure the functioning of the whole. This description captures what modern-day corporations were becoming by the turn of the twentieth century when Durkheim was writing.[7] Corporations, with their different departments, hierarchy, divisions of labor, and so forth, are highly specialized groups. Although Durkheim viewed them as organic solidarities par excellence, some corporations in recent years have returned to a more mechanical form of affinity through the use of mission statements and benefits packages that stylize their employee identities as "in and of" the company itself. In high-tech companies like Google or Facebook, for example, employees' sense of self may be rooted in the unusual lifeworld created by the new management approaches and working conditions (for example, casual dress code) of these organizations.

But, for other companies, particularly those controlled by private equity funds designed to quickly leverage company holdings for fast turnaround and sale, identity formation among human resources may be too expensive and unjustifiable to shareholders.[8] Instead, of greatest value to equity investors may be the fungibility of both workers and clients, understood in the context of proprietary higher education as faculty and students, respectively. Schools like the University of Phoenix, a publicly traded for-profit, hire few permanent faculty and instead rely on "practitioner" adjuncts marketed as teachers of the latest industrial skill sets. New Delta, as an ABA-accredited law school, could not follow this faculty model. It had, instead, the quandary of maintaining an obligatory, permanent, tenure-line faculty while hoping to attain for investors the benefits of employee fungibility. It resolved this tension, I suggest, through managed precarity.

Untapped Markets

When New Delta opened its doors in the mid-2000s, it was to join a stable of Law Corp proprietary schools in emerging markets. Law Corp management, along with outside consultants, conducted extensive research and determined that several metropolitan areas across the United States had unserved legal education markets. But these new programs were not the first in their jurisdictions. Market researchers had determined that extant law schools in the area were too selective for most of the students hoping to become attorneys there.

Until that moment, this selectivity had been considered by most legal professionals a good thing. It assured everyone that only the best of applicants were being admitted to study and eventually practice. In traditional law school admissions terms, the extant JD programs in the jurisdiction took in only students who scored around the seventy-fifth percentile of all LSAT takers. This, in turn, assured the public, consumers of legal services, that the law degree from Big State School of Law, for example, could be read as some assurance of quality. It also assured that students were admitted for only the right reasons. Federal student loan money could be readily secured by anyone accepted and if schools were in the business of generating the greatest revenue, they might have had an incentive to open admissions criteria to those likely to fail or unlikely to pass the bar.[9] Selective admissions criteria also helped assure that the existing law schools in the state remained well ranked under the universalizing hierarchy of the *U.S. News & World Report* ranking system. Whereas many have recently criticized those rankings and the gamesmanship carried out by several schools in pursuit of ascendancy therein, these rankings—and constituent student selectivity—have remained at least some general indicator of bar passage and reputational strength among legal professionals.

Even under such national restraints on admissions, the number of attorneys in the United States still grew during this period at a rate roughly double that of national population growth.[10] Nevertheless, as the need for legal services grew with the state's population, one emerging paradox was a disparity in access to legal services for rural and urban poor.[11] This was not unique to the state or area surrounding New Delta or other Law Corp schools. Across the United States, low-level legal tasks such as wills, divorces, bankruptcy, and so forth were becoming out of reach for many people for reasons of cost and geography.[12] Meanwhile, attorneys interested in conducting these types of services were increasingly limited by the growing size of student debt upon graduation. New graduates, already heavily attracted by jobs at high-paying corporate firms that did the most to train them in legal practice, were now even less motivated to open a solo firm in a poor urban or rural area.

All of this established a distinct problem of "access" within the legal community. But the question remained, "access to what?" exactly. Already, nonprofit nongovernmental organizations such as the Southern Poverty Law Center or Public Counsel, to name just two, had long catered legal services to marginalized communities. Staff attorneys at these organizations were indeed some of the brightest from high-ranking law schools; on recruitment, they became eligible for a variety of student loan relief programs that would offset opportunity costs for graduates not entering corporate law.[13] Attorneys in such positions have reported some of the highest career satisfaction rates of all working lawyers. If these organizations have been relatively successful at channeling law professionals into needed social justice positions, why not simply open more of them?

The answer lies in the interaction of private business and public finance illustrated by this story. Entities like Law Corp's parent fund, one I will call Venture Partners Group (VPG), entered the law school business to generate revenue for off-site investors. They discovered, much like the University of Phoenix before them, that the federal government was willing to provide easy credit for students to enroll in accredited higher education. Whereas UOP had long since captured the market for undergraduate education, the law school market was only recently opened up for financialization under new accreditation policy following a historic lawsuit against the ABA.

The case began in 1992 when the Massachusetts School of Law at Andover (MSL) sought national accreditation. Although a nonprofit entity, MSL had created a model of faculty engagement and pedagogy that strove to keep overhead costs low.[14] It used primarily practicing lawyers as adjunct faculty and put students to work on real cases, thereby maintaining low faculty salaries.[15] Unfortunately for the school, these practices created, among other things, a student–faculty ratio well in excess of the ABA maximum at the time.[16] On denial of its accreditation bid, MSL filed an antitrust claim against the ABA, which, although ultimately a failure, sparked an investigation by the Department of Justice (DOJ), which then filed its own suit in 1995. In its complaint, the DOJ alleged a number of "anticompetitive standards and practices" including, among other things, fixing of faculty salaries, unnecessary exclusion of graduates from non-ABA law programs, and, most importantly, summary elimination of proprietary law schools from accreditation consideration.[17] Early in the case, the ABA entered a consent decree accepting responsibility for many of the alleged practices and offering to remedy these.[18]

So the opening of ABA accreditation to for-profit law schools signaled an opening of *access* to vast public resources for private business. Law Corp, realizing the significance of this access, likely also understood that it might have difficulty selling the idea to equity investors more accustomed to investing in distressed commercial entities. Perhaps to overcome the dubious appearance of the business model, the company developed its systemwide "mission pillars" (see Chapter 2). Common among these is an implicit but clear mission to increase access to legal education and, by extension, access to legal services and access to justice.

Springdale School of Law

At its opening in the mid-2000s, New Delta was initially labeled Springdale School of Law,[19] after the city in which it was located. At that time, Law Corp officers hired a team of approximately a half-dozen legal educators and retired judges to build the faculty and curriculum for the school. The program began in a strip mall in a wealthy area of the city. Its founding dean was also a senior vice president for Law Corp who had taught at several low-ranked ABA schools and authored several casebooks. Within a few years, educators from other institutions such as Gonzaga, St. Mary's, and St. Thomas were recruited to help bolster the legitimacy of the program.[20]

The first dean touted the Law Corp schools as "fixing" what was wrong in legal education. As he described it at the time, "It's student-centered, it's very community-connected, and multiculturalism is the norm rather than aspiration."[21] This focus on student centeredness would remain with the institution throughout its growth. But the interest in multiculturalism, perhaps because of the ideological sound of the term and relatively conservative bent of the community in which the school was situated, was later dropped in favor of a more amorphous phrase: "the underserved."

The school graduated its first students in its third year of operation. That first group numbered only thirty-four and included both full- and part-time students, many second-career professionals, or those with daytime jobs throughout their studies. Over the next few years the class sizes grew, and the school hired more faculty. In several cases, faculty initially hired to teach "lawyering process"—known elsewhere as "legal research and writing"—were revetted through the hiring process and transitioned to teaching legal doctrine.

Faculty Recruitment

The law teaching "market" is highly unusual both as an employment marketplace in general and an academic employment marketplace in particular. Technically there are few set requirements for teaching in a law school other than the possession of some advanced degree. Although at many schools the JD is required, at a number of well-respected programs faculty teach with only a PhD in a related field such as politics or legal history.[22] Today, with a slump in hiring among the largest law firms—ones formerly responsible for training new graduates in actual practice capabilities—schools are under pressure to hire professors who can teach legal skills courses. Notwithstanding this recent development, law school faculty hiring in years past was surprisingly disjoined from one implicit aim—training new practicing lawyers—of legal education. Hiring committees were more likely to call back elite graduates with one well-placed esoteric published article than they were a seasoned litigator trained at a midlevel law school. Hiring practices also differed considerably from those found in the social sciences and humanities, where extensive portfolios showing research, teaching, and grant-writing prowess are routinely required.

For its first few years, New Delta recruited faculty through word of mouth, local advertisements, and professional networks. Most of the founding faculty were from the local community around Springdale. But, as the school expanded and approached its first ABA provisional accreditation, it needed to attain the national legitimacy that even fourth-tier law programs must. In the late 2000s it sent its first hiring committee to the AALS Faculty Recruitment Conference, otherwise known as the "meat market." The conference is a hiring-only meeting usually held in Washington, D.C., in the same hotel year after year. As some have said, it is the largest gathering of "highly elite educated young people running around in cheap Brooks Brothers suits." To get there, candidates would have had to submit a single highly stylized on-line application through the AALS. This application is not as rigorous as that required by academic departments; it asks for formal inputs of education, work, teaching experience and preferences, publications, and references.[23] References are checked only on selection for the campus visit in the next round. Meanwhile, preliminary candidates are invited for a kind of intellectual speed dating in the hotel consisting of thirty-minute appointments with each inviting school's committee. For the three-day event, the hotel is buzzing with generally young professionals racing to catch elevators to stand in corridors waiting to spar with veteran legal academics known as a group for their pugnacity.

New Delta's committee, however, approached the process a little differently. When I first met with them in 2010, following a very tense and unproductive meeting with one Ivy League law school, I found their lines of questioning and follow-up very refreshing. What were my ideas about law teaching, and how it could it be done better? How could my training as an anthropologist be of use in the classroom and beyond? Whereas other committees, attempting to mimic appellate court hearings, were likely to attack a candidate's research solely to test his or her defense skills, the New Delta faculty I met had a distinctly constructive approach. At that initial meeting, all the way in Washington, D.C., I asked them about the significance of Law Corp. What was it? What impact did it have on governance? Who was really in control?

The newly appointed dean was present in my interview; she took the lead while others chimed in. Law Corp, she said, was merely the holding company that owned their "consortium." This consortium was not unlike a university system with its branch campuses and flagship or nerve center. Each school was different, she said. Theirs, for example, had the most racially diverse faculty. And each was primarily autonomous, she continued, though governance was shared in certain matters. My concerns about a private corporation controlling an academic institution lingered, but I had heard enough to justify a closer look. Most importantly, I was admittedly very interested in the warm inquisitive posture of the faculty and dean amid the ravenous context of the "meat market."

A few weeks later I flew to Springdale for a campus visit and job talk. Shortly after the dinner already described, I returned to my hotel room and discovered I had forgotten to bring a tie. For some academic disciplinary hiring purposes, the full "suit and tie" might be overkill; but in the context of law hiring—this was not my first campus visit—I knew a lack of formality would be read as disrespect. I approached the hotel concierge to see where the nearest clothing store might be. By that time it was after 10 p.m. and, he said, most places were closed. "There is a Target store five miles from here," the young man at the reception said, face illumined by the blue light of a computer screen. I had no other choice; I asked him to drive me, picked up the most expensive tie I could find in the men's clothing section, paid the twenty dollars, and returned to my room after tipping the man for going above and beyond his job description.

The next morning, I walked the short distance up to the law school "campus," understanding that it was a freestanding graduate program without high expectations for a tree-lined, sprawling campus. But neither did I expect to find the strange arrangement in which New Delta then found itself. The school at that time had leased a series of office buildings around a central plaza adjacent to a large covered parking garage. At the center of its semicircle of buildings sat a massive twenty-story high-rise tower, "shaped like a Speed Stick deodorant," as someone later described it. In one of the low-rise outer buildings, a single suite was occupied by a small convenience store selling coffee, sandwiches, candies, and energy drinks. On the surface it had certain appearances of an educational center.

But a few minutes spent lingering in the plaza revealed a wider variety of people than that found on college campuses. Although some wandered through carrying backpacks or laptops, as many people carried small children, senior walkers, or nothing at all. Though New Delta occupied much of the surrounding offices and three floors of the tower, the remainder of the high-rise suites were offices for government and private companies ranging from the Internal Revenue Service to TD Service Financial Corporation—a company specializing in foreclosure notices and publication. These entities brought large numbers of nonstudents to the location, and the school made its best efforts to frame this presence as proximity to legal and quasi-legal services. Above all, some employees of these coexisting enterprises harbored resentment toward the relatively new law school and its students. "Suddenly they were taking up all the elevators, and slowing us down getting in to work," one IRS worker told me. Altogether, the stucco offices set along a major intersection next to a city light rail stop gave the new school a feeling of transience. Well before my visit, however, I was informed that plans were underway to move to a new, bigger, more permanent location in town.

This was reiterated when I stepped onto the campus that fall morning. I was greeted by some of the faculty who had dined with me the previous evening. They seemed happy to see me again and passed me off to an older male professor I will call Jesús. Jesús was the assistant dean for faculty scholarship and, I learned from the faculty web page, held an LLM degree from Yale.[24]

As he walked me around the campus poking into various classrooms, the law library, and an elevator or two, Jesús kept running into students and staff who appeared very fond of him. "Hey Jesús," a student shouted down the hallway, "we beat your team last week. You should've been there to save 'em."

"This is Riaz," he told some of the administrative staff. "He's our candidate for the morning."

"And they let *you* show him around!?" they responded chidingly.

In time, I learned more about this senior professor who seemed to be the life of the party. He was Mexican American and raised in the Midwest. He'd wanted to become a schoolteacher and applied to work as a substitute after college. On his first day of assignment in an elementary school, he once told me, he was walking across the schoolyard when some kids threw a dirt clod in his direction. Still young himself, he swung around and chased the kids down and put one in a headlock while demanding an apology. That, he said, was his last day teaching at that level. Jesús later attended law school at a university in the Southwest, practiced briefly, and then decided he wanted to become an educator again. He had nothing of the formality and affectation that many law professors exhibit; around the New Delta campus he would become a staunch advocate for student ethnic and political organizations—particularly the Native American Law Student Association. For example, he personally organized and arranged a "blanket ceremony" wherein faculty presented the school's first-ever Native American graduate with a ceremonial Indian blanket as a token of respect and well wishes.

"Why'd you go back to do an LLM at Yale?" I once asked him, comparing the apparent formality of that institution to his own laid-back demeanor—and apparently that of his current institution.

"I wanted to teach, and I knew I had to ramp it up. My JD wasn't gonna cut it."

I enjoyed talking to Jesús very much that day. He showed me the spot in the law library he and his colleagues had set aside to display "banned books." He spoke critically about the corporate school owners and their apparent watchdogs on the faculty and administration. He talked about the freedom there to research and write on any variety of topics, not simply the straightforward doctrinal scholarship that many law schools required for tenure. After my job talk, Jesús made sure I was given a plate of food and a moment to eat after everyone else already had. And after that, when he could have called me a taxi and rushed back to work, he insisted that he drive me, went to pull his car around, and ran its air conditioning for a few minutes predeparture to make the journey more comfortable. Inside he pulled off his blazer and revealed underneath a simple gray t-shirt. Jesús explained further that the faculty would meet to vote in the next few weeks. If there was a supermajority in support, I would receive an offer by Christmas. If only a simple majority, I would remain in contention through spring.

That ride to the airport and our ongoing conversation about legal education formality and radicalism was impressive to me. On the flight home I decided I would discuss a possible move with my wife. Barring that, our future lay in the hands of their faculty. Or so I thought.

"Talent Plus"

Most ABA law schools carry out the same cycle for faculty recruitment. In spring of the previous academic year, they constitute hiring committees made up usually of three to seven faculty members. In late summer many place an advertisement with AALS for its Faculty Placement Bulletin. On distribution of the first batch of faculty candidate names in August, committees begin poring over on-line AALS Faculty Appointment Registry (FAR) condensed CVs (curricula vitae) compiled from data entered into the on-line system. These one-sheets are an accurate representation of the minimalist approach to entry-level candidates' law teaching capabilities.

Law school hiring committees select candidates for their needs, arrange to meet them at the AALS-hosted "meat market" for speed dating, then make decisions to invite certain interviewees for campus visits. My own participant observation—including meetings with six committees ranging from Ivy League to provisionally accredited schools—suggests "elite" law schools may make such decisions after the initial interview based largely on questioning about research, whereas lower-tiered schools do so on the basis of research *and* teaching, or teaching alone. From there, four or five candidates per open position are invited to campus and, following a series of interviews, a job talk, and dinner, committees assess and rank their preferred candidates, hoping the top choice will accept an offer of employment by the time such decisions are finally rendered. This is where the process usually ends.

At New Delta, however, the process had one additional crucial step. Once the faculty committee had made its selection and sent it to the dean, the candidate then had to undergo a third-round phone interview with the management consulting firm Talent Plus, Inc. This firm devised a list of roughly fifty questions and conducted person-to-person recorded phone interviews, which were then assessed and scored. Questions included, "How do you feel about the statement, 'that's not my job'?" and "Describe a time when you felt you really helped someone." Throughout all of this, Talent Plus sought to determine for its clients the probability of its candidate being a good employee. In short, it tested for personality traits that lent themselves to easy management. In its own words,

Talent is a person's capacity for near-perfect performance. We identify people with the potential for near-perfect performance so clients can make wise decisions in the selection and development of their teams. When we identify talent, we transform lives. Talent Plus is the Leading Talent Assessment Partner with organizations committed to growth.[25]

This description differed considerably from one given by Edward, a former faculty member asked about the firm's role in the school's personnel decision:

RT: Can you tell me about Talent Plus? A recruitment tool/screen, correct? What was it screening for?

Edward: Talent Plus purported to ferret out those who did not comport with the organization's ideal characteristics . . . The premise was that characteristics don't change (after middle school). Either you are hardworking, or lazy. Either you are generous or miserly, etc. . . .

Law Corp would provide the baseline characteristics/traits of those it wanted; Talent Plus would create a system (a series of seemingly random questions) that help to distinguish those who share the sought-after characteristics from those who do not.

These efforts to seek out the most fitting employee comported with other ideological artifacts popular within Law Corp. A book administrators and senior faculty often recommended to new people was the strategic management best seller *Good to Great*. That work studied eleven examples of "great" companies and sought to deduce the key characteristics endemic to all. Number two on its list is "choosing the right people":

We expected that good-to-great leaders would begin by setting a new vision and strategy. We found instead that they first got the right people on the bus, the wrong people off the bus, and the right people in the right seats—and then they figured out where to drive it. The old adage "People are your most important asset" turns out to be wrong.[26]

This preoccupation with distinguishing between the "right" and "wrong" people pervaded much of organizational life at NDSL. Use of Talent Plus was but one conspicuous example of this broader effort.

Talent Plus first developed its questionnaire for clients using a bank of questions designed to test for particular psychological qualities. It then worked with the client organization to fine-tune these questions for particular local needs. An educational institution, for instance, might have greater interest in qualities of empathy, public leadership, and discipline. These questions were used for most hiring decisions throughout the Law Corp schools, and for faculty candidates—despite full recommendation through the faculty governance process—failure at this stage could be fatal. Some faculty resented this step being applied last in the hiring process at New Delta:

Edward: We questioned the whole process. How the baseline was determined. How Talent Plus's questions represented that baseline. What negative side effects . . . ? No real answers. Hostility, if anything.

The school president likened it to a lawnmower: "You can continue to hire the way we traditionally do it, or use this great tool to help. Look, I don't know how the lawnmower works mechanically, but I know that the lawn looks great after using it."

ISOs [Individual Strategic Objectives][27] were reputedly tied to continued use of Talent Plus, which was very expensive. [They] hired fourteen new profs one year and conducted over thirty-five Talent Plus interviews at approximately 1K [thousand] to 1.5K each.

RT: Geez, not cheap at all to mow the lawn. Do you recall what Law Corp's "ideal type" sounded like?

Edward: Good question. I don't. I do recall that Law Corp/Talent Plus selected a number of "ideal" employees and tested them in order to extract or
identify those qualities. Ironically, I believe Jesús was among those tested.

If it was so determinative, why was this step not applied first after the initial
short lists were created out of AALS? Earlier in the history of NDSL, this was
in fact the case. If so, then why change it to serve as a kind of administrative
override? Why have faculty spend so much time on candidate files only to have
certain ones removed at the last instance by an outside consultant? Would it
not be fairer to the candidate to give him or her this response before making the
trip out to Springdale? These concerns were articulated and sent up the chain
of command to Law Corp executives, but they were not directly addressed. Like
many things at the institution, this left a wide berth for speculation, leading
to one local theory that the corporation considered it cheaper to use faculty
time and energy vetting a psychometrically unhirable candidate than to psychometrically test all candidates before the faculty determined one-quarter of
them were worth hiring.

Separate from the hiring of new doctrinal law faculty through the AALS
national market, New Delta also carried out the unusual practice of continuing to hire from the local bar. Although this is common practice nationwide
for adjunct teaching in practical or specialized law courses—estate planning,
for example—it is unusual for the recruitment of permanent full-time faculty.
New Delta's penchant for doing this was mutually beneficial. For lawyers long
practicing out in the local community, law school "professor" would be a cov-
eted title to add to one's resumé because most in the legal profession and wider
communities do not understand critically how teaching assignments are made,
and they ascribe a level of legitimacy and erudition to this title. To the adjunct
teachers themselves, students unreflexively apply the title "professor" in regular
communications. To prevent confusion and maintain the prestige of permanent faculty, some law schools such as USC go so far as to forbid casual external
law teachers from using the titles "professor" or "adjunct professor." There, instructors must identify themselves as "lecturer in law"—although students still
refer to them as "professor" without hesitation.

At New Delta, casual instructors from the local community were indeed labeled "adjuncts," as "lecturer" became a conciliatory title reserved for academic
success counselors described later in this story. Uniquely, these instructors at
New Delta were often scheduled to teach core doctrinal courses, sometimes

including first-year curriculum: torts, property, contracts, and constitutional and criminal law.

Further unique to this setting, aspiring faculty from this reserve pool of ready teaching labor were occasionally hired on as full-time visiting or full-time permanent faculty. In general, this arrangement had the effect of what I term *upward casualization*.

Whereas regular labor casualization historically takes place "from above" with management or administrators deciding to hire contingent workers to save on fixed costs, upward casualization takes place in contexts where at least part of the workforce enjoys something like tenure or tenure eligibility. Unable to leverage extant workplace precarity to extract maximum value from this group, leadership may turn to employing a secondary group under conditions of precarity to conduct tasks previously assigned to the higher-paid secure laborers. By placing the new group in a position of precarity but offering the specter of upward mobility, management or administration is able to get it to do things that otherwise demand higher remuneration. Seeing part of their own work apportioned out to a lower-paid, lower-skilled cohort, the initial group with tenure or tenure eligibility may be pressured to work more or question fewer directives.[28]

This arrangement resembles but differs from the "split labor market" theory introduced by sociologist Edna Bonacich in the 1970s. There, Bonacich argued that ethnic antagonisms among labor resulted from management's use of ethnic minority newcomers as cheaper labor and undercutting of "white" labor's bargaining power in industrial conflicts.[29] For Bonacich, this structural arrangement incentivized formation of exclusionist movements and "caste" hierarchy among the working class in America. Upward casualization refers instead to the juxtaposition of two distinct labor groups with one holding something akin to security of position. Job security provisions for the one group prevent their forced attrition or reduction in wages, but the presence of a subordinate labor group appearing to encroach on the former's prestige encourages it to work more vigorously. The threat may not be an economic one, but it is a sociocultural one.

Workforce casualization has been a hallmark of neoliberalism. In higher education more specifically, the shift toward casual labor for teaching needs in most American universities has been the subject of vigorous discussion and debate. According to now widely cited statistics, 43 percent of U.S. university instructional staff in 1975–1976 were casual or "contingent" (for example, non–

tenure-track) workers. By 2011, this number had risen past 70 percent, so that full-time faculty with security of position make up roughly a quarter of all U.S. college and university teachers.[30] The detrimental impacts of this trend on higher learning in the United States have been the topic of substantial discussion elsewhere.[31]

For much of this period, law schools in the United States had been largely sheltered from the casualization of higher education labor. For decades, ABA Standard 402 had held that schools must maintain a student–faculty ratio of at least thirty-to-one and that anything greater than this created a "presumption" of inadequate full-time instruction.[32] This requirement was only recently removed by the Council of the Section of Legal Education and Admissions to the Bar—a move that was intended to foster differentiation in kinds and costs of instruction as advocated by high-profile reformists.[33]

Around the same time, the Standards Review Committee of the Section of Legal Education proposed alterations to Standard 405 on faculty professional environment. Whereas Standard 405 had been interpreted to require *tenure* for full-time doctrinal faculty, the proposed wording allowed for differentiation including "long-term contracts" as an adequate form of security of position.[34] The changes were meant to allow alternative teaching contracts to further promote reasonable differentiation—both in substance and in cost—within the law school market. One of the arguments for this arrangement was that it better democratized law teaching by allowing a wider variety of instructors face time with students. Yet there was strong reaction against this in several quarters. At Brooklyn Law School, for example, the faculty resolved that it

vigorously and unanimously opposes these proposed changes, on the grounds that they would: (1) Undermine the quality of legal education; (2) Undermine academic freedom in the legal academy; (3) Undermine faculty governance in the legal academy; and (4) Undermine the movement, long endorsed by Brooklyn Law School, to bring clinical law professors, legal writing professors, and library directors into full membership in the academy.[35]

There was also reason to suspect that any resulting cost savings from new, differentiated contractual arrangements, at least within the private equity for-profits like New Delta, would not be passed on to low-income and minority students without significant additional oversight on access to Title IV federal student loan moneys.

Although the proposed language failed to pass, NDSL began to capitalize on changing attitudes on Standards 402 and 405. At approximately this time, the school took measures to promote its academic success (study skills) counselors by extending to them the honorific title of "professor" and assigning them to teach substantive law courses—a move some felt used the new wording of Standard 402 without raising concerns among current and prospective students. Well before that, school administration effectuated casualization through the hiring of local nonscholar attorneys in their teaching stable. On at least some occasions, when tenured faculty were fired, their teaching loads and offices were filled by the unilateral hiring of visiting assistant professors, or "VAPs," from the casual adjunct pool. Under the New Delta handbook in this period, it is important to note, VAPs also had full voting rights. So, although at most institutions security of position was protected by *both* the tenure concept and faculty governance over the hiring of even visitors, at New Delta it was ultimately protected by neither.

If permeability between local adjunct teaching and full-time faculty was one factor in upward casualization, the presence of lawyering process faculty was a second. "Lawyering process," otherwise known as "LP," was a branch of law teaching in the Law Corp schools dedicated solely to the teaching of legal research and writing. Legal research and writing (LRW) is perhaps the most Manichaean of law school subject areas. It is immediately useful for practice. But students and instructors alike often dread it. The courses consist of instruction in access to and navigation of legal research tools; whereas formerly this entailed physical searches in the contents and indexes of court reporters, legal encyclopedias, treatises, law journals, and so forth, today it generally centers around on-line research using the proprietary databases Westlaw and Lexis-Nexis. These two services, owned by multinational corporations Thompson Reuters and Elsevier respectively, hold a practical monopoly over on-line legal information today. Both have developed refined search engines so that today's law student can simply enter search terms—without any special connecters or Boolean indicators as in years past—and generate a fairly efficient list of relevant information. The significance of all this is that, in the eyes of many, present day legal research training need not be as elaborate as it was in the days of print materials and library stacks.

Nevertheless, research forms only one component of the LRW classes. Its other feature is not "writing" in any common sense but rather a highly stylized, formulaic technical writing meant for clear, fast, and easy navigation by legal professionals higher up in the status hierarchy. In the case of legal *memo* writing—usually the genre taught in the first semester—the work product is intended to be written by law firm junior associates for entry in the client's file and with the purpose of instructing senior associates or partners on the issues and relevant authorities for any given case. The memo is intended to weigh both sides of a case and to evaluate the likelihood of victory if the dispute were to go to trial. Memo drafting is considered highly important yet somewhat menial work, and for this reason it is taught with a high degree of draconian scrutiny, revision, and repetition. Legal *brief* writing, the second skill usually taught in a follow-up semester of LRW, is not evaluative but rather persuasive. It is intended to instruct a sitting judge on the merits of one's own client's case and the weaknesses of the opponent's. For both the memo and the brief, the audience is a senior colleague traditionally owed great deference, and each is taught as a form of highly skilled supplication.[36] The second jarring thing about LRW for most students is that it is the only set of assessments and grades one receives for the initial four months of a law school career. Doctrinal classes, which are the vast majority of classes in the first year, are assessed by one single essay exam at the end of the term, and even final scores from those are not released until after the winter holiday vacation, in January or even February of the first year. Until that moment, first-year students, perhaps self-selected already for ambition and argumentative tendencies, still view themselves as bound for success. For this reason, poor scores in the early months of the first LRW course can lead to incredulity and hostility toward the writing instructor.

Perhaps partly due to this, many law schools do not use permanent in-house faculty as LRW instructors. On the contrary, many use adjunct teachers from the local bar for whom, as mentioned earlier, the privilege of calling themselves "professor" may be adequate compensation above the roughly $3,000 stipend they also get for their trouble each semester. Other law schools also understand the substantial value these teaching positions are worth to JDs not trained as academics—that is to say, lacking a PhD or other advanced credential—and hire cohorts of legal writing "fellows" to serve in the same capacity. Increasingly, given the scarcity of tenure-line jobs available, even JD/PhDs accept these positions for extended or consecutive periods. In many cases, then, the jobs are considered secondary to regular doctrinal law teaching, and they are staffed by casual teachers.

Law Corp schools were, in this regard, somewhat different than most. There, LRW instructors were hired as permanent faculty with one qualification: that their security of position was not protected by a system of tenure but rather one of progressively longer, presumptively renewable, contracts. A second qualification was that lawyering process material was drawn from a single common manual and used a website even for classroom instruction and exercises. It was, in short, a kind of "course in a box," a concept Law Corp purposefully developed in other ways discussed later in this book. Although their grading duties increased with the more frequent writing assessments expected in their field, their class sizes were mandatorily capped at twenty students each. For some of these reasons, LP professors were paid roughly 70 percent of what their doctrinal counterparts earned.

At a glance, the maintenance of a permanent LP faculty by Law Corp schools seems a great innovation. Legal research and writing, employers have reported, are the most important skills expected of new practicing attorneys.[37] It also made good on the conspicuous Law Corp mission pillar, "practice-ready training." For nontraditional second-career students especially, this practical approach was more sensible than the "liberal artsy" or policy emphasis of higher-ranked law programs. But this apparent commitment to student "value" had its limitations.

Notably, LP faculty had been vetted for the explicit role of teaching legal research and writing. Though some were hired from the AALS "meat market" described earlier, many others were hired from local communities. They were not, therefore, presumed to be on the same scholarly footing as those vetted through the hiring process for doctrinal teaching—these latter often brought publications, advanced degrees, or notable clerkship experience to that position. Despite this dichotomy in credentials, however, this division between doctrinal and LP professors was socially almost imperceptible. At faculty meetings, members of both groups commingled, sat together, spoke passionately, and voted. But, although doctrinal faculty paid little attention to the pay differential, LP faculty, I learned eventually, were acutely aware of it.

Partly as a result of this, LP faculty appeared to embrace Law Corp's opportunism regarding their position. These instructors were sometimes given opportunity to teach doctrinal courses, a move that would help them augment their teaching experience beyond the rote LRW subjects. What they did not publicly realize or object to was that Law Corp received the benefit of doctrinal student instruction at a cheaper rate than it otherwise would have. New Delta frequently considered LP faculty in its hiring searches for doctrinal faculty—even those targeting the AALS conference. Though it would seem counterintuitive to waste money on a national search when the school would consider and often hire internal, nationally uncompetitive candidates, there were two advantages to this. First, New Delta had already vetted these candidates through the Talent Plus psychometric evaluation. And second, this provided an incentive for existing LP teachers to support company policies in the hopes of one day being hired as "scholarly" law professors. During my fieldwork, four instructors were hired internally in this fashion prior to a large restructuring in teacher assignments and contracts, later known as Faculty 2.0 (see Chapter 4).

And so, although in part reflective of a commitment to "practice-ready training," the maintenance of a permanent in-house LP faculty corps maintained a second tier of faculty instructors, allowed this second group to be used in cost-saving ways, and signaled to noncooperative or dissenting law professors that they were readily replaced if a dispute with administration ever prevented them from performing value-generating services.

Student Recruitment

Although New Delta faculty were brought on board through a lengthy four-step process culminating in a psychometric evaluation by an off-site consulting agency, students were recruited at a comparatively low level of scrutiny. As at all ABA law schools, students were assessed based primarily on LSAT score and undergraduate grade point average (UGPA), but New Delta's minimum standards were lower than nearly 90 percent of all other schools. During the height of the law school "bubble" in 2011, amid the Great Recession, enrollments for the incoming NDSL first-year class were at a historic high. In that zenith year, the mean LSAT for the starting class was 150 whereas UGPA was roughly 3.0.[38] The total size of this group was nearly 450, although, as Chapter 4 describes, many of these students would transfer out within a year.

If the incoming indicators during peak enrollments were already low, pressures to satisfy equity investor return commitments, coupled with competition for fewer students, would drive them lower over the following years. Well before that drop, however, NDSL already had a program in place to enroll low-indicator students through an "alternative" admissions program, and it used ongoing orientation and academic success efforts to mitigate the risk that these students presented to themselves and to the profession.

The process often began shortly after the candidate took the LSAT. For some, this marked the first time a student heard about the school. A nontraditional student, June, explained this process to me. She was thirty-something with a young son and had been enrolled in law school elsewhere before. For personal and financial reasons, she was forced to drop out of her first law program and move back to her home state. There, she retook the LSAT and soon received the following correspondence:

Hi June,

I noticed that you live in Springdale and I thought you may be interested to know that a couple of seats just opened up for the Spring start here at New Delta School of Law. We are located downtown [sic] Springdale, on the corner of Bradley and Hampton Avenues. We are limiting the number of admits for this semester to keep the spring enrollment to around 50–60 students (compared to around 300 for next August). Orientation is January 15th and the first day of classes for the new students is January 19th.

Since you already have your bachelor's degree and LSAT, you could start at New Delta School of Law this January. Based on your 156 LSAT and 2.92 undergrad GPA, you may qualify for a Scholarship of $11,000 per year. I hope to see your application soon (the fee is waived through LSAC [the Law School Admissions Council]). Let me know if you are interested and I will send you a copy of the full-time schedule.

Jenny

P.S.: If you can't start this January, I can give you the direct link to our Fall application.[39]

June did enroll that January. And, as this letter illustrates, the spring term start was, along with part-time day and night programs, marketed as a great flexibility feature. Later, when administration mandated a move to trimester scheduling, this too was added to the marketing toolbox, offering students the option to finish in two years rather than three.[40]

Financial Aid as Sales Strategy

In recent years, for-profit colleges and universities have received significant attention for dubious recruitment and financing practices. Foremost among those has been the application of substantial pressure by financial aid officers.[41] I asked June and other students whether the school's financial aid officers applied any such pressure to them when the time came for filing and submitting requests for federal student loans. One student actually reported a woefully hands-off approach, saying that although no one pressured him, he wished someone had counseled him more about interest rates and borrowing the maximum amount. Like so many around the United States, this student said he would be paying these loans back for the rest of his life.

Other students described NDSL's financial aid officers with indifference or praise. Tomás, a first-generation (to both college and law school) Latino student, said the financial aid offering was one of the main attractions. I asked whether he experienced pressure in this regard:

> RT: Was there much selling on the part of admissions or financial aid to get you to come there?

> Tomás: Not much. In particular, I think it was more my desire to go to law school and not really ever thinking (or researching for that matter) the difference between law schools (I got into Thomas Jefferson and Whittier), and my first choice was University of San Diego (I was not admitted), plus not having anyone to tell me any different. I just went where I was offered the most fin[ancial] aid.

Emilia, a very bright forty-something Latina, also heard quickly from the school on taking the LSAT but described nothing untoward regarding the financial aid transaction:

> Emilia: From the moment my results were available, I began to receive emails from Jenny at NDSL. It was nice to know it was an option. . . . I knew that I at least could go there, and she was clear about the scholarship up front, and the amount actually went up the closer we got to summer.

> RT: And it sounds like they did not put any pressure to apply for federal loans in your case; is that correct?

> Emilia: I can't recall, but in reality I had completed my [FAFSA, or Free Application for Federal Student Aid] in February of that year already, and I also had submitted from Veterans Affairs [VA] assistance while in school. I was very proactive about financial aid . . . if anything, I was hounding them for an official statement. The VA rep[resentative] Bill at NDSL did remind me to apply for loans if I was not paying out of pocket. I don't feel it was pressure though.

Meanwhile, Melanie, the young Asian American mother quoted in the Introduction, did highlight a turning point in the law school's treatment of her:

Melanie: The admissions office seemed great in the beginning. They met with me during off hours because of my work schedule, and they really facilitated the entire application process. It felt like I was totally accepted to the club and that the paperwork was just a formality. Financial aid was great too. Bill really took the reins and walked me through everything—they were really accessible and helped me secure extra funding for day care, etc.

RT: You say "in the beginning"; what changed?

Melanie: After I was admitted, it felt like I had to track them down every time I needed something else. I mean, they were really helpful once I nailed someone down to talk to, but, when I was just an applicant, they seemed to pay more attention to me.

These observations, though based on a narrow sampling, suggest a possible distinction between the for-profit *law* school and other proprietary higher education contexts. Elsewhere, in the same period as this research, financial aid offices had been caught pushing new students to sign enrollment and loan documents using a variety of professional and personal psychological "pressure points."[42] In this case, students' own ambitions and belief in their own success—what others have called "optimism bias"—may have prompted them to incur tens of thousands in debt per year.[43]

"Scholarships" may have played a role in this process.[44] Offering undecided candidates several thousand dollars per year off the law school "sticker price" gave individuals a sense of a priori achievement and boosted their confidence in their ability to succeed in law school in general and NDSL in particular. For many, this confidence neglected an important feature of the law school assessment process. As Lawrence, a traditional white male student explained it,

As you know, the "C Curve" at our school placed the majority of students below a 3.0. Statistically speaking, only a certain amount of students could earn a 3.0 or above.

As this relates to the school and its appeal, the merit scholarship was a real trap for people. Because when the school offers to pay about half the tuition, you want to go to that law school. But, as a student, when you are subject to that curve, the 3.0 is much more difficult to maintain [compared to B-curve schools].

So, it is my belief the school offered these scholarships knowing: (1) it was an allure for students, and (2) those students wouldn't have the scholarships for long because of the imposed curve.

As Lawrence says, one could enter with an undergraduate B average and perform at the average level for his or her cohort and still, thanks to a forced curve, achieve mostly C grades. Worse still, performance at the C level for most NDSL students meant loss of these treasured "scholarships" and payment of the full tuition price in year two, necessitating increased debt financing. And, as students knew, full price was drastically more than in-state tuition at the much higher-ranked Big State School of Law. But the admissions strategy to offer discounted pricing up front worked because it played on individual optimism bias and often paid back when midrange students achieved C level grades, lost scholarships, and—unable to transfer elsewhere—were tied down as Title IV income streams for two additional years.

Orientations

Orientations play an important role in the transition from institutional non-membership to membership. As at any new academic institution, new students at New Delta were scheduled for a variety of orientation events and meetings. In most circumstances these sessions serve the function of providing usable practical information as well as acculturation to the new organization. Although the former function can be critical to the short-term efficiency of the institution, the latter may be more significant for its long-term survival and sustainability. In the fall of 2011, New Delta leadership chose, in time for the first expiry on initial equity investor capital commitments, to both move the school's location and dramatically increase it class size. From its campus, miles outside Springdale's city center, it signed a lease and moved to a high-rise in the city's bustling downtown. From a total student body of roughly 340 students in 2008, it grew to roughly 1,000 by 2011. And, to accommodate these new students, it hired new batches of entry-level faculty.

With so many changes entailing such rapid growth in human resources and clientele, it was conceivable that the school leaders would fear losing local identity or the highly stylized Law Corp–managed cultural core. Worse still, it would have been very possible that the influx of 450 new students in 2011, dramatically increasing the school's population, might alter levels of professionalism or diversity that Law Corp had sought to develop.

But there was, at least formally, a standardization process. Most students at New Delta went through a one-week new student orientation. Prior to the curriculum overhaul described in Chapter 4, this period occurred before the start of the first semester. It required students to complete homework and attend a pair of mock law classes to simulate the challenges of law school's infamous first year. Students learned the basics of case briefing and the IRAC writing method.[45] Orientation also introduced students to basic note taking and outlining, as well as the NDSL "culture."

In addition to this crash course in law study, students received instruction on professionalism. Presenters spoke on law school decorum and dress code. Of particular importance during this session was the topic of social media, with students advised to watch carefully their postings to Facebook or Twitter out of concern for how these might come back to hurt them when searching for jobs in the community. But because many of the NDSL incoming students were nontraditional recruits (such as paralegals or legal assistants) from the area, much of this was familiar to them. Administration also spoke about its successes in producing student outcomes. Finally, new students attended a welcome reception held on the top floor of the new downtown campus in a generic "lounge" area overlooking the entire city.

Students invited to the NDSL "orientation" were generally from three admissions categories. On receipt, all applications were sorted into four groups: "automatic admits," "discretionary admits," "discretionary denials," and "denials." In the first category were all those students whose formulaically combined LSAT and UGPA scores hovered near or exceeded the seventy-fifth percentile for the school. In the second were all those students below the seventy-fifth percentile. In this category were those students whose admission required faculty approval. Such approval was based on one of two things. In the higher quartile were those applications that were read (in theory) by a faculty committee comprising permanent faculty and staff. In the lower quartile were those applications deemed admissible on completion of an auxiliary preorientation mini law school course costing several hundred dollars at one time and later offered free of charge.

This program, known as AAMPLE, or Alternative Admissions Model Program for Legal Education, permitted select students to work around their low indicators by completing two sample law school summer courses. At the time of this research it was offered in standardized form at twenty-two law schools nationwide, with programs like NDSL drawing an increasing percentage of their students from this group of second-chancers. In theory, it operated on the belief that a subset of inadmissible law school applicants with poor LSAT scores might still succeed at the law school tasks of issue spotting and legal reasoning. Starting with an 11 percent acceptance rate through AAMPLE in 2005, NDSL progressed to admitting 33 percent of such students in 2008, and 80 percent by spring 2011. If successful in the AAMPLE program, students were admitted into the JD program and invited for new student orientation.

AAMPLE was one of the key tools in the New Delta "diversity" toolbox. It consisted of a separate, two-course session covering criminal procedure and negotiable instruments offered on-line through a web-based learning platform. It then used essay-style law school assessments. This in turn permitted the school to admit candidates predicted to fail while promising them the tools needed to avoid failure.

Out in the law school admissions discussion boards, talk of the AAMPLE programs around the U.S. was mixed. In July 2008, Top-Law-Schools.com user RonSantosRules wrote:

A.) Pay money to take two law school courses, study for 60–80 hours per week in an accelerated program . . . with the possibility of NOT being admitted to the school anyways (depends on the school with the success rate) and also NOT earn credit for the completed classes?

or

B.) Retake the LSAT, increase score, get into law school without forking over hard earned $ for classes that won't count anyway and maybe even get schools to give you money with a scholarship.

Seems like a no brainer to me.[46]

Then in April 2009, user Booya wrote,

Do not do it, retake the lsat, and spend the money on prep courses instead and go to a school without Aample! Avoid the tier 4 schools, they [sic] rip-off scams![47]

And in June 2009, user BkGirl22 wrote,

For anyone accepted via AAMPLE you should give it a try. I was admitted to a NY law school via AAMPLE and am in the top 10% of my class after my first year and I had only scored a 149 on the LSAT. For those who are not great at these sort of exams (SAT, LSAT) do not give up. Hard work pays off.[48]

With a large price tag (for most of its usage) and no guarantees of admission, this program played a potentially problematic role in the school's admissions system and federal loan program eligibility. Still, there were some success stories. In some cases, students predicted to otherwise fail out were admitted under AAMPLE, tutored by Academic Success Center instructors, and then graduated with GPAs well above 3.0. Though still exceptional, such cases were presented by the school as evidence of global success with the alternative admissions process. Similarly, several AAMPLE students passed the bar exam on their first try, and this too was widely advertised by administration on compilation of all passage data. Nevertheless, despite exceptional stories, some have noted AAMPLE students by and large had lower success rates both in law school and on the bar.[49] If true, this illustrates the larger problem of hegemony in this environment. As with the Law Corp schools in general, there are occasional success stories, and the question became how to make those speak for the majority of students passing through the program.

Innovating Self-Defeat

Both students and faculty were met on arrival to New Delta with a stunning variety of technological and practical teaching and learning devices, generally exceeding that found at most law schools and, certainly, in most higher education. The school referred to this element of its institutional identity as "innovation." This term, borrowed from the worlds of business and high technology, was already a buzzword in consulting circles. But, inside New Delta, it also served as an important infrastructural and marketing tool.

The school hosted the latest instructional technology. Each classroom was equipped with a computer terminal connecting an audiovisual projector, Blu-ray player, high-grade sound system, document camera, and, in large classrooms, a network of microphones so students could speak audibly in large spaces. Often the instructor would herself use a handheld or lavalier microphone amplified through this system. Several faculty used real or virtual "clickers," a technology that allowed students in a classroom to buzz in or vote on particular answer choices in real time. Many classrooms had videoconferencing technology, and most had video cameras and overhead microphones poised to record a course lecture either at the request of an instructor aiming to post his or her session on-line, or, as a few faculty speculated, to satisfy the curiosity of upper-level administration or corporation executives. Altogether, these classroom technol-

ogies appeared impressive and, compared to the more static permanent infrastructure of traditional school environments (such as library stacks and journal
subscriptions), they were relatively affordable.[50]

Law Corp ensured that each of its schools had top technological infrastructure, but it also created incentives for professors to develop "innovative"
teaching devices. In one example, the corporation offered bonus stipends for
developing what they termed a "Lesson in a Box." This was literally a teaching
module and script that one faculty member would develop for easy transfer-
ability to other instructors, other courses, and other schools in the Law Corp
consortium and beyond. Ostensibly, it was a "work for hire" and would become
part of the corporation's intellectual property. Most importantly, it would likely
prove useful if the company successfully lobbied the ABA to permit full on-line
JD programs to operate.

In the meantime, Law Corp executives had already spun off a new entity I
will label Law Corp Futures (LCF). Around the spring of 2013, Law Corp hired a
former top 50 law school dean to join its leadership in developing a new "initiative." LCF, this new initiative, would select "star" professors around the country
to offer certain law courses on-line to students of various schools around the
country. These courses could be taken as external credits applied to the student's law degree while requiring that the student pay enrollment fees at the
home institution. For a portion of this fee, albeit one much smaller than the
per-student cost of offering an on-ground summer class at ABA law schools,
LCF would contract with the home institution to offer the course as part of their
catalogue. After introduction of LCF offerings in the summer of 2014, the ABA
"liberalized" its Standard 306 on distance education, leading LCF to expand its
offerings to law schools the following year.

When introduced to NDSL faculty in a meeting in 2013, reactions to this
new subsidiary enterprise were not good. Following a presentation by the newly
hired director of this initiative, faculty raised the issues in a subsequent meeting. Why, some asked, was Law Corp, an entity that questioned institutional
prestige and hierarchy, developing LCF using "star" ABA law professors and
none of its own faculty? And wouldn't this simply lead to the replacement of
Law Corp faculty in sessions for which LCF credits were available to students?
These questions led to more than one tense confrontation between NDSL
faculty and leadership and would never be resolved before NDSL itself began

including LCF courses in its summer scheduling—in short, outsourcing part of its summer teaching load to its parent company.

But, well before this systemwide development, New Delta faculty were participants in their own precarity. At the other consortium schools, professors, it was said, appeared traditional in their approaches and more resistant to change. At New Delta, with its exceptionally young and racially diverse faculty population, change—particularly in pedagogical approach—was welcomed and often fetishized.[51] Instructional technology served this role as a speciously depoliticized inclusionary threshold factor in delivering the corporate mission.[52] For this reason, foresight on matters of "innovation," such as course information delivery or entire curriculum redesign, carried a low level of scrutiny and high degree of optimism. For example, young contracts and professional responsibility professors obtained an external grant to team up with students and software developers in the creation of an on-line virtual law office simulation game. In another example, a popular faculty member at New Delta who discovered the new on-line teaching method of Salman Khan and his revolutionary Khan Academy videos, decided to bring the "flipped classroom" technique to his colleagues at the school.[53] So popular was this new device at New Delta that Law Corp invited this instructor to present his discovery to the "sister" schools in its portfolio. The company's pleasure was understandable. But, given its contribution to the devaluation of its labor, the faculty's own enthusiasm was less so.

Much like the so-called lesson in a box, devices like the law office simulation game and "flipping the classroom"—fetishized as "innovation" by Law Corp schools—contributed to precarity in two ways. First, they helped reduce the classroom experience from one of "knowledge" development to one of information transfer. Second, they made human involvement in this process a matter of questionable importance. Many did not view it this way. For them this was a fresh departure from what is often described as a "hide the ball" approach in traditional Socratic law teaching. Innovation seemed simply a fulfillment of Law Corp's own corporate mission to "reinvent the future of legal education in the 21st century."

Faculty shared these devices in weekly meetings known as "best practices" sessions.[54] A professor would be selected to instruct his or her peers on the latest new technique he or she was using in the classroom ranging from technological applications such as PowerPoint or Prezi to classroom activities such as simulated negotiations or therapeutic attorney counseling. Other sessions might cover topics such as "How to Design Your Midterm"—a unique subject because most law schools at the time omitted any kind of interim formative assessment—or "Public Performance Rights on Video Materials"—also unique because a "fair use" privilege normally applying to higher education is void in for-profit institutions.[55]

Conclusion

New Delta School of Law's policies and practices for recruiting and retaining faculty and students created an environment of managed precarity—a condition of felt insecurity helping to create organizational coherence in institutions or businesses of moral instability. Whereas students and faculty were already engaged in contractual relations with the law school—the terms of which should have been readily identifiable and dischargeable—managed precarity added to these contractual relations another normative dimension playing on feelings of expendability, replaceability, and academic or financial attrition. These fears were in large part a function of increased "access."

Although many faculty recruited to teach at NDSL went through the national AALS hiring process, many did not. By maintaining instructor human resources of both kinds, the school preserved local feelings of teacher fungibility.[56] And although perhaps not created for this purpose, the presence of a full-time lawyering process faculty paid at lower rates (during much of this research) and periodically recruited over to the doctrinal faculty also served to create a climate of replaceability. Despite the formal presence of doctrinal faculty tenure, these contributed to job insecurity as a kind of casualization from below, or upward casualization.

For students, the mandatory grading curve and alternative admissions process had similar impacts. With many students offered generous financial aid to sign up for their first year, the school could count on making back its money in subsequent years when many of those students had fallen below the GPA minimums by virtue of a forced C curve. This reality likely played a role in the school's anxious institutional response to transfer attrition described in the following chapters. Besides this general source of precarity applied to all students equally, NDSL and other low-ranking law schools also used the AAMPLE alternative admissions program, which, although framed as a mechanism for admitting promising students excluded by rigid score index requirements, was viewed by some as a way of gaining access to more federal loan moneys while

appearing to measure potential success by other means. Not primarily concerned with testing the efficacy of AAMPLE, this chapter has viewed it as one
source for the ethnographically observable precarity described here.

In addition to simply owning and making available classroom instructional
technology and on-line teaching "tools," New Delta leadership promoted use
of these through weekly "best practices" sessions aimed at influencing teacher
choices toward greater use of media and communication technologies. Resisted
by some, these devices were embraced by many, making classroom instruction
less contingent on human instructorship. With the advent of Law Corp Futures
as a new branch of Law Corp designed to offer outsourced on-line pedagogy to
law schools broadly under new ABA rules permitting distance education, some
among New Delta students and faculty alike began to question where all this
was heading.

Chapter 2

"Charter Review"

Policy as Culture and Ideology

"**W**HAT do you think of when I use the word *culture*? I'm afraid you think it's code for something else."

One spring morning, to the surprise of those present, the dean raised this query in a small meeting with faculty committee leaders. Seated around a closed circle of tables in a room overlooking the city, the group hesitated. Finally, someone responded that culture is a "living thing," constantly changing to cope with its environment. Another said that culture has no "inside"—that it means what members of a community say it does around the "water cooler" or in the "faculty lounge—if we had one." But a third was most suggestive: "Every time I hear that word here I get nervous," she said. "Like, if I can't fall in line, I should start looking for another job." At New Delta School of Law, she seemed to suggest, "culture" was a gloss for something far more normative than shared symbols or practices.

Early on, anthropology asserted considerable authority in defining the culture concept.[1] The neighboring disciplines of sociology, history, politics, linguistics, and philosophy all laid claims in the decades since, but, beginning in the 1970s, cultural studies organized writers across these fields to denounce disciplinary limitations and biases in efforts to study such a transcendent concept. They highlighted ways in which anthropology had objectified native communities in the effort to isolate human culture in its putatively "savage" states and in turn facilitated the "civilizing mission" of European colonization. But even as overt colonialism retreated from Asia and Africa, anthropology continued to document and analyze cultures of geopolitically significant people amid the Cold War proxy wars, and foreign policy experts used area studies to classify and control behavior among subaltern peoples.[2] For critics at the end of the twentieth century, this all raised an important question: Was *culture* a legitimating term for the constellation of symbols and practices of any one community, or

was it a disciplinary instrument to establish behavioral averages, deter noncon-
formity, and control populations?

The emergence of "corporate culture" in the 1980s suggested an even more
complicated life for the concept. There, culture could mean both legitimation
and discipline in the context of financial and industrial organizations. Beyond
the descriptive "organizational culture" that referred to symbols and practices
of collective enterprise, *corporate* culture captured the managerial effect of defining and propagating a set of distinct company values. Distinct values, the following decades demonstrated, became crucial for corporate success in a global
market with increasing redundancy among ever more commodities.

After the financial bubble and market collapse of the late 2000s, some began
to see corporate culture as serving a different, more instrumental function.[3] As
Leonidas Donskis has written, "An instrumentalist approach to culture immediately betrays either technocratic disdain for the world of arts and letters or
poorly concealed hostility to human worth and liberty."[4] Banking firms originating subprime housing debt and selling it off to third-party buyers told their un-
derwriters that they were expanding access to housing for low-income families
and racial minorities.[5] Private creditors offering loans to low-income students
entering poor-performing for-profit colleges viewed their practice as expanding
access to education and the American Dream.[6] Corporate culture in these examples cloaked predatory business models in a veneer of social consciousness
and framed everyday company actors as caregivers to the uncared for.

At New Delta, talk of "culture" appeared frequently. In one context, faculty
described turf wars over scholarly research evident in other academic institutions and then described a more collegial environment among professors
at their own school. Intense scholarly competition, they would say, "is not in
keeping with our culture." In another context, personnel were subject to a formal peer evaluation in which groups of roughly five faculty and staff graded
one another through a lengthy evaluation form originally developed by school
founders. Administrators, all were told, then used final evaluation scores to determine promotions or merit pay increases. One poor evaluation could harm
an employee's chances for retention or advancement. On occasion, employees
offended by one another "retaliated" using this formal device and its consequences. Although this occurred infrequently, substantial gossip and innuendo
reverberated around the evaluation process as a result. Each of Law Corp's
schools partook in this annual ritual and, whether or not it was calculated to do

so, it generated a climate of suspicion and doubt even as Law Corp suggested it was meant as a tool for "continuous improvement." Faculty critical of this evaluative process and blowback were known to say, "We should change this . . . It's just not in keeping with our culture."

From these observations it might appear the school was host to organic and democratic conceptions of the word expressed in the first and second speakers at the beginning of this chapter: "culture is a living thing" and "culture belongs to everyone." However, by far the most significant deployment came in the third sense, one I will call *policy as culture*. In this chapter, I detail how Law Corp sought to cast corporate and institutional policies as part of a transcendent culture to secure the former as a kind of ideology, reconciling tensions in the company's moral posture. Through structured repetition and reflection, faculty and staff were encouraged to embrace "the culture" rather than dwell on their underlying business model—one that generated millions of dollars annually in subprime student debt and transformed those millions into off-site investor returns.[7]

In this sense, ideology is a taken-for-granted worldview that elides conflict and contradiction, often to the detriment of the individuals harboring it. Although traditionally it was the means by which actors were motivated to work against their own discrete interests or against the interests of their social class, some now suggest it is increasingly a justification for individual work against the very idea of "social" interests. Marx and Engels's early writings introduce the primary sense of ideology as false consciousness. In *The German Ideology*, they famously wrote, "The ideas of the ruling class are in every epoch the ruling ideas. . . . The class which has the means of material production at its disposal, has control at the same time over the means of mental production."[8] Whereas their concept flows from a materialist view of history in an era of industrial economic production, ideology in the for-profit law context would appear to reconcile a different tension: support for an educational model premised on high at-risk student indebtedness justified ultimately by rhetorical claims to serve social justice. The success of ideology in this environment draws equally from Weber's notion of ideology as *rationalization*—a fragmentation of the observable world through faithful application of religion, science, and bureaucracy.[9] As outlined in the following discussion and in other chapters, Law Corp deployed countless bureaucratic and quasi-scientific techniques to assure itself and its employees that they were serving educational and social purposes.

Finally, this discussion draws from Lukacs's update to Marx and Engels on the totalizing potential of ideology far beyond the economic life of individuals. For Lukacs, ideological formations have potential to structure all aspects of social interaction.[10] As indicated in the following pages, this capacity was important in ascribing meaning to the work of professors and staff, and it drove the corporation's effort to insinuate itself into the psychic lives of educators. New Delta's constant framing of its institutional policy as culture sought to secure the former as ideology in each of the senses just discussed.

The remainder of this chapter examines this framing in three separate sections. Describing what I term *mission culture*, the first section shows how Law Corp's clearly articulated charter and mission pillars served a pedagogical function in public gatherings and in visual artifacts placed around the school's interior space. Following discussions of the mission pillars, that section then explores faculty uptake of mission culture through a specific practice known as "charter review." The second section then explores *management culture*, a means by which New Delta pursued its mission through management techniques borrowing from popular psychology, psychometrics, and Fortune 500 business strategy. The first subsection there examines "emotional intelligence" testing and training, whereas the second looks closely at "continuous improvement"—a management mantra that stressed ongoing surveillance and auditing. Ultimately, goals pursued *in fact* through these techniques differed from the objectives articulated on paper in the charter. Finally, the third section outlines development of policy as culture in the paradoxical form of *counterculture*. I use that phrase in its popular sense of "culture against," but I also suggest administration not only tolerated formal rebelliousness from faculty, it appropriated this to soften the experience of for-profit corporate policy. Together these sections support a claim that the unique top-down law school culture of NDSL functioned to hold back community reflection on the moral hazard of for-profit legal education.

Mission Culture: The "Kool-Aid"

When the third speaker in this chapter's opening paragraphs talked bravely of pressure to conform, she was not without support from colleagues. As others described to me behind closed doors, New Delta faculty and staff felt pressured to not only conform but also to invest themselves at deeper emotional levels. As one professor told me, this expectation emanated from the highest ranks:

Well, every few years the CEO makes an appearance at the beginning of faculty orientation, no doubt to touch base and remind us that the mother ship still exists. I can only speak from my interpretation, but it could [be] his way of trying to connect with us . . . showing that he's a human being underneath the title. The faculty members who already *drank the Kool-Aid* were in awe: "OMG, how wonderful." What is completely inappropriate is that this is a public forum to employees by the boss. As such, the undercurrent is that as a good employee you must comply and drink the Kool-Aid too. And the CEO has publicly stated that he learned all this from some psychologist/family therapy guy who he hired to help his troubled son. I can appreciate that this may have helped you or your family, but what place does it have in the business world? I've heard from a colleague that there have been even worse presentations at the home office, where sexual abuse is discussed in graphic detail. Just not appropriate, and you have the pressure that you must join the collective to be a good employee.[11]

As many will recognize, "drinking the Kool-Aid" refers to the 1978 mass suicide by more than 900 members of the People's Temple cult at Jonestown, Guyana. There, an entire village of American expatriates believed cult leader Jim Jones's message that he and his people had been chosen for salvation, that the public and law enforcement in both the United States and Guyana were out to destroy them, and that they could escape this fate by taking their own lives. They did so by drinking a cyanide-laced drink—not in fact Kool-Aid, but a similar drink mix—on November 18, 1978. This remained the largest single loss of American civilians until the events of September 11, 2001.[12]

Alongside its popular meaning of everyday social conformity, "drinking the Kool-Aid" represents a larger political oblivion. It signifies the act of surrendering critical thought in the name of Utopia and a willingness to step into the unknown when a leader gives the order to. In this regard, it captures a goal immanent in all policy: the surrendering of certain individual agency and the commitment of compliance until the policy has been changed. But, in an environment like Law Corp's, problems emerge when two or more policies coexist and conflict.

The Charter

Every employee learned sooner or later that the company was a for-profit institution. This designation alone set a tone that was ever present. Even as school administrators argued that the designation was losing distinctive meaning in the context of higher education commercialization, the economic recession and fiscal austerity characterizing this period seemed to often force the for-profit mission back to the table.[13] On more than one occasion, for instance, faculty were diverted from teaching preparation and research tasks to attend extensive meetings to "brainstorm" solutions for waning applications, marketing outreach, and trickling revenue from private sources.

But as employees were forced to consider and address fiscal shortfalls, they were also encouraged to pay nearly constant attention to the Law Corp "charter." This document was a visual and textual representation of the avowed values of Law Corp and its schools. It featured a Greek classical-style temple with foundation, pedestal, three columns, and triangular pediment sitting atop these. The columns of the structure stood for "mission pillars" and were repeated discursively more often than any other stated values. Summarizing the charter in a section entitled "Our Mission," Law Corp's website read,

[Our] mission is to "establish the benchmark of inclusive excellence in professional education for the 21st Century." This mission is grounded in three pillars that include serving the underserved, providing a student-outcome centered education, and graduating students who are practice-ready. Achievement of our mission is a function of outcome excellence, process strength, innovation, humility-based leadership, and a culture centered upon personal authenticity, accountability, and commitment to results and the greater good.[14]

Artifacts found around the NDSL building reiterated these corporate values. In hallways connecting faculty offices, administration had installed large glass and steel wall posters listing virtues such as "Humility-Based Leadership" or "Accountability," illustrated with motivational images of mountain climbers on a cliff or goldfish in a bowl. Soon after hiring, new faculty were given Law Corp "tipcards"—a form of inverted rolodex with hard plastic pages repeating the values inscribed in the charter. Although Law Corp leaders intended that these cards sit prominently on all faculty desks—and many did—a number of professors left them in a drawer, unopened, with no intention to display them in their office spaces.

Law Corp considered service toward the three mission pillars essential in faculty evaluation, promotion, and tenure. Even skeptical professors had to reckon with them as they navigated bureaucratic techniques of the organization. Filing for promotion from assistant to associate professor required, as elsewhere, a lengthy compilation of documents and narratives showing prowess in teaching, service, and scholarship—though the latter was construed more loosely than at other institutions. Not only did this require formulating a narrative and offering supporting evidence, but it also required faculty to describe explicitly how they had supported the pillars.

Practice-Ready Training   Attention to practical skills was part of a larger historic shift in legal education during New Delta's infancy. Although law was still a relatively young "academic" discipline, writers had criticized its lack of practical legal training since at least the mid-1950s.[15] Much more recently, the 2007 "Carnegie Report" had issued findings on a one-year field study of sixteen law schools, noting that although practical training had improved since the 1950s, it still had not advanced quickly or widely enough.[16]

In its first pillar, the New Delta Charter called for "practice-ready training." But for faculty and administration, "practice-ready" meant more than just practical training; it meant that courses should prepare students to open their *own* law office on admission to the bar. This assumed, correctly, that many if not most graduates would choose or be obliged to enter solo practice. Several things about this were significant. First, solo practice work traditionally carried a degree of stigma in the legal profession. Though it earned some respect due to the entrepreneurial courage of "hanging up a shingle," solo practice was widely considered an avenue for those who could not obtain "jobs" on graduation or who could not survive in the competitive environment of midsized to large firm offices.[17] Although it bothered some students that their futures would be limited on graduation, to their great credit many simply did not care because they wanted to work in social justice or in their own communities. A second significant feature of this was resilience to certain shifts in the employment market during the economic crisis of the late 2000s. In that time, as others have explained well, the legal job market contracted, upending the traditional distribution of expertise.[18] With large firms hiring and training fewer new untested graduates, practical training in tasks such as motion filing, document drafting, and client intake had to be learned *prior to* rather than following bar admission. Because of this, during the Great Recession, Law Corp could report to its investors that its schools were partially insulated by its own practice-ready mission.

Already from its inception NDSL publicized this quality as a distinguishing feature in the market. Although ranked in the "fourth tier" of ABA law programs, it viewed one of its main competitors to be a first-tier school within the same metropolitan area.[19] The ranking difference already allowed the school to cast itself as a more accessible, antielitist institution; but it further sought to distinguish itself on strength in training future practitioners. Similarly, other fourth-tier schools outside the area were also seen as a threat, though it was not clear that many students choosing between similarly situated schools at this level would leave their geographic comfort zone anyway. Nevertheless, New Delta sought to distinguish itself from its local and regional school competitors by promoting its practice-ready mission. And, once enrolled, many students framed their choice to matriculate in terms of this distinction.

Instructors pursued practical readiness through increased technical training in the classroom. Academic Affairs required faculty to include one or more "practice-ready exercises" in their course syllabi and scheduled biweekly "best practices" training sessions in lieu of scholarly symposia or brown bag lectures on faculty research. In addition to the technological innovations described in Chapter 1, these focused heavily on implementation of practical exercises. In these sessions and beyond, professors exchanged classroom teaching ideas, including motion drafting and group exercises. As intended, these initially succeeded in distinguishing the school from others—especially higher-ranked "policy schools," where students rarely engaged in writing or assessment prior to the final exam. That ubiquitous arrangement, critics pointed out, placed *summative* ahead of *formative* assessment.[20] At New Delta, however, founding faculty decided early on that students should have more formative assessments as a matter of pedagogical opportunity and educational fairness. With this requirement, students could learn from mistakes and seek advisement. For the 1L students, this came in the form of mandatory midterm exams—a great departure from the sink-or-swim final examination of higher-ranked and traditional schools. For faculty, midterms meant considerably more exam development and grading responsibilities and less research and writing time. Yet, under New Delta's no-frills business model, this represented added value rather than a demerit.

Though many faculty supported the placement of student training above research, some resented this seemingly calculated decision to undermine their scholarly relevance in wider academic communities. Sensing this resentment, one Law Corp executive visiting a faculty meeting stated without irony how many critics the company had accumulated in the national academic community and how important it was to simply ignore them by only "seek[ing] validation among ourselves."

But faculty were not the only ones who questioned the "added value" of practice-ready training in its local implementation. Students often approached writing and group work expectations with skepticism or, worse, hostility. If for 1Ls midterms, written exercises, and group work were expected of all students, and if all 1Ls were required as at other schools to take four to five courses per semester, then the expectation to work on projects could produce significant added stress. Worse than this, many students viewed these "innovative" assignments as repetitive busy work.

They also disdained group exercises for another especially important reason somewhat telling of this environment. In small group work, students explained, one or two leaders often emerged to take charge of a project—drafting a contract for example. The remaining students, it was said, did little or no work. Leading students often discouraged contribution from their peers, perceiving them to be weaker thinkers. In many cases, the latter were the same low-income and minority students that Law Corp had distinguished its business model by including.

This resentment may certainly have been present at other law schools as well. But most unique here was its encounter with the greater diversity built into the school's stated mission. New Delta's low admissions selectivity—the very feature that allowed it to bring in more minority and lower-income students— produced 1L classrooms that were exceedingly wide ranging in intellectual ability, background experience, and work ethic.[21] Students raised in dual-attorney households sat beside first-generation high school and college graduates— itself alone an admirable feature. But, unlike higher-ranked programs where the abilities of these disparate individuals could be reasonably assured as uniform by strict selection standards, New Delta's unique combination of geographic and socioeconomic markets did not produce great uniformity among incoming students. Prior to the complete overhaul of the first-year curriculum described in Chapter 4, this problem was often passively alleviated by transfer attrition in the second year. For this reason, the very students who would later transfer as 2Ls harbored considerable resentment at being compelled into group work as 1Ls.

For those who remained past the first year, practice-ready training continued in the opportunities to work in the clinics and in the requirement to take a course in "General Practice Skills" as 3Ls. Clinics had been an important aspect of legal education since the mid-twentieth century and offered law students hands-on experience in specialized practice areas. NDSL's clinics served marginalized populations and were housed within its main building and one off-site location. Nevertheless, many viewed these clinics as low priority and underfunded. After several years without clinical leadership, New Delta hired a new clinic director to organize and expand existing services during the period of this study. Within months of her arrival, operating budgets were cut and support staff let go, and these gaps remained unfilled throughout this fieldwork. The new director requested greater resources and faculty support, but within two more years she stepped aside and the clinics were placed under the leadership of a doctrinal faculty member.

Beyond clinics, students were required to attend a special course entitled "General Practice Skills" or GPS. The course was designed to expose students to the "realities of practice in a small law firm," reflecting the way the school envisioned small firm practice as the most likely future for its graduates. In most cases, one in-house "faculty" member—a term applied with increasing looseness to a variety of instructional staff—led the course and coordinated a series of "guest speakers" in the form of practicing attorneys in the community. Students expressed anecdotally a lack of rigor and organization and felt dissatisfied by such a large requirement in what was to be their otherwise breezy final year. Some also resented being taught by practitioners rather than professors. As Keshia, the African American woman quoted in the Introduction, told me: "You cannot staff your law school with community lawyers. You need a stable group of professors who want to be professors, not do this on the side."

NDSL's emphasis on "practice-ready" training was a deliberate reaction to the traditional "educated citizenship" model to which most policy schools had aspired. It reflected a growing undercurrent among legal education reformers— like those who drafted the Carnegie Report—who felt faculty had been abrogating a responsibility to train practicing lawyers. And it promised to give students something tangible for their relatively high tuition costs.

But it also had two understated consequences that would come back to haunt New Delta following its first ABA accreditation. First, by endorsing the "practice-ready" emphasis, school faculty had tacitly accepted a mission somewhat at odds with scholarly research and their own career advancement. By promoting practice readiness over policy reflection, the institution, in what many felt was a calculated effort, marginalized traditional scholarship at a time when most would say its young faculty needed it most for career security and longevity.[22]

Second, it went generally unmentioned that "practice ready" and "bar ready" were entirely separate things and that there would be no future opportunity to practice law for students who failed to pass their state bar exam. In the early postfoundation years, when New Delta professors had relied most on traditional teaching methods and facilities, the school's bar passage rate was extremely high, often surpassing all others in the jurisdiction. After winning ABA accreditation, however, New Delta had rigorously implemented practice-ready training in every 1L class; after the school expanded and relocated to a more elaborate law firm–like facility, bar passage rates fell considerably. From their peak in 2008 to the time of this study, those rates fell from approximately 90 to approximately 50 percent. In the subsequent year it fell even lower to hover near 30 percent.

Student Outcome–Centered Learning   The second pillar inscribed in the charter called for a "student-centered learning experience." This too was a reformist choice made at the inception of NDSL. Creators felt that law programs in general had been built around faculty. Traditionally faculty delivered the key services, attracted publicity, and bolstered institutional legitimacy in national, regional, or professional communities. Administrations were sometimes cast as logistical support to this central component, and students seemed to occupy a third rung as they passed through the institution on a three-year cycle.

So, whereas at the old NDSL campus faculty offices were ensconced in a separate building apart from students, at the new building these offices lined the outer corridors of three floors with classrooms and conference rooms interspersed among them. Students could thus meander past faculty offices between classes, and in some cases they took this opportunity *during* classes when office hours of one professor coincided with the teaching of another. Faculty office doors were composite wood bordered by a twelve-inch wide, floor-to-ceiling glass pane, and curtain or shade coverings were expressly forbidden. This, it was hoped, would prevent professors from "hiding out" from students. In still another example, one human resources staffer describing the location of "employee" mailboxes to a new staff member was heard explaining: "You see, I say *employees* here. We're all the same. Faculty are no more important than we are."

Nevertheless, in the years prior to this study these efforts to reverse traditional institutional priority had resulted in distorted student expectations. Students, faculty reported, interpreted "student-centeredness" literally and were increasingly behaving as customers. Following complaints about student feelings of entitlement in office hours, exam review, and grading, NDSL administration modified the mission. "Student-centered learning experience" was thus changed to "student *outcome*–centered learning experience" with the goal of prioritizing academic performance rather than individual consumers and tying success to bar passage and job placement more than feelings of customer satisfaction.

Serving the Underserved   Finally, the charter proclaimed its third mission pillar as "serving the underserved." Here, the school vowed to serve racially and economically marginal communities through exceptional outreach activities and through ongoing daily business. Community outreach activities varied from clinical offerings on campus and the later advent of an off-site clinic serving the homeless, to presence at minority bar associations and conferences. Although in some senses most colleges and universities engaged in similar outreach, what distinguished New Delta's avowed pursuit of this mission was the claim to be "serving the underserved" through everyday, revenue-generating activities. In other words, "serving the underserved" would become a mantra—a metonym for how Law Corp wanted employees to view their efforts as they generated returns for off-site investors on the basis of student indebtedness.

Simply by admitting and attempting to train students with low incoming indicators, New Delta felt it was offering a valued service to the margins of society.[23] As Law Corp's CEO said on several occasions, most legal services were concentrated in upscale pockets of dense urban areas, leaving many in low-income and minority communities lacking access to an attorney. Opening their doors to students with low GPAs and LSAT scores allowed the school to attract greater numbers of students from those communities. These students, it was said, would then return back and open small firms to serve the legal needs of their demographic groups. Admitting and billing those students for three years of law study at approximately $43,000 per year was thus itself conceived as a way to provide a valuable social good: "access to justice" through access to legal expertise.[24]

Not surprisingly, this approach had been a running theme among for-profit higher education more generally. Private equity owners used it to attract investor capital by casting the overarching mission as a socially conscious one. As one former Fortune 500 CEO put it, "I invest in bonds and other things, invest in all these widgets . . . I invest in a school. It's education-for-profit. I like this investment more than any one I got."[25] In this way, the phrase serves two rhetorical functions. First, "serving the underserved" supports the presumption that education—legal education in this case—is an intrinsic good. "The more training we offer people," entrepreneurs and policy makers seemed to feel, "the better." This echoed a presumption already underpinning expanded access to higher education more broadly.[26] It was supported in turn by an axiom that further education always brings a return on investment in the form of greater income, though this has recently been questioned, particularly in the context of for-profit colleges and vocational-technical training.[27]

Second, "serving the underserved" glossed an inherent danger in capital accumulation more generally: the need for perennial growth and market expansion.[28] Legal professional job opportunities, I have already mentioned, narrowed considerably throughout the Great Recession of the late 2000s.[29] In this environment, attracting new students to law school and satisfying capital investors with promised returns necessitated a new narrative for growth. That narrative, repeated in meetings and in public relations, came to be "serving the underserved."

"Charter Review"

Faculty and staff sentiments about the mission pillars and charter were ambivalent. Most generally supported the three stated objectives. For some, these goals had proven important in their decision to join New Delta. If faculty remuneration in professional schools seemed to be greater than in other higher education contexts, the mission promoted as socially conscious and student oriented forestalled misgivings about significant student debt burdens and sought to cultivate faculty satisfaction from every day's work. But many drew a distinction between the true mission values as envisioned by faculty and the ultimate institutional practice of those through administration protocols. As one professor told me,

I realized in my time there that missions mean different things to different people, and, if they are framed vaguely enough, they can be twisted to encompass almost any meaning. I did not expect [New Delta] to hew closely to the stated mission. The odd thing about it is that I believe strongly in how the early faculty articulated the mission. It was just clear early on that the school did not believe in the same things that the faculty believed in. However, I still thought that, through faculty governance, something the ABA Standards and our faculty handbook provided, that the faculty's conception of the mission would be what was most important.

Faculty tended to believe the three pillars should guide New Delta internal policy irrespective of the impact this would have on revenues. In the debates about curriculum reform addressed in Chapter 4, this understanding proved decisive in resistance to new integrated courses. But well before school administration pushed for those changes headlong, it was already apparent to some that administrative interest in the three mission pillars may have been superficial. As evidence of this, they cited the near-daily practice known as "charter review."

Under this practice, corporate policy required allotment of introductory time at nearly every personnel meeting for a recap of the Law Corp charter document and a call to speak about one of the core values as it "resonated" among employees.[30] Often taking up five to twenty minutes of meeting time, this ritual was often accompanied by a PowerPoint slide or hard copy circulation of the printed charter document. In describing what resonated that day, employees occasionally referenced the first two pillars described earlier: student outcome-centered experience and practice-ready training. But, by a large margin, the most commonly cited mission pillar in these public reflections tended to be "serving the underserved."

A staff member—a career services officer, for example—would raise a hand, the dean might call on that person, and she or he would say something to the effect of, "I'm going to have to go with 'serving the underserved' today. In career services, we have partnered up with immigration clinics around the city in a new program to match 2L students with pro bono opportunities so they can accumulate hours and give something back." Or a faculty member in turn would say, "I'm thinking about 'serving the underserved' because we're holding training sessions for our students to go out into at-risk high schools and conduct student moot court exercises. This could be a great way to reach out to new people and get them thinking about a law career."[31] Following one or a number of these pronouncements, the dean would respond "that's just great" and then transition to the next item on the meeting agenda.

As a matter of institutional policy, this ritual was required to kick off all employee meetings at New Delta and allowed faculty and staff an opportunity to share information about new developments and activities. Yet, for two reasons, it represented much more than that. First, beyond the charter review, meeting agendas already included a section on "good news reports." Second, it often served as public reminder about the content of the three pillars. If a copy of the charter was handy, someone circulated or projected it onto a screen. If one was not present, senior faculty or administration publicly reminded the group of its content.

With these two observations in mind, I suggest that charter review served an important pedagogical function in the daily operation of NDSL business. It instructed faculty and staff not just to keep these values in mind but also to frame their work within the walls of the institution as *foremost* for the good of students and of the community. Its most prevalent usage was to emphasize "serving the underserved" above other priorities. This emphasis, and frequent public reiteration, in turn, related directly to the business model. The more New Delta drew revenue from vulnerable students—those with low undergraduate academic indicators or from poor backgrounds—the more it sought to remind its personnel that their mission was ideologically praiseworthy. As one professor told me:

They review the charter because they read in a report somewhere . . . that that is what successful organizations do. . . . It reminds me of twelve-step programs. Reading the steps to recovery happens at the start of every meeting. For me serving the underserved points to helping those who traditionally would not have had access to legal assistance or a legal education [that is, minorities]. Nothing wrong with that. It becomes a problem when we overemphasize it and especially when we start admitting students who likely won't make the grades or pass the bar. If we're going to admit these students, we have to do everything in our power to help them succeed. Hard to do when data show that, for example, more one-on-one help works, but they schedule us for 100 [person] sections.

During my own meeting observations, few if any personnel openly questioned the mission pillars or charter review. But, during closed conversations, current and former faculty spoke very critically about their ideological roles and intended impact on personnel. Some likened this to common daily rituals of religion or patriotism:

I'm not sure the charter mattered. It was like saying the Lord's Prayer. Words repeated without connection to the substance or their significance. Mind control of the . . . I don't want to say weak and insult any of my colleagues, but to me charter review was ceremonial, like the Pledge of Allegiance or Star-Spangled Banner at the start of a sporting event.

Another employee viewed this as one of the corporate governance tools: a mobilization of workplace psychological research findings:

The school wanted others to believe its mission. If you say it loud enough, perhaps it's true—or at least others will think so. [With respect to] serving the underserved, the school did very little other than constantly refer to the percentage of minorities enrolled there.

Given the importance of faculty in delivering the company "product," this closeted self-awareness was startling. Equally surprising, some faculty believed that their expectations of serving broader social justice ends had been manipulated—that the mission pillars had been used successfully as a recruitment tool and that they themselves had been insufficiently critical at the outset. As one said,

The mission pillars are what brought me to the school, I really felt I was doing something really different to actually help "transform" legal education; in theory it all sounded good, but the application was destructive to me, to my self-esteem, to my ability to help create the school I thought we all wanted. I feel bamboozled, like they got me in the door with the promise of this incredible opportunity, but then it turned into a nightmare; I felt like a pawn being used for their own purposes, but they wouldn't tell me what those purposes were (maybe I was just naive), and in the end, it was the "bottom line." Dinero!

As these informants suggest, a significant aspect of charter review and its greater ideological role was its coercive tendency, a quality that places it on par with ritual in other key anthropological studies.[32] There, participation as spectator or as agent in the practice is often an important requisite to membership in the community.[33] But, in traditional tribal contexts, the coercive tendency of ritual is both disciplinary and legitimating. Although it restricts the range of behavior available to a tribal member, it also gives that person a place in the structure of the tribe and meaning for its existence.[34]

At NDSL, charter review may have had a similar dual function in an environment where this was badly needed. As this section has argued, it served a pedagogical function by instructing participants on how to view the practices of everyday activity in the organization—activity that, as shown in later chapters, became increasingly linked in a time of austerity to ultimate revenue. But, at the same time, it instructed employees how to make meaning of their place in the organization. They were offering a community service through education. Business experts, some came to feel, just happened to have devised a way to make money from this. Charter review facilitated this distancing and, for the most part, served its disciplinary and emancipatory functions well in that regard.

But for some professors like Rose, the ideological process remained incomplete:

"Serving the underserved" is a mantra for a couple of reasons. One—it means absolutely nothing—so we all put the lens we like on it—what is serving, and who are the underserved? For me, it means something very different than it means to [the CEO], but I feel good about helping to serve the underserved so long as [I] look at that phrase through my lens. But the meaningless[ness] of this statement is true for all mission statements; they are designed so no one could object to them. Here, this particular focus allows [Law Corp] to assume the moral high ground. If you object to anything they are doing, you must be one of the oppressors, because they are "serving" "underserved" communities.

If faculty and staff recognized an apparent meaninglessness in the Law Corp mission, this did little to hinder institutional techniques justified by its pursuit. So far, building on informant accounts, I have shown that New Delta expected employees to invest in the company on deep emotional levels. Whereas this account has focused on the discursive features of policy as culture, the next section turns to the organizational techniques employed in its pursuit.

Management Culture: Chasing "Zero Defects"

If the development of mission culture served an explicit ideological function, *management culture* served as its bureaucratic complement. That is, once individuals subscribed to the stated mission of New Delta and its parent company, they still had to be organized into a functioning bureaucracy. Rather than rely simply on an organic solidarity where each individual would bond with others by playing a role complementary to the larger whole, the school cultivated solidarity with the corporation through a suite of cultural tools borrowing from popular psychology and business management. Another means by which employees were to make meaning of their work environment, these tools, I suggest, also facilitated easier management of personnel.

"EQ" Testing and Training

Emotional intelligence, or "EQ" as most referred to it, was a system of evaluating and improving an individual's response to the social environment. It was based on a hierarchical view of human emotional responses and aspirations to reach "higher" levels on this spectrum. Although its origins lay in academic psychology, the concept was popularized by Daniel Goleman in his 1995 bestseller *Emotional Intelligence.*[35] Goleman then applied it to the corporate workplace in his 1998 *Harvard Business Review* article, "What Makes a Leader?"[36] There, he argued that although necessary for individual success in a corporate organization, raw intelligence was less determinative than emotional intelligence.[37] "It's not that I.Q. and technical skills are irrelevant," he wrote:

They do matter, but mainly as "threshold capabilities"; that is, they are the entry-level requirements for executive positions. But my research, along with other recent studies, clearly shows that emotional intelligence is the sine qua non of leadership. Without it, a person can have the best training in the world, an incisive, analytical mind, and an endless supply of smart ideas, but he still won't make a great leader.[38]

Leadership, in this context, may be a floating signifier. The hierarchical structure of a corporation means that successful advancement through its ranks is by definition a progression from being managed toward managing and from strictly following corporate policy to in some measure creating it. It is a progression from less to more agency in the organization—even if behavior near the "top" is tightly governed by the small group yet still above, compliance affords an opportunity to govern the behavior of the much larger group below. Leadership, then, is a term for a category containing the various qualities requisite to advancing in this structure. It is not necessarily the general quality of being able to direct groups of people. That quality, seemingly exhibited by tenured faculty who were later fired during NDSL's adjustment to the new market, proved to be more liability than virtue.[39] The goal of EQ in this environment, then, seemed not to be promoting the tendency to rally colleagues' support behind new ideas or policies but rather promoting an eagerness to seek advancement in the organization. It pursued this in two ways.

The first was "testing." As described in the previous chapter, Law Corp used an important personality testing service to screen employment candidates prior to hiring them. For faculty recruitment, this raised significant concerns about governance, intellectual freedom, and cultural bias. But, well after being hired, employees were subject to emotional intelligence assessment.

Second, faculty and staff were then required early in their employment to complete emotional intelligence "training." This training began with a psychometric test—an online EQ evaluation developed and scored by an outside consulting firm. The consultants screened for emotional responses to workplace "conflict" using a long series of questions. They then issued a report showing each individual's personality on two line graphs: one evaluating a person's conflict response behavior (such as silence, aggression, and the like) and the other showing key behaviors from other individuals that would tend to provoke negative responses.

Individuals then came together for on-site training over several consecutive business days and included large and small group activities designed to reveal individual vulnerability with intent to cultivate trust among the collective. It also came accompanied by significant amounts of printed material, including research findings, activity worksheets, and inspirational aphorisms from thinkers ranging from Marcus Aurelius to Joseph Campbell. Some of the more significant features about these materials were the prevalence of heuristic visual illustrations and the prominence of Law Corp's own brand name throughout. The company seemed to make very clear that this was *its* tool and part of *its* culture.

Visual aides featured prominently in the EQ training literature. They appeared as embedded PowerPoint slides with familiar shapes and clip art, arrows, labels, and bullet points. One illustration appeared to use the face of two monkeys, one thoughtful and one sad, to visualize the manner in which people responded to stress. Another illustrated a continuum using three clip art squares with labels like "occurrence," "sentiment," and "response," all connected by arrows.[40] Details of these diagrams and flowcharts notwithstanding, their greatest significance was in their attempt to concisely map the inner dimensions of the human minds making up Law Corp. Unlike efforts in geography or anatomy, this emotional mapping was not verifiable—neither to science nor to lay individuals. If this were not an accurate vision of the human mind, employees of Law Corp would not soon find out. But, once such visuals were distributed and EQ training had been completed, it no longer mattered how employee minds looked from the inside. To the ideal EQ subject, the training and materials *became* the manner in which inner emotions were visualized— they replaced prior conceptions of the preemployment Self with a new, "emotionally intelligent" Self.

In some ways, this outcome was true whether or not the employee audience member "drank the Kool-Aid." During sessions, trainers asked employees to reveal inner thoughts such as "What events shape the person I am?" or "What am I afraid of?" Under this expectation, and with administrators in the room, everyone complied. And yet, although some revealed highly sensitive information or described childhood memories, others deliberately remained superficial in their revelations. Many, if not most, faculty in these settings completed the required tasks with an ironic wink and a smirk—knowing very well that they must go through the motions of EQ training but wanting to get on with their jobs and guard against encroachment of the workplace into their psychological lives. Even holdouts found themselves using emotional intelligence language ironically after the training to describe office conflicts and sentiments. Although meanings may have been transfigured, EQ concepts had permeated the language of New Delta.

With so much time and money spent on the trainings, it was surprising to many that Law Corp continued to enforce its EQ policy when participants so overtly subverted its demands for personal authenticity. This resistance seemed to strengthen the corporation's resolve to impose the training on its people. It also provided an alternative means by which to assess performance. Said one former staffer, it allowed,

[The] leadership [to] focus[...] on personality versus job performance. I can think of at least two people that did a very good job but were let go because they had challenged the authenticity of the EQ culture. I think leadership was threatened that if [the CEO] found out that employees view it more as a façade than a true culture, that they'll lose their jobs.

This meant that deployment and assessment of EQ concepts were not limited to specific training sessions and rather permeated Law Corp and New Delta meetings and performance evaluations throughout the entire year. For faculty like Amber, this became uncomfortable:

Meetings were routinely called in which EQ concepts were identified, explained, and then "practiced." During these sessions, employees (not just faculty) were encouraged— I am awa[re] of none [who] refused—to divulge personal information about specific failures in our lives, about things we are most embarrassed about, and character flaws that we notice in ourselves.

Administrators closely integrated emotional intelligence with the charter and mission pillars described earlier. Pursuit of the three mission objectives, leadership said, required EQ work from all employees. From this close integration, faculty often made the small jump to conclude that EQ training and its practices were expected of them but not administrators and that expression of the leadership's faith in the ideas of emotional intelligence was disingenuous or worse. Amber continued:

The people who buy into EQ and tout it the most are the people who don't practice it and need it the most. Also, some of this culture is just plain not appropriate for the workplace. The CEO should not be doing PowerPoint presentations about the "five cycles of shame." Also, they often don't do things because it's heartfelt and they truly believe in it. They do it because they read in some Harvard report that if you do this thing you get more productive employees.

Suspicions ran in both directions. Some faculty and staff saw imposition of these practices as hypocritical. "I think they viewed the faculty as not wanting to practice the EQ culture," one staff-member said. "However, I think they missed the whole point that the leadership wasn't really practicing the EQ culture. . . . I had issues with this." And whereas faculty suspected administration of using emotional intelligence as a kind of upholstery for its management culture, administration suspected faculty of trying to undermine its success. To overcome this, administration attempted to incentivize cooperation by rewarding EQ above scholarly achievement, pedagogical skill, or popularity among the students. Although administration remained suspicious of faculty buy-in to management culture, there were some it felt genuinely supported and practiced what their EQ training had told them. This created a divide between those who could "see through" management culture and those who could not. Failure to see through was—among the community of former litigators and judges—a weakness in the eyes of some. Amber spoke poignantly to this:

Personally, I believe that the professors who buy in are deep in their own dysfunction and don't get that its not appropriate. It's a business, after all, not a twelve-step program. But, as we've all heard, data point to our profession (the law) as containing some of the most unhappy people.

Continuous Improvement

A second noteworthy feature of this unique corporate–educational management culture was adherence to what the company labeled "continuous improvement." This concept, inscribed into the Law Corp charter, was considered a *personal* value; it meant that individuals were to solicit feedback and incorporate it into their day-to-day performance. In an email expressing a complaint about the handling of a student file, one employee might "utilize" his EQ training to express a vulnerability such as, "I too have made this mistake before," and then proceed to express disappointment with the other's timeliness with the file. The second employee might then respond in writing, "Thank you for the valuable feedback and opportunity to improve my performance." Integrating EQ with continuous improvement in this way, leaders hoped, would create a gentler, more adaptive work environment. But, beyond securing the well being of personnel, it was also intended to reduce so-called defects.

For decades leading up to the foundation of Law Corp, reduction of defects had been a long-standing industrial corporate strategy. In that tradition, Law Corp's CEO began suggesting that its employees—professors included—train in Six Sigma, a management system developed by Motorola in the 1980s and popularized by Jack Welch at General Electric (GE) in the 1990s. According to GE literature, "The central idea behind Six Sigma is that if you can measure how many 'defects' you have in a process, you can systematically figure out how to eliminate them and get as close to 'zero defects' as possible. To achieve Six Sigma Quality, a process must produce no more than 3.4 defects per million opportunities."[41] The goal of this training, in short, was to achieve near-perfect production in industry.

Similar to East Asian martial arts training, Six Sigma training proceeds through multiple levels of expertise or "belts" ranging from "white belt" to "black belt." To achieve these ranks, trainees sat for a certification exam. Thus, the white belt is "certified" to participate only in local problem solving, having only a simple awareness of Six Sigma concepts. A black belt leads problem-solving teams and trains their members. Below the black belt is the "green belt"—an individual in charge of data and analysis support to black belts and responsible for her or his own green belt subteams. As of 2012, at least 10 percent of all Law Corp employees had been certified as green or black belts in the Six Sigma hierarchy.

At a glance, it would seem that a process management tool developed in one industrial technology manufacturer and implemented at others would be ill suited for the education sector. After all, Motorola produced communication devices (among other things), and General Electric produced toaster ovens (among other things).[42] This difference was not lost on faculty and staff.

And yet, Law Corp seemed to assiduously apply Six Sigma process management to push continuous improvement within its ranks. Because education itself is intangible, however, the corporation seemed to focus most on continuous improvement of its main service providers—its faculty. To this end, professors were asked to submit annual "work plans" outlining objectives for the year in areas of teaching, service, and scholarship. As a matter of policy, they were then subjected to two annual performance reviews for administrators to gauge whether work plan objectives had been missed, met, or exceeded. Wary of this, senior colleagues sometimes advised junior faculty to understate their capabilities in the submitted work plan so as to reliably state at year's end that their objectives had been "exceeded." Unless this could be demonstrated, new professors were told, problems would arise in promotion and tenure reviews. Junior faculty heeded the advice.

Counterculture: Marketing Rebellion

Subversion of work plans and performance reviews points to one final variant of New Delta's effort to transform policy into ideology. With the density of policy as culture established through observations of Law Corp's mission and management cultures, the question then became what happened to outliers—those who resisted meanings and practices established as a matter of policy. In this brief final section, I sketch out postures of resistance on the part of school personnel and describe the fate of some of those individuals over time as both New Delta and Law Corp responded to the market changes outlined in depth in Chapter 3.

In its early years, from the time of foundation to the time it received full ABA accreditation, New Delta appeared hospitable to a discourse of counterculture, particularly among faculty. It not only tolerated and celebrated plurality of thought and opinion as a form of "diversity"; it staked its fortunes on the virtues of rebelliousness and resistance in legal education.

Law is a profession founded on status and hierarchy; law schools, therefore, have long chased rankings and prestige. Against this trend, Law Corp—opening its doors near peak saturation of the profession—marketed its schools early on as antiestablishment and antielitist. It hailed its teaching as "innovative," developed classroom infrastructure using the latest audiovisual and online technologies, and questioned the validity of national ranking sources such as *U.S. News and World Report* largely on the basis that its student demographic profile emphasizing minority and "nontraditional" students rendered its schools incommensurable with other fourth-tier and regional law programs. It also encouraged its faculty to view themselves not as mainstream academics with their "noses in books" but as engaged teachers more deeply invested in students. On this account, New Delta was perhaps the most avowedly antiestablishment of the Law Corp schools. Its faculty, for example, was more racially "diverse," with a larger ratio of African American and Latino/Latina professors than any other school in the country.[43]

Recruitment of nontraditional professors and staff tied in to other nontraditional practices. In its early years, for example, New Delta changed locations several times within a short period, never permanently purchasing property but instead leasing various buildings and spaces. Rather than creating a sense of impermanence, these moves seemed to generate among personnel a feeling of freshness and flexibility in those years. Similarly, at one of its early locations just prior to the enrollment rise and fall described later, the school's law library hosted a section called "Banned Books," where librarians collected political, legal, and cultural texts once deemed unsuited for public consumption by the U.S. legal establishment. The idea for this conspicuous display had emerged from faculty who viewed their role in this unusual academic environment as one of "speaking truth to power." Administration received that critical posture openly early on when it targeted state power and cultural hegemony in legal history and profession, but it reacted caustically when it challenged New Delta and Law Corp policy shifts amid the later economic downturn.

In recent years, the school also hired faculty engaged in new developing fields of study such as *comprehensive law* and *therapeutic jurisprudence*. Faculty in these fields developed new courses and hosted or attended conferences with titles such as "Lawyers as Peacemakers" and "Rebellious Lawyering." Those professors embraced a view that law was more than traditional litigation and that it should be shifted from conflict pursuit to conflict prevention—from "going to war" to "keeping the peace." Extending this approach, some New Delta professors even set aside classroom meeting time for group meditation or assigned weekly "reflection journals" as a graded assessment. Meanwhile, one criticism among teachers, even within school walls, was that these unusual teaching approaches, developed in an environment committed to "serving the underserved," were experimenting on minority and nontraditional students—precisely those already at risk of not passing the bar or finding a job even under traditional educational models. How, some asked, would they be properly *socialized* as lawyers when their education called into question traditional attorney socialization as such?[44] That criticism notwithstanding, these newer soft-law approaches were well intentioned and well received, and they marked the law school environment as one interested in progress more than tradition—as institutionally countercultural rather than mainstream. But at NDSL this meant that counterculture may have been appropriated in school policy for its ostensible marketing value and that it may ultimately have been less authentically *counter* than many faculty, staff, and students felt at ground level.

Conclusion

Law Corp's business was premised on rapid growth and increasing revenue from student tuition. Based on this model, it had been able to attract private equity investors and large capital commitments to acquire one school and open two others in a period of just a few years. Law schools, many seemed to acknowledge, were cheap to operate and required very minimal marketing. Everyone stood to benefit from a law degree—most of all financially. If funding a three-year course of education to attain that degree required obtaining another loan, most students were willing to oblige. As Law Corp realized early on, this was especially true among minority, low-income, and nontraditional students for whom the symbolic importance of professional membership heavily influenced the "rational choice" calculus to enroll. To attract and accommodate more of these students, Law Corp schools began with relatively low admission standards. A few years into the Great Recession, however, they lowered these further to absorb the significant decline in student applications. As they did this, class sizes initially increased, top students transferred out at higher rates, and bar passage rates fell. Seeing this, faculty and staff grew increasingly wary of the Law Corp business model to take on as many students as possible with significant risk that they would never achieve incomes to fulfill their debt obligations as they had first imagined or been told. Most Law Corp employees—former lawyers in particular—had chosen education as a career to "give back" what they had been given, and yet they increasingly took note of the moral hazard exhibited by the company and its decision making.[45]

In an effort to offset this moral hazard—or perhaps offset its visibility to employees and the community—school leadership cultivated policy as culture. Here, that phrase has referred to corporate policies that shrouded themselves as community practices, values, or "culture." Through this process, Law Corp sought to convert institutional policies into common sense or intuition, not only in daily business but in deeper emotional senses that reoriented employee experience of the social world around them.

This reorientation was pursued in three ways I have called mission culture, management culture, and counterculture. Under *mission culture*, New Delta imparted with near religious recursivity the mission pillars and its charter. Displaying a visual representation of these values, asking employees to "resonate" with them in public meetings, and distributing desktop "tip cards" all encouraged employees to see the school through these categories. Foremost among those, "serving the underserved" became a mantra.

Under *management culture*, Law Corp turned to psychological and business management practices to create a smoothly functioning bureaucracy based on interpersonal diplomacy and precision. This was pursued through emotional intelligence and through application of industrial techniques such as Six Sigma. Combined, these signaled a commoditization of the employees themselves. Because neither students nor education could be considered fungible objects or "widgets," the institution appeared to reduce the "defects" not of products but producers. To do this, it sought to identify bad employees through a barrage of data collection tools from personality testing applied at recruitment, to emotional intelligence testing applied in training, to employee work plans and reviews applied annually, and finally to peer evaluations conducted semianonymously but often leading to greater conflict and suspicion.

Finally, styling and marketing itself as an alternative or antiestablishment program, New Delta embraced *counterculture* early on to escape the U.S. national rankings obsession. In this way, it attracted faculty and students who themselves were nontraditional in legal education, but it also sought to upend traditional academic hierarchies by deemphasizing faculty scholarship and shifting professors away from the center of school life. While doing this, it also marketed itself as a place where *students* rather than faculty were at the core of the school's mission. And yet, once admitted and financially committed in the program, many students would report feeling that the administration and business office moved first, with other stakeholders expected to "fall into step."

These observations illustrate further the role of ideology in neoliberal political economy. Against its increasingly transparent production of moral hazard, Law Corp relied upon ideology to extend the life of its business. Although its critics objected that this was shortsighted, the corporation's objective was revenue, not social sustainability or moral equanimity. Offering its investors high returns for relatively short commitments of capital, its deployment of policy as culture prolonged life through the Great Recession. From a simple, functionalist perspective it "worked"; it allowed the corporation to expand quickly ahead of declining enrollments in a prevailing regulatory atmosphere of "let the market decide."

Viewing policy as culture as a form of ideology, one is reminded to ask whether ideologies are by their nature *all* bad. Is ideology a kind of "false consciousness" in the Marxian sense, or is it the "necessary logic" of social organization in the Weberian sense? One response may be that ethnography—fieldwork case study—is not equipped to select and generalize a choice between these. We can experience and document ideology at one site but reproducing such experience through encounters with others is another matter—one fraught with investigative challenges. On the other hand, New Delta shows us that at a single site ideology can accomplish both; it can work as *both* false consciousness and necessary social logic. Ideologies are "false" in that they promote individuals to act counter to their own intentions or interests. But they are "rational" in the way they give those individuals a place in their world and a reconciliation for conflicts they themselves may be complicit in perpetuating.

Chapter 3

The Legal Education Moral Economy Bubble

O NE morning in April 2009, a respected partner in the Washington, D.C., law firm of Kilpatrick Stockton brought a gun to work. Despite career highs such as appearances before the U.S. Supreme Court, he had been asked to leave his position with no courtesy period to find new opportunities. That morning, perched in a fine office chair typical of a D.C. partner, he fired the .38 caliber pistol into the right side of his own head and died instantly.

On a single Thursday in February earlier that year, six American law firms terminated 800 employees.[1] Of those, 320 were licensed attorneys, and the remainder were permanent support staff. Over half of the "reduction in force" that day came from just two firms: Holland and Knight and DLA Piper.[2] For the entire month of February the nationwide total would reach 2,000 people.[3] By the end of 2009 it reached 10,000.[4] Among nonlawyers, these numbers, cold and distant in their "roundness," may not mean much. Weren't there too many attorneys in the world? And weren't they a nefarious bunch—quick to overbill vulnerable clients already in distress?

The meaning of the so-called Bloody Thursday layoffs went far beyond basic concerns of supply and demand or just desserts. They indicated wider economic collapse reverberating around the world at the time. As countless others have described, financial misfeasance on the part of large banks operating under looser regulations in the early 2000s led to a credit bubble that—pushed by the fall of home prices beginning around 2008—burst under the stresses of actual value assessments.[5]

The resulting law firm layoff stories might be grouped into at least two model narratives. In the first, the layoff was a *disaster*; it caught the attorney by surprise and yanked him or her violently from a comfortable (albeit all-consuming) routine of corporate legal work bringing in nearly $200,000 a year—enough to afford two luxury car leases and a home in many expensive markets. Caught off guard with car and mortgage payments, laid off associates awoke to the realization that the law degree they held was no guarantee of stability and affluence of the kind that had made law school drudgery survivable. In the second genre of layoff narrative, ejection from Big Law was a *blessing in disguise*. Although the associate position secured two or three summers earlier had been a great source of comfort in the face of massive, six-figure student loan debt, it was never in fact what that person *really* wanted to achieve or spend his or her days doing. That associate's real dream may have been to start a business, serve the homeless, litigate for the environment, or, in the case of at least one Los Angeles attorney, manage and promote indie music bands.[6]

The 2009 layoffs represented what many considered the beginnings of a vast "structural" change in legal professionalization. The firms discussed in the preceding paragraphs, along with several hundred similar large ones, had been greatly responsible for the practical training of thousands of American attorneys over the previous decades. Recruited from the upper tiers of the *U.S. News* rankings, new attorneys in those firms left their law schools with high grades but without knowing the real practices of professional law— activities such as client counseling, motion drafting, contract negotiation, or deposition taking.[7] On receipt of "summer associate" job offers—ones usually leading to full-time postgraduate employment—law students typically went through intensive training in legal research and writing and any number of the lower-level litigation and transactional tasks listed earlier. Schools, the accepted logic went, produced legal thinkers. Firms, it continued, produced lawyers. Though many of these new recruits would never be promoted through the associate ranks, and many more would never make partner, most castoffs would land on their feet in the many smaller firm and corporate counsel jobs that uniformly demanded big firm experience for the formative reasons just described.

Opening three brand-new law schools in the years prior to this upheaval, either Law Corp executives failed to anticipate that the legal services industry would collapse as quickly as it did, or they did not envision themselves vulnerable to the impacts this would have. Insofar as it dramatically expanded operations long after the impending storm had arrived, Law Corp decision making appeared counterintuitive. In this chapter, I describe the feverish growth of New Delta in the years following onset of the Great Recession. This sudden growth, leading to logistical problems inadequately prepared for, had immediate effects on the 450 new students brought in as first years in 2011. Nevertheless, difficulty meeting investor obligations—likely more than observable concern about logistical or pedagogical limitations—would quickly impose a limit to this large burst of entrepreneurial expansion.

Structural Change versus the Law School Lifeworld

Commentators predicted that the loss of high-paying—particularly entry-level—work was a permanent structural change in the law industry. Accepting that premise, some went further to say this portended worse, not for those who would have obtained those jobs but for those who never could have hoped to. Loss of the highest-paid positions would cause a domino effect sending higher-achieving graduates looking for work in lower-paid or public sector areas. This in turn would push students outside the top twenty or thirty law schools in the United States, and certainly those outside the top 20 percent of graduates emerging from all other schools, out of competition for those jobs. Although similar downswings had come and gone in recent decades, 2009 appeared different in its threatened permanence.

The dualist picture this assumed was already a reality. Law graduate incomes had already sorted themselves into a "bimodal distribution"—a distribution with two distinct averages: one clustering around $160,000 a year and one clustering around $60,000.[8] If in prerecession years this bimodality corresponded loosely to a division between "high" and "low" law school tiers, today graduates of the top programs can be found in both clusters, whereas more graduates of the low ones are found outside legal services entirely.

If the new realities represented a permanent structural change, how were its effects experienced and negotiated by people within schools, firms, and the profession? Social scientists have long grappled with this distinction between *structure* and *agency*. Structure, on one hand, is the large, sometimes global framework in which individuals are organized, shaped, controlled, and disciplined. It is the web of relationships—personal or institutional—in which people's movements and decisions are governed by sets of rules and possibilities. Agency, meanwhile, is the capacity for individuals to decide for themselves and act independently of outside control. In our modern world, who we are is determined by a combination of both of these—though the ratio likely depends on variables like nation, race, and economic standing. Structure, therefore, is only ever one-half of the story.

So-called structural change in the legal profession must be understood with agency also in mind. This should take into account local experience and individual decision making—aspects of what the German social theorist Jürgen Habermas called the "lifeworld."[9] In the lifeworld of New Delta, any effects of structural change were held at bay for the first few years of the Great Recession. There were two main reasons for this. First, if Big Law was collapsing, it would take a year or two—depending on the local job market and graduation rates—before the domino effect from this would be felt in small firm and public sector practice areas where NDSL graduates historically found work. Second, the same ambient economic scarcity—the Great Recession—giving rise to a decline in Big Law work was also a major factor in people's decisions to return to higher education for advanced degrees.

Take, for example, Emilia. A young mother of a college-aged son attending the nearby Big State University for undergrad, Emilia was in her late thirties and a diligent student. Emilia had been working at a mortgage company where she began as an administrative assistant and was promoted quickly, first into client services and then into management. In the end, without even a bachelor's degree, she was making good money and living well. Once the housing sector imploded, however, people like Emilia were first to be let go, and many returned to school in the hopes of finding careers that would restore their high standard of living. While completing her bachelor's degree, she said, "I heard of New Delta through a paralegal friend. I mentioned law school to them a couple of years before I finished undergrad . . . 2008 or so, after the mortgage industry collapsed and I went back to school. They said it would be quicker but not ABA-approved . . ."

As Emilia's case suggests, law schools and higher education in general become attractive to people during economic downturns. In times when the national economy experiences a loss of jobs and significant reductions in force, laid-off employees and unemployed job seekers tend to use the opportunity to return to school to build their "human capital."

In the case of law schools, this "recession bounce" had been a historically recurrent phenomenon. As some have shown, law school applications made jumps during each of the last two unemployment highs in the United States.[10] Typically, the explanation goes, law is a reliably lucrative industry and so-called opportunity costs of further education are lowest when unemployment rates are higher. Candidates laid off or excluded from current employment can decide to return to study without great concern that they are giving up significant earning potential over the three years required for the JD. Finally, when hiring is slow, the three-year waiting period is often sufficient for job market recovery and expansion; compare this to the one- or two-year time for completion of an MBA, or nine years for most humanities PhDs.[11]

So realities "on the ground" inside New Delta were potentially shielded from wider market forces. Under normal conditions, legal service industry contractions would take some time to have an impact on law school applications, whereas wider economic forces removing moderate-to-high income jobs (for example, mortgage officers or appraisers) from the economy would normally increase demand for legal education. Business officers at the school responded accordingly. Several decisions illustrated this; each of them presupposed not only sustained enrollment levels but significant increases in student demand.

The first was the spring 2011 signing of a ten-year lease on a new high-rise building in the heart of the city's downtown. This decision acted almost as synecdoche—a part that captures elements of the whole—for all of New Delta business practices in this period. The reasoning may have proceeded as follows: around 2005, equity investors were promised high returns for capital commitments of roughly five years each; the signed agreements did not require profits to be generated from the initial years of operation; as the maturation of these agreements approached around 2009, school officials were asked to begin maximizing revenues; to do this, ABA accreditation was essential for drawing in Title IV federal loan dollars, as was rapid expansion in student enrollments; to accommodate more students, as well as establish the school in an area more accessible to the legal services and city, state, and federal judicial facilities, the school would move downtown; this move could itself be introduced into marketing materials as both a distinguishing feature relative to nearby state and out-of-state law school competitors and as a sign of confidence in lasting financial strength for those questioning their own enrollment choice.

A second decision reflecting a perceived immunity from economic contraction was the concurrent drive to hire several new faculty and nonfaculty instructors in the same year. Whereas most law schools hire only one or two faculty, if any, at a time, New Delta made offers for the fall of 2011 to twelve—six in permanent tenure-track doctrinal positions and another six in permanent legal research and writing positions, as described in Chapter 1. This ambitious hiring round was necessary in part because of then-strict ABA guidelines on student-to-faculty ratios;[12] it therefore reflected informed confidence that the new incoming class for 2011 would nearly double the size of their next largest cohort.

Further suggestive of this sustained confidence was another hiring round of nearly similar volume the following year—only in 2013 was faculty recruitment placed on hold in response to projected falling enrollments.

These examples indicate that business officers did not apply the long-term critical strategic thinking typical of corporate operations. A former staff member described this apparent shorter-term thinking:

New Delta has always had an aggressive growth plan so that the investors could make their money back quickly and more. Even when the market went south, Law Corp insisted on increasing enrollments to predownturn projections . . . it's as if they totally ignored what was happening in the economy. . . . This also explains why Law Corp is offering crazy incentives to students, like $10,000 if they are academically dismissed in the first year or refunds if they don't pass the bar the first time. . . . The goal is to get the students in the door so they can get the money. So what if they have to pay a 136 LSAT $10K if they don't pass the bar when they got $50K or $60K in tuition each year? They still made a boatload of money.

For those inside at the time, however, between residence in a new state-of-the-art facility, a greatly enlarged first-year class, and a near 50 percent increase in faculty size, life at New Delta appeared to remain sunny well into 2012.

Thunder and Lightning: Public Scrutiny, Transfer Defections, Waning Applications

During the calendar year 2012, three forces coalesced to darken local skies. The first of these was a sudden jump in public criticism, the second was a rise in transfer attrition, and the third was an ultimate drop in law school applications across the nation.

In January 2011, *The New York Times* published an article by business and law journalist David Segal that some have listed as a turning point in public opinion regarding U.S. law school economics. Entitled "Is Law School a Losing Game?," the piece began in dramatic fashion,

If there is ever a class in how to remain calm while trapped beneath $250,000 in loans, Michael Wallerstein ought to teach it.

Here he is, sitting one afternoon at a restaurant on the Upper East Side of Manhattan, a tall, sandy-haired, 27-year-old radiating a kind of surfer-dude serenity. His secret, if that's the right word, is to pretty much ignore all the calls and letters that he receives every day from the dozen or so creditors now hounding him for cash . . .

Mr. Wallerstein, who can't afford to pay down interest and thus watches the out-standing loan balance grow, is in roughly the same financial hell as people who bought more home than they could afford during the real estate boom. But creditors can't fore-close on him because he didn't spend the money on a house.

He spent it on a law degree. And from every angle, this now looks like a catastrophic investment.[13]

So began the introduction of many American readers to the world of debt-financed legal education. For those seeking to attend schools of higher educa-tion in the United States, there are three primary means to financing tuition, supplies, and room and board. One is to pay cash, drawing on some large pool of resources such as personal savings, parental savings, or collateralized debt such as a second mortgage. Another is to borrow from private creditors such as banks or credit unions. And the most common is to borrow from the fed-eral government directly through one of several guaranteed loan programs.[14] In the case of New Delta, because it was unaccredited by the ABA for its initial five-year existence, student financing could come only from private sources in those years.[15]

Unlike most industries, where creditors make actuarial calculations regard-ing the degree of risk before assessing interest rates and lending out money, higher education lending makes no such inquiries. The assumption underly-ing this omission is that education always leads to better outcomes, that these outcomes have greater cash value, and that therefore education is always a good investment.[16] Historically in American society this assumption has proven correct.

For law students it was especially true. The cost of attending an ABA-accredited school, though always expensive, invariably brought a dramatic payoff over the long-term life of the JD graduate. Recent research even amid the downturn still placed this added lifetime value at roughly $1 million.[17] This meant that, traditionally, the federal government has been very willing to lend or to guarantee private lending for anyone wishing to study law, even for the price of a midsized house in some states. This did not vary with respect to the school chosen. Under historic and current Department of Education policies, the key concept is "access"; consideration for any alternative scheme taking prestige or outcomes into account would be considered a limiter on educa-tional access. More to the point, it would delimit the educational opportunities for lower-performing students—potentially those most in need of the support.

This emphasis on "access" was a key feature of federal education lending policies that emerged in the post–World War II era with the GI Bill and continue well into the present. It led to one significant and dubious result: a great percentage of federal dollars for these programs wound up financing studies at many of the worst educational institutions in the country. In recent years, for-profit colleges and universities have received greater scutiny for taking taxpayer money while offering questionable degrees to students too vulnerable to know better or transfer out.[18]

But New Delta and Law Corp public relations (PR) made focused efforts to distinguish themselves from the for-profit colleges featured in those scandals. In the early years, they did this through heavy emphasis on the school "mission pillars." These institutional values emerged from a high vertical structural source and translated through the imposition of emotional intelligence standards into what I termed "policy as culture"—an ideological construct through which employees were encouraged to articulate their day-to-day activities not as revenue creation but as justice achievement.

So long as the unique educational niche serviced by New Delta was at the law school level, these "cultural tools" were relatively successful in maintaining a stable institutional environment. For-profit colleges like the University of Phoenix, DeVry, or ITT Tech[19] were already identifiable as predators, but New Delta could more easily distinguish itself as participating in the "learned profession" of law. I questioned several of my research participants about this proximity and distanciation. The first was Nevina, a former faculty member:

> RT: Is New Delta comparable to the University of Phoenix or DeVrys or ITT Tech—all being for-profits?
>
> Nevina: No, I don't think so. . . . Students at a [graduate] program have proven they can finish a course of study (they all have a bachelor's degree in *something* from *somewhere*) . . . That's different (however slightly).

Another informant, Lawrence, was a high-achieving student who—although otherwise critical of New Delta leadership—also felt that it was exceptional as a for-profit aimed at legal training.

> I think it is different for now. But I suspect Law Corp will die out or go national like those other schools. But I'm not convinced a legal education will ever be minimized the way those other schools have minimized the liberal arts.

Despite this early exceptionalism, New Delta could not long sustain its distance from for-profit colleges as the public debate about the value of a law degree unfolded. Segal's article, cited earlier, followed by several more in the same outlet, increasingly challenged the notion that a JD would bring certain payoff sufficient to sustain its price tag. Others at New Delta picked up on this loss of distinction. One former student, Fred, who transferred out after his first year, said,

I would group New Delta-like law schools with those other schools. I read the other day that private [for-profit] schools in the United States account for 13 percent of students, but 33 percent of [federal] financial aid each year goes to that 13 percent of students. I take away from this that those students are not getting the same bang for the buck as other students. That financial aid money is disproportionately going to private institutions, at the expense of graduates being saddled with huge debt.

For Fred, the distinction between proprietary colleges and law schools broke down at the level of financial aid receipts and revenues. Another informant, Kate, spoke from the position of a former faculty member who had long harbored skepticism about this exceptionalism. For her, the school's programming and admissions practices seemed a priori as bad as the notorious for-profit colleges. Once she was hired, Kate felt executive decisions seemed to put business needs ahead of educational ones. For her, this did not reflect on the business model in general but rather on its implementation by local leaders:

As for for-profit schooling, I believe there can be a place for it, but not to what it has turned to at the law school. I think after [the second] dean took over, he brought credibility to the school, and the legal community took note. Plus, nearly all the retired judges wanted to work there! The example of the law school has [since] turned into another University of Phoenix; what it tried to distance itself from it has become, a school that accepts anyone, not because the student has the ability to succeed or because the school could possibly help underserved communities but because it needs to make a profit. . . . I don't think we are any different from those schools; they are in the business to make money from people who cannot get into school anyplace else . . . or they promise to get the student through a "regular" program, quicker, faster than anyone else, exactly what the law school is promoting!

So, internally, practices used in pursuit of the revenue-generating mission were, for some, identical to what people worried about among the key predatory institutions in higher education. But, back on the outside, public debate on the value of the law degree exacerbated New Delta's difficulty maintaining the distinction. Whereas expensive legal education was once justifiable on the basis of future income, now, even at the highest levels, this virtue was questioned. Additionally, notwithstanding any change in employment outcomes, law schools at all levels had raised their tuitions in extreme amounts over the previous decade.

These two trends would be written about by the legal academics Brian Tamanaha and Paul Campos.[20] Although different in their tonalities and approaches, both produced accessible, widely read polemics against the contemporary value of the U.S. professional law degree. Tamanaha's 2012 *Failing Law Schools* hit the legal academy hard.[21] It was a revealing look behind the curtain:

> What I write in these pages will affront many of my fellow legal educators. I reveal the ways in which we have repeatedly worked our self-interest into accreditation standards, from unnecessarily requiring three years of law school to writing special provisions to boost our compensation. . . . I argue that law schools extract as much money as they can by hiking tuition and enrollment, while leaving students to bear the risk, in the first instance, and taxpayers thereafter.[22]

Following the book's release, Tamanaha was invited to speak before a variety of academic and policy audiences around the country, and he initially obliged. The ABA, for instance, was interested in harvesting any reform proposals. But interest quickly gave way to acrimony. Legal academic audiences began to take issue with the claim that their job performance was inefficient or that their scholarship bonuses—amounts ranging from $3,000 to $20,000 for one summer's worth of research—were too large. Seizing on this as an attack on their scholarly output, some accused Tamanaha of "anti-intellectualism"—despite his many theoretical books and SJD (the only truly "terminal" academic law degree). More importantly, the book appeared just as applications and enrollments had begun to fall, and some labeled it the "last straw." But as Tamanaha later told me, he and other colleagues had been writing about law school tuition for years, and the Segal articles had already appeared one year earlier to a much larger audience.[23] Yet in at least one case a university president announced a series of cutbacks to faculty research funding at his own campus law school, allegedly after reading the book.[24]

A key feature of *Failing Law Schools* was an alterregulatory[25] argument. Thanks to regulatory capture, Tamanaha said, law schools were overly restricted by ABA accreditation standards—particularly those requiring faculty tenure and faculty research.[26] The costs associated with meeting these two require-ments, he said, are some of the largest obstacles to keeping student tuitions low. Retraction of ABA standards in these areas, or indeed removal of accreditation requirements entirely, would permit "differentiation"—the emergence of dif-ferent kinds of law schools that might specialize in policy research or practice training. This argument has been echoed by others including Paul Campos in his similar 2012 polemic and Clark Neilly in a 2011 talk at the National Lawyer's Convention.[27] Lighter regulation, the argument goes, will permit the emergence of "economy class" law schools as alternatives to the "Cadillac" or "Ritz-Carlton" model allegedly required under current ABA rules.

But, as Bryant Garth has pointed out, this two-tiered or "hemispheric" model has already partially existed. Citing Heinz and Laumann's ambitious 1980 study, Garth invokes the empirical case of the midcentury Chicago bar divided neatly into hemispheres of "high" prestige and income attorneys practicing in large corporate firms and "lower" prestige and income lawyers practicing in small and solo offices around the city.[28] Perhaps more importantly, the division grafted neatly onto a similar division between white Anglo-Saxon Protestant attorneys and other "ethnic"—that is, primarily Catholic and Jewish—practitioners in midcentury Chicago. In those years, prior to full formation of ABA Standards on accreditation, ethnic aspiring attorneys were tracked into lower-tiered prac-titioner schools such as John Marshall and DePaul, clearing the way for their mainstream white colleagues to enter and graduate from the top schools in the region such as Chicago and Northwestern.[29] Attorneys graduating from each of these hemispheres of legal education tended to cater their practices to mem-bers of the same ethnic and socioeconomic communities, such that their for-tunes were tied to wider possibilities shaped by ethnic segregation and business opportunity in Chicago.[30]

This arrangement resembles the moral economy espoused by New Delta. There, executives embraced the "access" model on the stated belief that theirs was the best way to diversify the legal profession. Other law schools, they said, particularly those chasing *U.S. News* rankings through hypercompliance with ABA Standards, had failed students of color and those from poor backgrounds. For these executives, there were not 200 plus rungs on a national rankings ladder—there were only two, those that aspired to rise in prestige, and those that catered to students, especially those from marginal communities. The school embraced the model of legal education hemispheres even within the existing ABA regulatory framework. More importantly, with its stated goal of "inclusive excellence for the 21st century," it viewed itself—its parent company, really—as a dominant force within the nonprestige hemisphere.

But from midcentury Chicago to modern-day Springdale, there was always a dilemma with this antiestablishment division. Once school marketers convince the public that their vocational model of legal training is better for diversity students, they are also convincing it to accept that this is where such students "belong." Policy and philosophy schools in the *U.S. News* "top tier," they suggest, are places for abstract intellectualism and perhaps not suited for members of ethnoracial and economic minority communities. The question then becomes why such students would accept this deterministic, vocational–scholarly segregation.

Having worn several different hats in legal education and legal profession research, Bryant Garth is an ideal addressee for such a complex question.[31] I asked him directly whether a hemispheric approach to legal education made it easier for proprietary law schools to take advantage of students from marginal communities and whether he felt such schools were indeed improving "access" to the legal profession:

They are absolutely not gaining access except in the rarest of instances to the lucrative careers, but there's a part in me that also says, if you interview these people in fifteen years, which we've done a lot of—not from for-profits, but sometimes for-profits, but mostly from other schools—that the prospects of the students are similarly bleak, and the students are happy with their choice to become a lawyer. They're the first in their family to [earn a] law degree. So I don't think it's a fraud on the consumer; I mean I think that's the elite perspective on it, that it's fraud on the consumer; I don't think so.

It is worth pausing on this documented satisfaction students, especially those from low-end law schools and with more limited career prospects, exhibit toward their earned law degree. Should reported satisfaction be the end of the story in a case where the financial burden incurred to achieve it is so great and distributed in its social impact? Law's professional hegemony, after all, derives not from its standalone superiority as a knowledge base or career path but from wider assumptions about these among practitioners and clients. Does the happiness minority graduates report signal the absence of professional hegemony or a more complete hegemony among those potentially most harmed by the augmented student debt load? The answer directly implicates the responsibility borne by accreditation experts.

> RT: People criticize the current ABA accreditation because it forces a model of "Cadillac" law schools. . . . Do you have any insight on that, this idea of a more bifurcated, dualist profession?

> Garth: I'm opposed to that. I'm opposed to that as a matter of—from putting it as a solution. Inevitably we're getting there, but right now it's porous enough that there's some mobility; some from the lowest-ranked schools worked their way into large law firms, because what happens is they become the first intellectual property lawyers, they become the first bankruptcy lawyers, they take careers that are marginal, which then become valuable, and so they—the first-generation entertainment lawyers and then they get rewarded, so you have Southwestern partners in top-100 law firms in Los Angeles as you do Stanford graduates. But they didn't get in there in the same way—they got in there through the back door rather than through the front door, and so you have that; so, I don't like the form of bifurcation, which is what people want to do. This is what Tamanaha wants to do; he wants to have the class of researching schools and the class of nonresearching schools, and I think that that makes a kind of an apartheid model of legal education, and for years I opposed that even though inevitably if we go the way we're going you have to—Harvard can keep adding more and more clinics, more and more resources, more expensive professors, and the Whittiers and whatnot of this world can't do that.

> So you end up with a market bifurcation, but it's much more nuanced than it would be if you had just the two models, and then remember we already have two models in a certain way: California has state accredited schools, has an online school or two, and has nonaccredited schools that are much cheaper; there are no frills, and the question is, who is going there? Are people with good credentials looking for that low-cost alternative? No, it's the people who can't get into anything else who could go there.

Transfer Attrition

Back inside New Delta, the public critiques began to hit home. The PR dilemma of law schools and for-profit colleges had been separate reasons for concern. But New Delta's status as both made its position particularly worrisome. In late

2011, the school hired a new public relations expert. I asked one former employee why that role had been created at that precise time:

> Employee: I believe she was recruited at the time because of the negative
> publicity of for-profit law schools, and the president of the school felt that
> marketing could help improve enrollment. Also, because they were consid-
> ering the name change.

> RT: What kind of negative publicity was circulating at that time?

> Employee: The poor investment of a law degree was compared to the debt
> acquired . . .

Public relations efforts may have helped to continue recruiting external students for a time, but they were not sufficient to reduce transfer attrition among
first-year students intimately familiar with the school's offerings. Student transfer rates had historically remained low in American legal education.[32] The many
reasons include loyalty to a particular school or area, likely loss of scholarship
money, problems of transferring course credits, and loss of second-year opportunities such as law review membership or on-campus interview meetings. By
the spring of 2013, however, transfers among ABA law schools reached an all-
time high.[33]

One reason for this was growing importance of *U.S. News* LSAT reporting in
the determination of school rankings. Ranked heavily on the incoming LSAT
medians they reported to *U.S. News*, law schools did not have to include incoming transfer scores into those calculations. In their effort to expand while
maintaining their rankings, ABA schools began welcoming more and more
lower-scoring students as transfers during the second year. Another factor was
the growing realization among even higher-ranked schools that they could soon
see a drop in applications and yield rates. The single strongest indicator of this
was LSAT examinee numbers. In any given year when there was a change in the
number of LSAT takers, this was taken as a signal of a change in applications
numbers the following cycle. Watching this particular storm cloud looming, law
schools viewed transfer acceptances as a way to brace for financial declines expected over the coming years.

In 2011, New Delta moved to a new building, hired 50 percent more faculty,
and enrolled substantially more students—many of whom came out of the
school's AAMPLE program. The contemporaneous numbers were a great sign
for the financial well-being of the school and for its capacity to fulfill financial

obligations to investors. For faculty in that year, teaching the larger number of students was generally a good experience; the larger pool brought in more high-quality students who would have succeeded at other schools but for a mistimed application or a deceptively low LSAT score. The presence of these students that year exaggerated an already existing bimodal distribution in background knowledge, literacy, and analytical abilities. For the students themselves, the experience of sitting in large classes with some who could analyze cases sharply but others who, they reported, could scarcely read, was disheartening. Thanks in part to a "forced curve," such students rose to the top in their classes, scored highly, and were ultimately well poised to transfer. As one student told me, "I think the transfer rate supports the premise that our class was an exceptional one. Of the people I considered the top of my class, I'd estimate eight of ten left for Big State." Although many such students would have transferred regardless because of prestige, some did so on the basis of educational quality more so than perceptions about status.

Botero was a high-performing Latino student with a background in engineering and interest in policy, and he was one of those enticed to New Delta by an introductory scholarship. He performed highly in his first year and described to me his reasons for wanting to transfer at the end of it:

RT: And so you came to NDSL and did very well immediately. Did you feel that it met your needs for policy discussion?

Botero: It did . . . to a certain extent. I felt the law books certainly met that need. Reading case law opinions opened up a new world that, honestly, I did not know existed. It was a true pleasure to do most of the readings. Additionally, I felt most of the faculty was really good. I loved their teaching, and I especially enjoyed talking about the public policy behind the law. However, I also felt some classmates did not contribute to my learning as much as I wish they did. Some did not contribute out of shyness, and that is understandable. However, sometimes I felt some did not contribute because they simply did not get it. That was a little frustrating for me. As rude as it may sound, I often asked myself why many of them had been admitted to law school.

Despite these feelings, Botero did not transfer, citing the generous financial aid preventing him from accruing debt and a female student with whom he had grown close.

Other students in this period cited different reasons for wanting to transfer out. Some, like June and Melanie, quoted early in this book, enrolled at New Delta thinking in advance they would transfer if eligible. Initially, such students were great for New Delta's sustainability. But once the school budgeted for these students as income streams over three years, their threatened departure was felt as a catastrophe. As student Lawrence told me,

These for-profit schools were designed for overflow students, much like myself. But when the dust settled and spots opened at more prestigious institutions, people flocked toward them. They resisted transfers because they were losing money by the bucketfuls. Every student who left was about $40,000 less for the school per year. The loss in revenue must have been tremendous. Plus, you're losing your best students. Herein was the conundrum: How do you stop good students from leaving your school if you refuse to provide the education they need? If they don't want to stay, you must try and force them to stay.

The administration, therefore, sought to discourage student efforts to transfer. In the first instance, it required that all students seeking release of their transcripts to other law schools—a requirement of all transfer applications—first meet with the dean to discuss their reasons for leaving. Early on, this meeting was treated as a mere formality. Later, as the applicant market tightened, the dean reportedly became more inquisitive in meetings with students, asking questions such as, "Has any faculty member encouraged you to leave?" In the second place, the school emphasized the big fish/small pond narrative to encourage high-performing students to remain. It warned them that their chances for long-term opportunities would fall if they left. Students like Melanie, who had recently transferred, did not react well:

New Delta doesn't do the students or the community any favors talking poorly about the risks of transferring and our inability to do anything better than government work. When I was interviewing for my 1L summer, I was number five in my class, and the career service department made me feel that working for the city was the best job I'd ever get. It was disheartening. When I got to Big State, the first interview they got me was for Greenberg Traurig. The second was for Skadden. They really believed that the sky was the limit for me. *Big* difference.

Those leaving New Delta for higher-ranked schools were often ecstatic. They were now accepted into a more elite club of attorneys with higher prestige, incomes, and life chances. But arrival in the new environment put their first-year education into proper perspective. Life at NDSL had not met their needs; this justified the move to restart socially, incur greater debt, and encounter all-new professors. But, if New Delta had been truly inferior in training them, then they too would be inferior in this new, more elite environment.

And yet, although students reported greater intellectual challenge at the new institutions, they often reported doing well after their first year. The professors at New Delta, they said in retrospect, had prepared them well. The rest of the experience left more to be desired. As Melanie said,

My husband and I both figured NDSL was a diploma mill and would probably be pretty easy for someone like me. Turns out that NDSL was actually challenging, and after a couple of months of my husband referring to NDSL as a "diploma mill" I actually began to get offended. With the exception of the writing program and my property professor, I was highly impressed by all of my professors. I felt that I got a great education, and, when I transferred to Big State, I actually felt well prepared (except for in the writing department, where I feel Big State kicks our butt).

When all was said and done, roughly 20 percent of the fall 2011 incoming class at NDSL transferred at the end of the first year. By far the largest recipient of transfers was nearby Big State School of Law, while another public university elsewhere in the state was a close second. Of those transferring, most were from the upper 20 percent of the class that year. This fact would eventually have an impact on the school's first-time bar passage rate two-and-a-half years hence. Meanwhile, many of these transfer students succeeded beyond expectations in their new higher-ranked law schools. As Melanie continued, "The administration and faculty [at Big State] have really been impressed by many of the transfers, and some of us have really learned to assimilate into their culture."

For many NDSL faculty, the transfer problem was no problem at all. Most professors were happy to write letters of support even if this meant losing their best students; they did so acknowledging that their actions would benefit the students in the long run. This produced a detriment to their employer and thus their own long-term employment, and seemed dually an effort at moral reconciliation and a tactic of resistance in an environment so controlled by management. But not all resisted in this way. Some felt they had offered an opportunity to students when no one else had and that student intent to leave was a sign of extreme disloyalty. In some cases, top students who worked closely with certain professors described being "cut off" in communications once their wish to transfer was announced. In similar cases, some professors held a blanket policy of denying recommendation requests from students seeking to transfer. In still other cases, a different camp of faculty—themselves growing concerned over the school's increasingly revenue-driven practices—made deliberate efforts to write as many recommendation letters for transfer as possible to give the maximum number of students a chance for success in a nonprofit educational environment. These requests often went to faculty in first-year courses: torts, contracts, property, civil procedure, and criminal and constitutional law. In 2011, for example, as a first-year professor of a two-semester torts survey course, I instructed roughly 180 students from both the full- and part-time programs at New Delta. From that group, I received letter requests from over thirty students and granted all of them. In the following year, after enrollments had already begun to decline, I had approximately half the number of students in classes and received almost exactly half the number of letter requests—again granting all of them.[34]

Faculty involvement in the increasing transfer rate was not missed by school administration. In April 2012, it hosted a "Transfer Attrition Faculty Brainstorm Session." There, faculty were called on to share ideas on how to stem the outflow of high-achieving students and, thus, prospective bar passers. Various suggestions emanated from the discussion. Notably, some suggested higher scholarships to compete with the public tuitions of Big State. Others suggested a new honors program that might offer special courses to high-GPA students. Still others suggested graduated tuition rates that might taper off as the student advanced. Notably absent from that faculty-led discussion was any talk of curriculum change—significant in that this would become the ultimate solution implemented within one year and that in the short run this would accelerate students' search for the exit doors.

Nontransfer Attrition

Beyond the group of high-achieving voluntary transfers, New Delta, as an avowed admitter of marginal students from ethnic and economic minority groups, experienced a share of involuntary attrition—loss of students for academic and disciplinary reasons. In the case of academic attrition, the policies and procedures were, initially, straightforward in their similarity to other institutions. Although neither the ABA nor ED explicitly required it, New Delta academic standards called for a minimum GPA of 2.5—the equivalent of a C average—to remain in "good standing" without qualification. Some students

Table 3.1.   NDSL academic standing levels by GPA.

Cumulative GPA	Status	Consequence	Appeal rights
2.5 and above	Good standing	None	N/A
2.0–2.49	Academic alert	Optional ASC counseling	N/A
1.41–1.99	Academic probation (one semester)	Mandatory ASC counseling	N/A
1.41–1.99	Academic probation (after one semester)	Dismissal	Petition for reinstatement Appeal for rehearing Appeal to dean
0–1.4	Automatic dismissal	Dismissal	None

felt the so-called forced curve meant a good number would be precluded from reaching even this low bar, but that perception was erroneous. The forced curve limited only the number of A's and B's that could be finally distributed; it did not "require" faculty to assign any D or F grades. This forced distribution often had the effect of compressing scores toward the middle, that is, toward the C range. Students deserving of D's and F's in "absolute terms"—in terms of total points or writing quality expected—were therefore usually helped by this policy.

Nevertheless, a subset of students each term fell below the 2.5 threshold and were placed on "academic alert" (Table 3.1). Students on alert, those with GPAs between 2.0 and 2.5, were sent to the academic success department to receive optional counseling on legal study skills and class engagement. Those below the 2.0 threshold were placed on academic probation and required to regularly visit academic success counseling (ASC) for guidance. ASC instructors helped the students to create a plan for improvement and required the students to further meet with their own professors for added feedback. If, after one semester on probation under ASC counseling, the student was still unable to attain a 2.0, he or she would be dismissed from NDSL with a right to petition for reinstatement citing exceptional circumstances. A student who had less than a 0.4 GPA improvement to make was usually reinstated, although this practice varied based on circumstances. If denied reinstatement, the student had rights to appeal for a rehearing before academic standards, or to the NDSL dean directly.

Faculty familiar with the academic standards process reported to me feeling that it tracked closely to numerical predictors of bar success. In a period of high enrollments and thus high admissions standards, this faith in the GPA's predictive quality may have been well founded. But as enrollment "shortfalls"[35] began to be addressed by lowering admission standards, even the 2.5 may have been too low to safely predict bar success under the school's forced C curve.

Moreover, faculty reported a tendency of the standards committee to err on the side of reinstatement. "In my experience," someone told me, "the committee operated from a bias toward generosity."

To understand why, I would suggest, one need look no further than the ideological edifice, described in detail in Chapter 2. There, the business model—naked of any cultural rearticulation—appeared inherently in a state of tension. But dressed up in the "mission" talk of student centeredness and service to the underserved, it was more palatable; it gave low performers a first and second chance to prove themselves while breaking down obstructions to access in an historically elitist, exclusionary profession. The second chance afforded failing students academically attrited by New Delta conformed to the same logic that justified school admissions and business practices more generally. In the Introduction, I described this as a form of inverted "social abandonment."

Finally, disciplinary encounters caused attrition for yet another smaller subset of students. Although these cases were initiated first by a faculty or staff member in front of the student honor court for disciplinary censure, they seemed to disproportionately ensnarl the same marginal or nontraditional students that defined the school as "diverse." In several cheating cases, for example, part-time students reported for violations by an adjunct instructor were also working mothers who had been out of school for some years; a social attitude they exhibited toward collaboration and mutual support in completion of assignments was thus inimical to the individualistic, competitive format of traditional professional law school.

In another case, a Latino student was reported for leaving a final exam room with a copy of his exam essay prompt sheet—a definite violation of the strict rules imposed on law school exam administrations. When I spoke to this student privately, he explained to me that the criminal law fact pattern tested that day told of an inner city landlord who assaulted his own nonpaying tenant. This story, the student continued, was identical to a run-in his own mentally challenged father had had in his home city one year earlier. Distracted by the similarity of the stories, the student lost concentration when concluding his exam and placed his materials, laptop, notes, and the exam prompt in his own backpack before leaving. Realizing the mistake a few hours later, this student turned himself in to administration. Meanwhile, after the professor was informed, a decision was made to bring the student before the Honor Court. There, he chose not to tell his side of the story.

"Why?" I asked him later.

"Because I didn't want to use my father's sickness as an alibi," he said, "and I didn't want them to feel sorry for me." At the conclusion of his proceeding, the student was placed on probation. Distraught and demoralized from these events, he performed poorly in his second semester and was automatically dismissed at the end of the year.

Exceptional though these cases were, they tended to implicate the most precarious of students. In disciplinary hearings, some brought their own attorneys to make defensive oral arguments against the associate dean of academic affairs serving as "prosecutor." During a brief ten-week period during which I observed the school honor court, *all* of the eleven disciplinary cases implicated nontraditional or ethnoracial minority students.

Notwithstanding the public relations problems attached to both law and for-profit higher education, and notwithstanding the dramatic loss of full-paying debt-financed students due to transfer, academic, and disciplinary attrition, New Delta's explosive growth finally ran headlong into a dramatic drop in student applications and enrollments. If first-year enrollment in 2011 was at 450 students, by 2013 it had fallen to 310. By 2014 this number was 262. This decline paralleled larger trends in legal education across the nation at the time. According to widely cited numbers available from the Law School Admissions Council, LSAT takers—the most relevant number for predicting applications—fell from 171,000 in 2010 to 105,000 in 2013.[36] The expected nationwide fall in applicants materialized; from a high of 100,600 applicants in 2005, the number fell to 59,400 in 2013.[37] As the loss of LSAT takers and applicants both predicted, enrollment yields—the number of students actually enrolling in ABA law schools—fell from 52,500 in the fall of 2010 to 39,700 in the fall of 2013.[38]

Although applications and enrollments both fell considerably during this period, they did not do so at the same rate. As this suggests, law schools competing to fill their seats with smaller pools of applicants had to admit students with lower incoming indicators to maintain basic enrollment levels. Here, schools were faced with a conundrum: remain selective and admit fewer students while taking a budgetary hit or relax selectivity to admit the same number of students and maintain existing budget projections. In the former camp, UC Irvine in California was forced to cut its incoming class size nearly in half to preserve the relatively high numbers it established for itself by an initial offering of "free tuition" to the inaugural class. One of UCI's main goals had been to enter the

U.S. News "Top 20" within its first few years, and refusal to relax standards was one major requisite for staying on track for this goal. Perhaps because of this move, the school premiered in 2015 at a still-impressive number 30 in the *U.S. News* rankings.

In the second group, lower-end law schools like New Delta in the *U.S. News* "unranked" fourth tier had little to lose by relaxing standards. For these fifty or so law schools, a drop in scores would not register in the rankings (though it would in ABA reporting), and this would permit maintenance of existing budgetary practices for an interim period until the law school application rates recovered in a few years. For most of these schools, the choice was probably one regarding "comfort" related to nonessential costs such as faculty scholarship bonuses.[39] But for New Delta and other Law Corp schools, flexibility with regard to admissions was an absolute necessity. Without this, they could not pay out the projected returns on investment promised through capital commitment agreements. As the Law Corp president told a group of faculty early in 2013, investors were soon coming up on the maturation point at which they could demand returns or, by right, remove their capital entirely, leaving the school effectively bankrupt.

The first signs of trouble appeared in 2011 just as the school relocated to its new larger building. At that time, this move was considered "just the beginning" for growth. Administrators projected enrollments for the next few years to reach well above 500 students per incoming class—one of the highest volumes among ABA programs and close in size to that already observed at other Law Corp institutions. The problem was that LSAC numbers already predicted a slump. Rather than discussing or reflecting on this ostensible disconnect, faculty and admissions staff were asked to work silently toward existing goals. As a former staff member told me:

This is how crazy it got: they weren't even allowed to say . . . Like, they have these numbers from LSAC; they can provide the number of test takers you have and the number of people that are actually applying to school. You have good hard data from LSAC. But they weren't even able to say the number of applications are down; they didn't want to hear that.

They thought that translated to "we weren't going to work as hard" rather than "no, this is just a reality." Or, right around the time there was a lot of publicity coming out regarding the lack of jobs, the employment took a dive, lack of jobs, and so did the pay in terms of law students in comparison to what it had been in the past. [They] weren't able to say that. It was kind of like living in a bubble. It just got really weird. So I know what they wanted to do was just throw more money at it. We'll give more scholarships, we'll give more scholarship money . . .

But actually I remember . . . the president [saying] his thing was 40 percent increase each year. That's what the investors want to see. . . .

For executives to maintain predownturn goals in this way, admissions standards would have to be relaxed. Whereas, prior to ABA accreditation, schools had to carefully observe a floor LSAT of about 148 (approximately the 36th percentile), after accreditation they were freer to breach this threshold. One informant described learning of tense moments from the initial ABA accreditation hearing:

[They] knew during the preparation that they were going to ask, "Hey, would you ever sacrifice quality for quantity?" [They were] told that when that question came up that the former dean and CEO would handle it. Of course the question came up, and they both assured the ABA, "Oh, no, we would never sacrifice quality for quantity." In fact, I don't know if it was the CEO or the former dean, but those are records to prove it right.

One of them said, "I don't ever imagine a scenario where we would go below 148 for our bottom LSAT unless it was based upon a program like AAMPLE." That's important to remember. Fast forward to October 2011.

By 2011, the school was taking in Title IV loan money. It had been operating at a deficit but was now in a position to balance its budget as well as begin paying off investors. For these to occur, given the most current LSAC numbers, standards had to be altered.

But any such decisions would historically have had to go through faculty. Under New Delta's own faculty handbook at the time, professors maintained governance over matters related to curriculum, academic standards, and admissions. The question then was whether faculty at the fledgling law school—a generally independent body led by senior professors somewhat self-conscious about their role as guardians against the capitalistic impulses of management— would acquiesce to any such changes. According to some, school administrators anticipated resistance:

[T]he dean came in and said [they've] got to get our numbers, we have to get our numbers, and you're going to have to go down on the students that you admit, and [they] said "Okay, well, you're dean. The faculty need to approve a new policy. Once the faculty approve the policy, let [us] know, and [we'll] do it in accordance to what you tell the faculty to say," which the dean wasn't really happy about . . .The dean said . . . "You don't need to go through the faculty. You just do it."

[They] said, "Well, faculty, they're not going to be happy with this." There were certain faculty members like Jesús, Oscar. Those two in particular, they were always concerned about our numbers and where we were heading as they started seeing a slight decrease, right? Everything, you know the school prides itself on being transparent, so everything was open. Somebody would ask [them] for the numbers. [They] could share numbers. It was not a big deal. That's how it should be. They're faculty.

. . . [They] thought we were supposed to be transparent at the school. [They felt] like you're asking [them] to lie and be deceitful about it, not deceitful but to be deceptive by hiding this from the faculty . . .

In the end, the numbers *were* relaxed gradually. In 2011 the school median LSAT was 148, and median GPA was 3.05. In 2012 those numbers were 145 and 2.96 respectively. By 2013 they were 144 and 2.88. Faculty and students alike reported noticing the differences:

There had been lots of complaints from faculty members about the quality of the students. [They] said, "You're dean of the school. If you want to bring in students that are below our policy, then [we] think you should be signing off on their admission letters or have the faculty change the policy. [We] don't feel comfortable doing that because [we're] going against the policy that we have in place."

At this point the dean said, "No, I don't want you talking to the faculty about it. They don't need to know. They don't need to be involved. I'm going to pull back what they do on the admissions committee."

Despite these tactical admissions decisions, gains on the business side were not realized. Even as admissions numbers were lowered, enrollments declined for reasons already articulated. But, worse than this, academic standards for existing students fell with dropping admissions standards. The same financial demands rendering every applicant more valuable to Law Corp also rendered existing students more valuable. Academic attrition, the dismissal of low-performing students before graduation, and certainly before the bar examination, declined; with this, so too did bar passage.

Academic success counselors, meanwhile, had the onerous responsibility of trying to tutor these students to understand legal analysis and doctrine. Many of these instructors were the "front line" between low-indicator law students described in marketing as "underserved" and the company's underlying mission to generate revenues by sustaining those students at minimal competence. One employee described the developments from close up:

> Employee: In my opinion it should have been predictable, and [we] relayed this to the administration on more than one occasion that, as incoming LSAT scores went down, bar passage would go down as well. But academic attrition would not. It would remain constant even though admissions standards decreased, when, really, in order to maintain academic rigor, if you are going to lower your admission standards you should if anything need to strengthen the curve in order to ensure that only students who are capable of passing the bar exam are graduating from law school.

> RT: What about the argument that "we are expanding access to the profession"?

> Employee: You're only expanding access to the profession if you're getting them past the bar. And I think the numbers bear out that, since they have expanded admission, they have not been successful in maintaining their bar pass rate. And that should not surprise anyone.

Conclusion

The period from 2011 to 2013 saw realities at New Delta shift from feverish growth to basic maintenance. Through this evolution, indications of the unique moral economy at work rose to the surface. The law school's insulation from wider changes in the U.S. economy wore thin. Where previous recessions had brought new waves of applicants to JD programs around the country, this time the "recession bounce" was very limited. During a period of apparent optimism, New Delta business administrators made several critical decisions to commit the school to larger overhead expenses, including a ten-year lease on a new building and a new wave of faculty hiring—as many as twelve at one time—to accommodate a projected 550 students per incoming class. Following a peak in the fall of 2011, this number slumped by fall 2014.

In addition to the drop in new applications, the law school experienced large waves of attrition—mostly from student transfers but also through academic and disciplinary dismissals. Transfer attrition became especially problematic in light of the new overheads, and it was made possible by a growing practice among ABA schools to poach students from lower-ranked programs without the added costs of vetting those students, dropping their 1L LSAT and GPA standards, or risking still lower bar passage rates. Academic and disciplinary attrition also became increasingly problematic in this period for the ostensible reason that the school was admitting increasing numbers of students—via the AAMPLE program and lower incoming standards—struggling to manage the academic and professional rigors of an ABA law program.

Responding to these factors, New Delta began lowering admissions requirements still further. School administrators mandated admissions officers to accept what were previously presumptively rejected applications. Shortly after, the dean of admissions was fired, ostensibly for opposing the pressure, and the entire Office of Admissions was reorganized to report directly to the school president—a Law Corp appointee.

Decisions about admission were increasingly motivated by business need. In the years prior to 2012, faculty insistence on baseline quality standards—already among the lowest of ABA programs—had posed no significant problem because student applicants at those levels were still relatively abundant. As recruitment "competition" for those numbers grew fiercer, faculty interest in student preparedness became increasingly at odds with the commercial objective. School valuation of students took on an increasingly economic character, while faculty valuation remained obstructively rooted in academic merit. As shown later in this book, these combined to make school valuation of *faculty* increasingly a matter of commercial viability.

That syllogism was made real in the fall of 2012 during a visit by the Law Corp CEO. At a meeting before faculty, he showed PowerPoint slides and discussed the model on which the school was based—one where the income stream of student tuition dollars was the "only" source of sustenance for the three Law Corp schools. Encouraging the professors to think of new solutions for recruitment and revenue creation, the CEO then expressed, for the first time, the possibility of a *reduction in force*—the contractual term for fiscally necessary layoffs inscribed into each faculty employment agreement. A RIF, as it became known for short, would be very "undesirable" and a "last resort," the CEO told the group. At the same time, he said, now was the time to decide who was on board with the school's mission and who wasn't. With this last turn of phrase, he clicked a button on a handheld remote advancing the PowerPoint to a new slide showing a stock photo of an American highway sign with the word "Exit" clearly visibly in white letters over a green background.

Chapter 4

Law School 2.0

Marketing Integration, Educating Investors

"**E**ARLY on, we heard the investment period would be about ten years," a former faculty member told me. "When we're there, and I'm sure those investors or large corporate investors are saying, 'Where's our money?' They're going, 'There's a lot of reasons, and you can see why we can't give you your money back right now.'"

Most ordinary businesses deal in risk. Whether publicly or privately owned, they offer products or services to a consuming audience betting on the probability that their offerings will remain in demand from one day to the next. When businesses borrow money to grow, they usually do so betting that demand will *increase* from one day to the next. But private equity firms are different. Theirs is a form of ownership offering capital at the outset of a new venture or entering to purchase a business years into its operation—often when it is on the verge of fiscal collapse. In either scenario, the private equity industry is primarily made up of a few dozen large firms specializing in industrial sectors. Most importantly, equity firms are not designed to hold onto such companies for more than five or six years. In that time, their goal is to maximize value by lowering fixed costs (for example, workforce) and raising prices.[1] In many cases during the mid-2000s, such firms began to borrow extra money against the value of the companies they had just acquired simply to pay themselves and their investors "special dividends"—effectively imbibing equity rather than infusing it.[2]

When VPG founded Law Corp, it did so to own and operate the first of three proprietary law schools. The first such school was acquired from another proprietary institution. The second and third schools—New Delta being one—were subsequently founded by Law Corp itself in the following years using the same profit model of aspiring law students, ultimate Title IV federal dollars, minimalist facility costs, and technology-based economies of scale. ABA accreditation, most I interviewed said, was a key part of this model; it was prerequisite to eligibility for federal money, a key to unlocking the national market of law students, and a marketable symbol of academic rigor. So long as accreditation remained likely, investors in VPG's Law Corp venture would be easy to find and easy to satisfy.

In the face of looming fears that economic downturn might complicate this plan, Law Corp officers could point to historic data showing that demand for legal education was, in effect, "recession proof." By 2012, as the last chapter showed, this claim of immunity from market decline was untenable. For the first time in recent memory, applications began dropping, and schools near the bottom of the *U.S. News* ladder were projected to be the first to fail. Investors in any private equity firm that had been promised immunity against such a turn of events would likely have been disturbed. Knowing this, Law Corp officials were eager to soothe. But, to do this, something new—or at least new looking—was needed.

Law Corp executives formulated a plan for their three schools to reposition themselves in the national law school market. Their faculty, they decided, would reinvent the law school experience in the spirit of the long-standing company charter but in a fashion more programmatic than anything ever attempted at the company. The name for this new campaign would be simple: "Legal Education 2.0." In this chapter, I suggest that Legal Education 2.0's emergence had less to do with substantive improvements for law students than calming wary investors. Indeed, its content and day-to-day implementation would be nearly irrelevant to the fulfillment of its underlying purpose. That purpose was not only to create a distinctively new and effective "product" but to help rebrand the Law Corp schools in a way that could sustain the "recession proof" claim officers needed to maintain investor capital commitments through the admissions slump of the early 2010s. Legal Ed 2.0 was, for those on the ground, intended to sell legal education not to prospective new students but to private equity investors squeamish about this sector as part of any investment vehicle. Finally, so as not to appear to unduly interfere with academic curriculum and standards, Law Corp officers hired teams of third-party business consultants to muster evidence, administrators assembled ad hoc faculty committees, and these committees then "proposed" the new program as if it emerged organically from among New Delta legal educators themselves. As I maintain, these events illustrate one of the key dilemmas within the Law Corp model: how to make a school implement business policies developed far outside education circles without allowing the bones of capital to show through its increasingly thin academic skin.

"Legal Education 2.0"

Legal Education 2.0 was an attempt to accomplish this goal. The name alone carried a significant symbolic load. To begin, it referenced the information technology industry where software programs, applications, or "apps" are updated and resold year after year. Such serial updating is quite often framed as ongoing improvement to the product.[3] Aside from the technological reference, the label Legal Education 2.0 indexed something generally "new." The number 2 serves this purpose perennially well because its only purpose is to distinguish the modified object from all that came before.

Finally, the name for this new program carried the historical weight—even if negatively—of "legal education." In the United States, the history of teaching and training professional lawyers has evolved through four major stages, one of which does not even involve law "school" as such. In the first stage, ranging roughly from the original settlements of British colonists in New England to about the time of independence, American lawyers were relatively rare and learned their craft primarily on the job. As trade with the home country grew, travel back to England to study in a proper law firm or at the Inns of Court became a more prestigious avenue to joining the bar.[4]

The second stage came with the outbreak of war between the colonists and England. At the outset of the American Revolution, travel and communications with England were cut off, and, with it, so was metropolitan legal training.[5] In this period, American legal teaching and study began to grow with the foundation of the first U.S. law faculty at William and Mary College.[6] Meanwhile, the profession began to grow in size and respect as a homegrown elite community taking charge of the leadership in building the new institutions of governance in the new country. A growing number of aspiring attorneys took up apprenticeships in law offices—though the conglomeration of attorneys into large firms was still to be seen.

In the third period, beginning roughly around the Civil War, American law began to shed its direct English influence and, with it, the English style of "reading" law. In 1870, Harvard scholar Christopher Langdell implemented for the first time the "case method"—a system by which the academic student of law was trained by reading select cases to induce rules and apply outcomes to new variations of facts. In 1878 the American Bar Association was established, and within two decades it formed the ABA Section on Legal Education and Admission to the Bar. And then, in 1900, the Association of American Law Schools (AALS) emerged. With the advent of new oversight institutions, American legal education saw greater standardization in requirements for admission and graduation. By 1905, the AALS, for example, mandated its member schools to require three full years of study. Later, it would also expect a completed undergraduate degree of all incoming law students.

Finally, in the fourth and modern era, the U.S. legal profession and law schools were witness to increased competition. In 1971, American law schools uniformly began granting the JD or Juris Doctor degree instead of the LLB—which had been a holdover from the English system and, although literally a bachelor's degree, had long been a graduate credential.[7] In competition culturally with the socially prestigious guild of American medical doctors, the legal establishment elected to rename its terminal professional degree a "doctorate" of jurisprudence. Today some, but not all, state rules prohibit lawyers from referring to themselves as "doctor" except in academic or foreign contexts.[8] Beyond interprofessional competition, legal education came to be characterized by institutional competition among schools. The greater saturation of programs inspired rankings, and the now ubiquitous *U.S. News and World Report* rankings rose to the fore as the leading authority in this effort. Learning the *USNWR* methodology, a growing number of schools then began investing in areas the magazine deemed indicative of quality—areas such as library size, for example. Finally, amid this competitive and resource-demanding environment, schools also began costly marketing campaigns to raise institutional prestige and national public awareness. According to some, this was in part due to ABA accreditation standards, first implemented in the 1920s, which homogenized law school offerings around the core first-year curriculum, a model of faculty as tenure line teacher-scholars, and an emphasis on legal doctrine and policy over skills and clinical training.[9]

Consultants

Against this backdrop of legal education history, and with a desperate financial demand for marketable industrial renewal, Law Corp executives called for change to the status quo. Up to this point, despite its self-marketing as a practice-ready law school, New Delta taught and assessed its courses according to a largely traditional model. Students studied the same combinations of subjects, faculty were split into doctrinal and skills teachers, students were assessed on a forced grading curve, and classes were graded with relatively few examinations—though more than at most other ABA programs.

At Law Corp headquarters, company officers, in collaboration with top school administrators, determined that each of their three schools should change both their curricula and faculty contractual models. But, for both of these to occur, faculty at each of the schools—operating under a handbook that seemed to enshrine traditional models of faculty governance, particularly over curricular matters—would have to be persuaded.

In October 2011, Law Corp sent to New Delta a team from the management consulting firm McKinsey & Company. McKinsey was itself an elite organization recruiting young associates primarily from Ivy League colleges and top business and law programs around the world. Its job was to quickly research any organization that hired it, develop "solutions" to render them more efficient or profitable, and present clear evidence to these clients that their services would work.[10]

Following the weeklong semester break, New Delta faculty were invited to a special meeting. Whereas standard meetings took place in the school lecture halls, this meeting was arranged in a smaller classroom with movable desks and chairs. On the agenda for the day, New Delta administration was to introduce the group of consultants dispatched from McKinsey. At least one Law Corp officer was also flown in and present for this exceptional gathering. The topic for the meeting was "Five Year Strategic Growth." Law Corp executives, pleased with the school's move to a new building and expanded first-year cohort, wanted input from both consultants and the faculty on how they might grow their class sizes from 450 students to the targeted goal of more than 575. The consultants, a group of four associates in their early thirties, made a presentation to faculty on the strengths and weaknesses of the New Delta program. Near the end of their slide deck, the most junior associate of the group clicked through a series of slides quickly and concluded, "So that's kind of the Holy Grail of education right now; what is the 'value-add'?"

Faculty were a bit perplexed. "Can you go back to your last slide?" I myself asked when he had finished.

Seemingly dismayed, the associate scrolled backward. On his penultimate PowerPoint slide were listed areas of improvement—ways the law school might better "maximize value"—including certain language listing the rearrangement of faculty tenure as a plausible device. This language was never mentioned in the verbal presentation. "My apologies," he said, before explaining that this was just one of many possibilities the team was proposing to their client Law Corp. Following the formal presentation, the group took a short break and returned to the room to find the tables removed and the chairs organized in a large full circle. With a faculty of roughly forty professors, the circle barely fit around the circumference of the small room. The consultants stood on the outside of this circle, still near the front of the classroom, facilitated the discussion, and took notes as it unfolded. New Delta administrators were eager to solicit input from *everyone* around the room. Faculty members could pass, but few did. Most had brief suggestions and expressions of gratitude and hope for the leadership of the institution and the consultants visiting. But several did not.

"I think we really need to pause and take a collective breath," said the senior faculty leader known as Oscar. "We have just moved to a new building and grown our class size significantly. We have just taken on more than ten new professors. Many of us still have not moved into teaching in this new location. If we keep thinking about growth I think we are going to lose sight of student needs and see a drop in the high-quality teaching we've so far developed here." Others around the room echoed this concern. When Jesús spoke, he made a similar plea: "We need to put the brakes on. All we're hearing about is 'more growth, more growth.' We need to grow into the school we've already created."

During my own turn, I spoke awkwardly. I reiterated the sentiment of colleagues like Oscar and Jesús about basic scholastic resource oversights. "For new professors at the new building, there are still basic resources we don't have in place. Things like a pencil sharpener for example. . . . Maybe first we could have someone in charge of resources before creating new programs and new titles to administer those." At the time ignorant of the separate organizational duties of administration, I was unaware that such a resource manager was already present. In direct response to the event, I received a cryptic message one month later.

On my arrival at the old campus to collect student final examinations for grading, a group of four or five administrative assistants, still working at the old location prior to the big move, were sitting in their workspace talking casually. When they saw me arrive, someone made a joke, the group laughed, and then their senior supervisor left momentarily. They released my boxes of exam print-outs, I signed paperwork documenting their collection, and I was preparing to leave. Suddenly, the supervisor returned smiling. In her hand was a new, un-opened, automated pencil sharpener. "Here," she said, "this is for you, we heard you needed one!" The group erupted into chuckles.

"Can I keep this?" I asked, surprised by the reminder of a comment made in closed discussions weeks earlier.

"Yes," she said, "we got one for everybody."

This incident, like the signing of the new lease described in Chapter 3, can be read as another indicator of institutional culture: it emerged out of a closed discussion among faculty about the exigencies of strategic growth and ambition in a fledgling educational environment. New Delta was already searching for new "value adds" to its educational venture when it had not yet met basic needs generated by its latest commercial expansion. The pencil sharpener in this example was then a low-cost symbol of the traditional school environment; it was a kind of equalizer between well- and poorly endowed school environments. As many adults educated in the Western world will recognize, a single sharpener often stood bolted to the wall in primary classrooms from the poorest to the wealthiest areas in the land. Confronted with high-level management consultants, polished quantitative data regarding stagnation and growth opportunities, and a quick PowerPoint presentation on the need for more, faculty expressed the need for reflection and soul searching. Supporting this, the absence of the most primitive technology was striking.

Meanwhile, the intrusion of outside consultants to identify problems and solutions was perceived by some faculty as a slap in the face to the educational experience and skills they themselves had accrued through decades of combined teaching and research. Law Corp, it turns out, had been hiring such consultants for a long time to advise business and marketing matters. As one former administrator told me, the company was, "notorious for hiring consultants at the drop of a hat." With Legal Education 2.0, however, the organization for the first time had to use consultants to try to convince its professional educators to change how they did their jobs. A former faculty member described how consultants entered this world:

That crept up on us. I mean it started out, I believe, with some people coming in from a group called McKinsey. Again, these people are probably consultants, but I do not think they . . . had their genesis in legal traditions, frankly. You're bringing in a plumber to do an electrician's job, kind of way. It started out with that, and I often wonder what provoked . . . and then that's when we had all these meetings, and we were dividing up into groups, and then we were writing stuff on a white board, and, again, all of this was sold to us under the guise of to help our students, to reach the ones who are really struggling and blah, blah and to remain competitive and all of that.

A lot of us had our misgivings from the beginning because, again, we are part of the law, the legal tradition, and my own personal feeling about all of those innovative things was always, "Okay, we can change, but how about the bar exam?" The bar exam is what makes someone a lawyer, okay. Until the bar exam changes, you really can't do too much as a legal curriculum. You really can't, because then what are you training the students . . . How are you going to teach them to pass this bar exam in order to then enter into the profession?

As this suggests, the arrival of consultants was experienced among faculty as jarring. On one level, all lawyers are, on completion of some benchmark, experts. For some that benchmark is the first year of law school alone. For others, the threshold is completion of law school itself. For still others, the feeling of expertise comes on completion and passage of the bar examination itself. And finally, for still another group, legal expertise does not begin until they have begun or completed a few months in their first legal professional job. There, the distinct professional tasks of advising clients, drafting documents, or appearing in court all function as rites of passage after which new initiates finally feel they have arrived in their professional habitus. For this same reason, many practicing attorneys look down on law professors—many with little or no practice experience—with suspicion. But in this environment, even where most professors had been practitioners and judges, the consultants were felt to displace local expertise. "They dismissed everything the faculty was saying," one professor said. "Had us going through all of these exercises, making us believe that our input was really valuable, and none of it was ever put to good use, right?"

In other contexts, the company used consultants to achieve specific internal goals. Talent Plus, the expert human resources personality testing company, was one example of this already described in Chapter 1. In another related case, Law Corp hired a group called Nobi (an acronym for "Nothing But Objectivity") to study the underlying causes of transfer attrition out of its three schools. According to its own materials,

Nobi is the latest evolution in the performance improvement industry utilizing Statistical Designed experimental methods. Nobi's Scientific Advisor is . . . a leader and authority in the field of statistical design with a management and organizational integration. About a dozen veteran professionals round out our team, averaging two decades of experience. . . .

Together, they serve clients worldwide, within most industries. From R&D to manufacturing, increased sales to customer satisfaction, improving education to healthcare, retail sales to complex end-goal web optimization. From customer retention to reduced rework and increased efficiency, we are among the best in the world at what we do: unlocking counter-intuitive answers for our clients. By using technically sophisticated, highly proven, powerful methods—especially in multi-channel optimization—Nobi, utilizing simultaneous designs, is able to deliver an easily understandable and accessible implementation model.[11]

Nobi's emphasis on statistical modeling—and the appeal this held for Law Corp officers—was striking. On one hand, the individual student choices to transfer away from New Delta and its sister schools seems to be something easily discerned through qualitative investigation. Then-current policy required each transfer applicant to meet with the dean to acquire his or her own transcript, but this method of data collection on transfer motivations was highly flawed: students would likely never disclose negative feelings toward the school administration, faculty, or curriculum while sitting one-on-one with the top official. But this could have been easily remedied with the use of independent qualitative researchers, or even faculty, to conduct similar exit interviews with students in private and keep anonymous records on transfer motivations. Above all else, a qualitative approach would have captured the *meaning* (or lack of meaning) of New Delta to its own students as they deliberated about leaving.

Instead, in May 2012 the school received representatives of Nobi in another special faculty meeting. There, the consultants explained their methodology—a perplexing series of steps to isolate, gather, and process statistical data from a survey administered by the school among a sample of former students. There, the team leader described the elimination of "noise" in the data, quantitative analysis and standard deviations, and interpretation of their results. To the group of law professors, this was a far more "successful" use of consultants. Quantitative data, they seemed to feel, could be trusted over and above the business strategy recommendations of management consultants.

Finally, consultant teams were used by Law Corp in its accreditation and reaccreditation bids at the American Bar Association. Here, the consultants were not so much experts with transdisciplinary expertise but well-connected former regulators. Hired on as contractors during the accreditation efforts of each of its schools, several of these former ABA officials would eventually be appointed to Law Corp's own "National Policy Board." For some faculty, the porosity between consulting and regulation was a big problem. For others, these accreditation consultants were very effective. One faculty member told me how their use became valuable during the reaccreditation process. He felt hiring of these outsiders was a sign of great commitment and acumen on the part of New Delta leadership:

They had built a library; they hired teams of experts, consultants, which really impressed me. To prepare for site visits, we practiced; we had mock site visits with deans from other schools that used to be on accreditation teams. It was like preparing for trial to moot court in coaching. It was great. It was a great learning experience of how to do it and do it right. They didn't skimp on spending the money. . . . I was pretty impressed with the business acumen of the school.

With the need for a kind of marketing renewal supported by outside consultants, three further steps were required for New Delta to achieve the 2.0 mandate set forth by Law Corp. First, it had to cultivate the new program as a revolution from within—a kind of organic rebirth prompted by faculty innovation rather than offsite corporate policy. Second, under the ABA and New Delta's own model of "shared" faculty–administrative governance, it had to permit faculty deliberation and adjustment to the proposed plans. Finally, it required a direct democratic vote on the part of full-time faculty to pass the new program with the apparent legitimacy of a faculty initiative that held student learning foremost in mind. But, as the remainder of this chapter describes, completion of these steps proved more challenging than business and administrative officers foresaw.

First, the dean of New Delta selected faculty members to populate two new ad hoc faculty committees. Other committees, it should be noted, had all been appointed by the dean following informal expressions of preference on the part of professors. Historically, these committees included subject areas such as academic standards, admissions, and international programs, to name only a few. Appointment to these bodies required no specific prior competence and sometimes reflected what appeared to be deliberation to split up faculty cliques or voting blocks. Chairs of each committee were also directly chosen, served two-year terms of engagement, and in later years reported directly to the dean in separate committee chair meetings where this smaller group would report committee activity and receive special announcements prior to the full faculty forum. In the early years, faculty committees—as an important portion of the governance process—were open to full-time faculty only. Later, beginning in approximately the fall of 2012, the dean began also appointing noninstructional staff to these groups as well. This staff included librarians, career services officers, and academic support teachers. Speculation held that this move may have been intended to dilute faculty opposition to or collusion against Law Corp decisions as well as to generate more labor from noninstructional staff.

To some, faculty chosen for these bodies appeared to be those who had historically supported administration decisions in the past. As one professor said:

I think the faculty members on the 2.0 committee were specifically chosen because the admin[istration] believed they could get what they wanted out of them—and what they wanted was more money. I have no doubt that the local administrators had ISOs that linked compensation to achieving the objectives of Law Corp's high-yield profit goals. As [one member] admitted, even the faculty members of the 2.0 committee were promised compensation if they got the faculty to vote the changes [in] it. That is why those changes were critical.

The two new committees of roughly five members each were constituted in the spring of 2012 just prior to the summer vacation. They were asked to meet over the summer to develop a proposal on how the faculty could reinvent the current law school offerings at New Delta. The two groups each had their own specialized area within the Legal Ed 2.0 proposal. The first, consisting of senior faculty, was charged with Faculty 2.0. The second, consisting of more midlevel professors, was to develop Program 2.0—later redubbed Curriculum 2.0.

Faculty 2.0

Faculty 2.0 was the name given to a reform that would rearrange faculty contracts, employment obligations, and security of position. It was not the first appearance of these ideas, but it was a well-timed amalgamation of them. By attaching this to the curricular changes simultaneously being developed, Law Corp could potentially attain a very well-tailored contractual arrangement to make more efficient use of labor in what it considered the most "value-generating" activity: teaching. This, in turn, was made possible by new proposal interpretations of the "tenure" requirement for accreditation emerging out of the American Bar Association around the same time.

As already explained, New Delta faculty were formally divided in two distinct camps from the school's inception. In one were the doctrinal law faculty, similar to what one would find at any ABA law program. These faculty were paid an introductory base salary of approximately $90,000 and were expected to produce a modicum of scholarship and advance through the ranks of promotion and tenure under the NDSL faculty handbook. Over the years, scholarship came to be interpreted increasingly loosely, with some professors producing one journal article prior to promotion, and others simply a newsletter or blog posting. Promotion under the NDSL Handbook meant a move from assistant professor of law to associate professor of law, but this "promotion" did not entail a grant of tenure nor a salary increase. All faculty annually received salary "merit increases" in varying amounts between 2 and 3 percent, depending on budgetary capacity. Tenure, meanwhile, was granted only on promotion from associate to full professor of law. And a posttenure review was to be completed even on tenured faculty in subsequent years. Each of these steps was to be reached at roughly three-year intervals, though in several cases it was postponed due to lack of minimal scholarly achievement.

Most nondoctrinal law faculty were known as lawyering process or LP faculty. These professors taught legal research and writing—a role reserved for adjuncts in most other ABA schools at the time. They were compensated at the base rate of roughly $60,000, a difference that was well known among their group though not their higher-paid counterparts. Occasionally, LP faculty could be asked to teach overload doctrinal courses for extra pay, and many in the past had applied for doctrinal jobs and been hired by their colleagues over competitive external candidates. LP faculty contracts, meanwhile, did not specify a system of tenure but rather promotion through several stages and then a series of presumptively renewable longer-term contracts. Given the presence of post-tenure review on the other side of this divide, the distinction for purposes of job security became rather faint in practice.

Still, the initial Faculty 2.0 proposal that ostensibly "emerged" out of committee took aim at this distinction and especially salary differences accompanying it. During its formation, faculty talked often about the problems of "siloing"—the overspecialization of professors both among doctrinal subject matter and among legal doctrine and skills. A major theme of the parallel Curriculum 2.0 proposal was also "integration," the combination of legal writing into doctrinal courses and doctrinal courses into one another. A single professor, some LP faculty began to say, should already be teaching *both* legal doctrine and legal writing. To achieve this, the wall between doctrinal and lawyering process would have to come down.

At the same time, Law Corp did not seem to want more tenure-track faculty. Despite the offering of tenure at full professor and the attenuation of security of position by posttenure review, Law Corp officials appeared to view tenured faculty as a risk. These professors, it was feared, could potentially work less, produce less scholarship, oppose corporate policy, and worst of all mobilize junior colleagues against the administration. These sentiments were increasingly familiar; they echoed a spirit of neoliberalism rampant in corporate discourse since the late 1980s and higher education more recently.[12] Fundamentalist in their support for free market enterprise and opposition to worker security of position—such sentiments had roots in Anglo-American political economy. For private equity–owned industries, they were especially important: for this market to work, owned companies needed to be fungible as commodities, capable of value differentials and trading. Fluctuations in a company's value, in turn, could be effectuated only by altering the ratio between fixed costs and revenues. In the case of higher education, one of the largest fixed costs is faculty payroll. With tenure in place, there was little room to reduce this cost.

Meanwhile, some law school reformers outside NDSL were waging a simultaneous attack on the tenure concept. These challenges, various in their content and form, all claimed to share a common purpose of reducing the cost of a legal education. For most, this was a matter of moral hazard: law school tuition had long outgrown the utility of the degree offered by most institutions, and law faculty compensation had grown bloated and self-congratulatory.[13] Commentators like Daniel Polsby (former George Mason University law dean), and James Huffman (former Lewis and Clark law dean) suggested a root cause of this nonmarket behavior to be the ABA regulatory requirement that its accredited schools include tenured faculty.[14] Others were quick to point out that the tenure "requirement" is in fact an example of regulatory failure—a result not of any clear-cut high-altitude norm but of law professors running the ABA Council of the Section of Legal Education and Admissions to the Bar and interpreting its Standard 405 in favor of a uniform tenure requirement.[15]

Following considerable discussion in 2012 and 2013 about revising Standard 405 to relax the tenure requirement, the ABA decided not to change the relevant language. Under existing language allowing for non–tenure-track teachers, however, Law Corp saw new opportunity to improve its costs. As it put some of its faculty to work integrating curriculum for marketing purposes, it put others to work "integrating" faculty.

The ultimate Faculty 2.0 proposal included removal of distinct titles; all faculty would be "professors of law." In place of doctrinal and LP faculty, the committee then proposed faculty "tracks": those already on and choosing to remain on the tenure track would remain unchanged, whereas those electing to leave the tenure track, or those former LP instructors now integrated into the "unified" faculty, would be given the choice to join the "teaching track." Teaching track faculty, they were told, would receive the same base pay, they would be asked to teach fifteen to eighteen credit hours per year instead of the standard ten to twelve, and they would neither be expected to complete—nor be compensated for completion of—academic research or scholarly writings.

One additional idea emergent during this proposal stage was the use of academic success staff—study skills instructors hired directly by the school without faculty vetting—to teach as contract professors as well. This aspect of the proposal appeared in several PowerPoint slides during Faculty 2.0 committee proposals. On at least two occasions, faculty raised this as a concern. In one case, Oscar flagged this issue, stating that these study skills instructors were hired to prevent at-risk student failures and that any such conversion of their job duties would encroach on that critical purpose. In other cases, some raised the concern that these instructors had not been selected for academic rigor, research, or doctrinal teaching prowess. Moreover, they said, application of the title "professor" to this group would dilute the significance of that title for regular faculty needing to command larger classrooms, maintain student diligence, and enforce rigid rules on professionalism and academic integrity. "Don't worry," faculty were told by a senior member of the committee (later promoted to Law Corp headquarters), "no one is going to take away your titles." In the years after this change, however, some like Sonia noted a difference:

What happened with the curriculum is that they also, in an effort to buy loyalty of certain people in the institution, for example, folks who were hired to be academic success lecturers, all of that also came into play. Where because they needed to have their loyalty, they brought them in as a Trojan horse, if you will, where they . . . through the back door without going through a process, they put them into the classroom to replace some of these faculty members. Therefore, these people were not even qualified to teach the skill that they were hired to teach in front of these students who were struggling, and now they were being called "professors." . . . The quality of teaching has gone down because they have done that.

Finally, the most significant feature of the Faculty 2.0 proposal was its proposal for pay equity. As specified, "teaching track" faculty would be expected to complete more hours of teaching and no scholarly writing. In exchange, they would receive "pay equity"—the same amount of salary earned by their doctrinal tenure-track colleagues. Before the Curriculum 2.0 reforms were fully realized and implemented, this seemed like a great deal for then-LP professors. Above all, this great deal would have a direct and undeniable influence on their democratic process when time came for faculty governance to vet the new 2.0 changes. For LP professors, as one told me, a vote in favor of the proposal would be worth an immediate $30,000 and this may have been decisive.

> Carl: We were offered "pay equity," sort of. So we would be moved up from a base salary of $60,000 to a base salary of $90,000.
>
> RT: Okay. That's huge.
>
> Carl: Um, it is huge, although it's actually not pay equity in the sense that if you've been there for three years and you were tenure-track then you would make, you could be making more or much more than $90,000, whereas we were kind of starting over at that base. But . . . it doesn't really matter.
>
> RT: Plus, you guys were working more hours for that same amount.
>
> Carl: Yeah, yeah, yeah.
>
> RT: Do you think that kind of incentive was determinative in the way the voting went . . .?
>
> Carl: I don't know. I mean I think that it was important to writing professors that if we were going to be asked to teach doctrinal law classes that we be compensated at the same rate as a doctrinal law professor. . . . And so that was important, right? Because there's no reason I should teach criminal law and get paid less than someone else teaching criminal law. You know? That doesn't, that doesn't really make sense.

Although Carl confirmed the value of the pay raise promised as one result of a favorable faculty vote on the 2.0 proposal, he equivocated on the immediate role such a sizeable increase had played in the voting process. Other faculty were more decided on that subject. In at least one case, another described separate meetings in which New Delta administration promised then-LP professors that their vote would be in their own best interest. Making instrumental use of extant faculty divisions, administration seemed to play to professors' feelings of relative deprivation. Another professor, Hilary, spoke frankly about this:

RT: Did you support the changes that were ultimately put in place?

Hilary: The ones that were ultimately put in place? No. I felt like it was eliminating legal writing, and I think . . . Even if I didn't teach legal writing, I think that that is such an integral part of being an attorney that you shouldn't combine it. I did not agree with that at all. I did, however, vote in favor of it because after multiple meetings with the LP staff and various people having meetings with [the] dean, [the associate] dean and some of the [other] people—I can't remember their names at this moment—basically we were assured that, one, we'd get a lot more money . . . I also knew that all of my friends and I . . . deserved to be on the same pay scale if we were going to be teaching the same thing. . . . As a group we all decided that we would vote in favor of it because it's more money, the same level as all of the other faculty members, and, also, part of the deal was LP was going to have a lot of input into these new classes to ensure that the writing wasn't pushed to the wayside. Those were the reasons that I voted in favor of it. The way it ended up, I don't believe it was actually what I was actually voting for.

New Delta administration's assurances were telling for several reasons. They revealed possible insincerity in expressions of will to "unify" faculty. During the ultimate voting process, then-LP faculty were separated off in a "block," invited and hosted in several separate meetings, and offered benefits uniquely suited to their position. As a group, they amounted to roughly twelve faculty votes. Later, one frustrated doctrinal faculty would describe this in an anonymous survey administered in the fallout from the 2.0 changes as a form of "bribery."

Second, administration's strategy to make faculty self-interest instrumental here reflects a degree of insincerity behind Legal Education 2.0 more broadly. If these reforms were intended for the best interests of students and their learning, faculty vetting and voting might have been left to extant governance processes. Instead, administration played to some instructors' desires for greater salary to procure votes in favor of the ultimately corporate-mandated policy changes.

As if to confirm this, Law Corp made a final decision toward the end of 2012 to solicit the final proposal from Faculty 2.0 committees at all its consortium schools. In the meantime, committees had engaged in countless hours of research, deliberation, proposal drafting, and conferral with counterparts at the sister schools. In the fall of that year, committee members at New Delta asked the dean in front of a full faculty audience when the faculty proposal would itself come before a full vote. For some the reply was chilling: "employment contracts were a business matter not a faculty governance matter—Law Corp would take the proposals under advisement and decide soon how to proceed." Meanwhile, the dean and others were meeting with the lawyering process faculty in preparation for the vote on the new curriculum. At the same time, they began approaching faculty individually with the goal of encouraging them to embrace the new "teaching track" option for faculty contracts as an alternative to the "burdensome" expectations of scholarly tenure. To the extent there had been any ambiguity as to the purpose of the Faculty 2.0 reforms, this active solicitation to relinquish prospective tenure as an unnecessary burden confirmed what some later asserted in a very public lawsuit against the school for wrongful termination: that the underlying goal of Faculty 2.0 was little more than the reduction or full elimination of tenure in favor of a more fungible, and thus marketable, property for private equity trading.

Program 2.0

Over the summer of 2012, a second committee was assembled to gather input, deliberate, and generate a proposal for curriculum overhaul. Like the Faculty 2.0 committee, though to a lesser degree, those chosen for this group appeared to be professors closer in communication with the dean. Initially, there were questions about its meeting schedule, time commitment, and additional compensation. Beginning in May, both the faculty and program committees were expected to attend weekly meetings with Law Corp officers and its consultants. The program committee established a web page for faculty input and information on the changes, although most professors went off for their respective summers, conducting research, traveling, or spending time with their families.

In a series of focus group meetings conducted during the late spring and early fall terms of 2012, the committee solicited input on the major goals for the overhaul. Out of those meetings, the largest reform suggestion became *course integration*—a combination of discrete law school subject matter into larger conglomerate courses. This move, some faculty argued, would better simulate the "real" practice of law. This idea was not unique to New Delta reforms. In 2007, the Carnegie Report concluded that seven reforms were necessary to the lasting relevance of American law schools in a changing market for legal services.[16] Among those, course integration featured prominently. This suggestion, it should be understood, ran counter to a century of legal academic tradition. The classic division of law school subject matter into torts, contracts, property, civil procedure, and criminal and constitutional law had arisen in the 1870s at Harvard under the direction of Charles Eliot and Christopher Langdell.[17] These discrete core subjects had already taken shape thanks in part to publication of treatises by William Blackstone in England in the 1760s and James Kent in America during the 1820s.[18] But, rather than reading and memorizing treatise materials the way students are required to do in the code-based systems of Europe, American law teachers began lecturing on legal doctrine using the now-infamous "case method." Emanating outward from Harvard Law School through both scholarly hegemony and faculty recruitment patterns favoring its graduates, the case method quickly became the dominant methodology for teaching law in the United States. Within decades of its ascendancy in professional training, legal education was characterized by the twin features of divided subject matter and case method teaching.

Following two years of fieldwork, the Carnegie Report concluded in 2007 that divided subject matter gave students a distorted picture of the legal profession.[19] Most practitioners, its drafters felt, would have to be able to cross several practice areas in handling litigation and transactions for increasingly complicated client entities and their disputes. A breach of contract claim between two corporations, for example, might likely entail aspects of contracts, torts, and agency. All such cases would require knowledge of civil procedure. The filing of lawsuits in any of these areas—indeed the bread and butter of litigation—was legal research and writing. The training of law graduates in legal research and writing at big metropolitan law firms—and thus deferral of significant skills training until postgraduation—had been common practice in the United States. The Carnegie drafters, meanwhile, identified the inequality and unsustainability of this structure. Solo and small firm practitioners, those accessible to lower-income clients, would get only the requisite training and experience through risky on-the-job training and experimentation. For those 20 percent or fewer of graduates obtaining big firm jobs and the training they came with, for-profit corporate clients paying fees to large firms were shouldering the main costs of imparting these skills. Law schools, the report said, should therefore also integrate more practical "skills" into the doctrinal classroom.[20]

After considering faculty input and consulting a variety of reform proposals circulating in legal education research, the committee embraced course integration as the core feature of Program 2.0. The move would adhere to Law Corp's mission of practice-ready training, and it would help distinguish New Delta as the "innovator" it promised to be.

In August 2012, faculty reassembled for a new orientation period. On the heels of its last major hiring campaign, professors were joined by approximately eight new faculty in both doctrinal and legal research and writing. Significantly, an additional faculty colleague scheduled to have joined them changed his mind in the middle of orientation and quit. The CEO, it seems, had flown in to address a separate meeting for new teachers, wherein he presented new data about the coming admissions slump and attempted to rally newcomers around innovation and reform. The survivability of the school, and faculty positions within it, depended on professors' involvement. On hearing that news, this one individual abruptly resigned. In an email addressed to the dean and forwarded to faculty, he described misgivings about the business model and leadership. Having left his family in another state and having only rented a motel room for the month, this new hire clearly had approached initiation into the organization cautiously. For some existing faculty, news of this reversal was not surprising. That same month, faculty received more bad news. Student transfer numbers away from New Delta had reached their all-time high. New admissions numbers for the incoming fall class were significantly lower than projected. And questions about pedagogy emerging from within had prompted academic affairs to hold a special meeting on "teaching rigor."

As the program committee presented details about the new curriculum, faculty learned how the integrated courses would affect their teaching. The committee proposed combining torts with civil procedure, contracts with property, and legal writing with criminal law. Torts, they suggested, was simply litigation in state or federal civil courts. Torts, most faculty said, would be an easily grasped, recognizable topic to combine with the dry abstraction of procedure. Contracts, they added, were often drafted or litigated in relation to property claims, and this too would be an "easier" topic to combine with the more conceptual property course. And criminal law would be the easiest doctrinal context through which memo and brief writing could be taught.

If this were simply a matter of mixing two subjects in the same amount of classroom time, the proposition would have been easy. But, to make these combinations work, courses that had been generally three units per semester would be combined into single five-unit courses. For this reason, one full unit from one subject, or perhaps one half unit from each, would need to be dropped. Professors then would have to decide, in collaboration, which potentially bar-tested subtopics to eliminate from their materials. At the outset, faculty were told they would maintain full discretion over such choices. Questions to be decided individually included whether to offer primers on each separate subject at the outset of a course, whether to alternate between subjects in a single period, week, or month of teaching, and whether to join efforts with other professors already well versed in the traditional divided subjects.

In the latter case, professors would be given the option to "team teach" the new integrated courses. An instructor well versed in property, for instance, might partner with an expert in contracts, design the overall course and assignment schedule together, and then alternate lecturing depending on the scheduled material. In turn this raised two new potential problems. First, how would any given course be credited as the work of any one teacher? Second, how would faculty—especially those under the proposed "teaching track" contracts—meet their higher credit hour obligations?

Many became squeamish about the proposed changes. Already in an email to colleagues in May 2012, senior professor Jesús had expressed concerns that the plans were not sufficiently "faculty driven." In time, despite clear language in the handbook requiring faculty stewardship of curriculum, professors felt New Delta administration was not genuinely committed to faculty involvement. At the August 2012 orientation meetings, the committees offered the first detailed presentations on the new proposals. Following these sessions, faculty were invited to breakout discussion meetings to comment on the strengths and weaknesses of assembled ideas. In one such meeting, New Delta's chief career services officer moderated the conversation. One of the few nonfaculty members of the committee, the officer had worked quietly in career services for several years following his own successful practice in a local big firm's corporate law practice.

"What about a pilot program?" someone asked him. "Why do we want to experiment with new teaching and learning on full-paying new law students who don't know what law school should teach them? Why not set aside a pilot class to test the new program with fully informed matriculates, perhaps a discounted tuition rate, and informed consent to collect data on their performance and learning challenges under an 'integrated' system?"

"We don't have time," he responded. "Our public relations department is *already chomping at the bit to market this new program*, and if we wait another year we'll lose our competitive edge."[21]

With the marketing purpose of Legal Education 2.0 effectively confirmed, faculty and staff connected this to wider developments in New Delta's public relations "reinvention." That fall, the office of the school president began circulating information about an impending name change. Already in its brief history, the school had shortened a previous name when it moved from its original location in a city suburb to the central location where it grew and received accreditation. In the meantime, marketing consultants had determined there to be ongoing confusion between the existing name and that of another for-profit college. With the move to the new downtown building, the reinvention of the curriculum, and the reconceptualization of faculty "tracks," the law school would rebrand itself under a new name accompanied by a new website. Following a series of surveys on the name, a popular high-priced advertising agency was hired to help select the final moniker and accompanying logo.

Conclusion

The manner in which demand for a new curriculum emerged in 2012 speaks volumes about the interaction of business model, corporate policy, and shared governance in the Law Corp system. Already interested in devising a five-year strategic growth plan, the company had engaged costly services from one of the premier management-consulting firms in the world. In doing so, it accessed the growing influence of consultants on higher education management and the increased interest in education on the part of private consulting firms realizing there is money to be made in marketizing this sector. The introduction of these consultants into the law school environment dealt a blow to faculty governance at the level of institutional power and individual confidence.

As an instructor named Myra summarized:

It just seems to me that the way the school is run, and this is a good example just with relying on all these consultants, is very much like a corporation, and it doesn't seem effective to me. We're an institution of higher education, we're not a corporation, so to impose corporate-like structure has only seemed to result in disgruntled employees, in my opinion.

With the onset of the law school admissions slump beginning in mid-2012, the role of McKinsey & Company seemed to shift from one of strategic growth to one of damage control. Legal Education 2.0, the consultants' brainchild, was presented to faculty with the support of substantial evidence suggesting the need for market differentiation in the bottom tier of ABA law schools.

Though initially a McKinsey proposal, the 2.0 idea had to be transferred from outside consultants to internal human capital. To this end, appointed ad hoc committees met to solicit "input" and generate proposal content for presentation back to faculty in the fall of 2012. Some openly described this as a corporate mandate and felt they saw through this recursive vetting process. The proposals, they said, did not truly emerge from the faculty and, in substance, benefitted Law Corp far more than students or faculty.

The ultimate proposal for Faculty 2.0 included alterations to the tenure arrangement whereby a group of doctrinal law professors would be shifted onto "teaching track" contracts, relieved of scholarly expectations, and precluded from earning tenure within the school. The dean's open advocacy for faculty adoption of this new contractual arrangement indicated what the institution hoped to gain from this reform: a greater ratio of income to payroll obligations. Meanwhile, integration of lawyering process teachers into the core faculty with a grant of "pay equity" became a powerful bargaining chip for administration. LP faculty were told separately that they would each receive an additional $30,000 if the new faculty arrangement were adopted but that this was contingent on a successful vote favoring the new Program 2.0 changes. Ultimately, a faculty vote on the separate Faculty 2.0 proposal was canceled ostensibly to preserve this bargaining position under the reasoning that faculty employment was an HR, not faculty, prerogative.

Bringing the curricular Program 2.0 proposal to faculty vote was not simple. Senior professors complained that they were being prevented from studying the need for curricular changes and from crafting a well-tailored proposal to change in the areas that would benefit students. Out of the planning committees came the idea to combine doctrinal and writing courses. In lieu of direct evidence of the pedagogical value in this move, some asked for a pilot or test program to evaluate the benefits of this move. In open "discussion" meetings designed to solicit faculty input, such requests were rebuffed by noninstructional staff, including one official who echoed sentiments from the marketing department that the curriculum changes had to be publicized as soon as possible.

In light of these events—well before voting took place—some had concluded that these innovations were intended for the benefit of Law Corp investors more than anyone else. In the absence of any evidence that "innovations" such as course integration or team teaching would benefit students, administrators instead argued for the *recruitment* benefits of the new program. But some like Myra were highly skeptical of this claim both at the time and in retrospect:

As far as the marketing department's concerned, maybe it was about marketing to prospective students, but I've got to tell you . . . from an admissions perspective, I would be shocked if we got any students in the door because we marketed this integrated curriculum. That's not why students choose a law school. It just isn't. And certainly in our case it's not. We're the only law school in the state that's going to accept people, for the most part, with LSATs in the 130s now, 140s, and 150s. Big State and U of Springdale have medians in the 160s. They'll take some people in the 150s, but not many. For people who can't move, we are the only option, and for people with a low-end LSAT score, we're the only option.

It isn't about, "We're being competitive and marketing the school curriculum," and, "Hey, we can now compete with Big State." It's not possible. For the marketing department to think that this has really made a difference to incoming students, I think that's just not true, but that's their thing. I think this is all about the investors. I think it was telling the investors, "We're doing something different, and we're going to be a market leader because not many schools are doing something like this." Yeah, absolutely, I think it's, if you want to talk about marketing, I don't think it's really about marketing to pro-spectives, as it was marketing to the investors. Do you remember one of the other things, I don't know who mentioned this idea, but we at least bandied about the idea of only integrating, like doing one course, either a test course idea, or let's just do one course, see how that works? It was like, "No, no, no, we . . ." You remember? . . . "We have to do the whole curriculum, that's what we have to do."

Chapter 5

Shared Governance in the Proprietary Legal Academy

I N the weeks leading up to a final faculty vote, Legal Education 2.0 appeared in flux. The side of the proposal aimed at professor retention and promotion was submitted to an offsite Law Corp "steering committee" for approval, but its drafters were told it was a personnel matter and would no longer require even *their* input. Meanwhile, the deans met with lesser-paid lawyering process faculty—a group then consisting of roughly twelve out of a total forty faculty members—to assure them that a "yes" vote for the curriculum change would mean both a "unified faculty," as they had long hoped for, and "pay equity" amounting to a $30,000 per year individual raise.

Concerned faculty raised the alarm that the changes proposed, including integration and minimization of key bar-tested first-year doctrinal subjects and dispersal of legal writing instruction across other coursework, would prove harmful to the students. This harm, some said, would combine with falling admissions standards to exacerbate declining bar passage rates. Initially surprised that administration was not more interested in their concerns, faculty soon felt they were never intended to be active participants.

In Chapter 4 I suggested that this arrangement resulted from the very origins of the 2.0 reform campaign. Those origins lay not in homegrown determinations that the already marginal students of New Delta would learn or pass the bar better under a new curriculum. They lay rather in an apparent fear at Law Corp headquarters that investors might remove their capital amid wider talk of "crisis" in legal education. This "crisis talk," coupled with clear evidence of declining applications and growing transfer rates at New Delta, called for new marketing content that could assure investors Law Corp would remain a safe property in which to grow their money.

In this chapter I describe in further detail how school administration conveyed this as an imperative by mediating faculty democratic deliberation and ratification of the 2.0 proposal. This includes a retelling of the process by which the reforms were ultimately passed and the direct impact this had on faculty governance, academic freedom, and basic feelings about respect and dignity among educators in this unique law school. Above all, I suggest that Law Corp officers succeeded in securing a reform agenda by framing the debate as one between tradition and innovation. In this framing, despite the relative youth of both the school and its professors, law faculty were depicted as married to tradition and inherently resistant to change. Select professors—particularly those chosen for the proposal committees—were embraced as reformers, whereas others—especially critics of the proposals—were painted as "bullies." In this hardening of positional interpretation, student well-being, much like legal knowledge itself, became an indirect object made instrumental in the larger battle over governance of the institution. Most significantly, this framing succeeded in allowing both Law Corp leadership and New Delta faculty to neglect underlying tensions appearing between private investor profiteering and publicly financed, professional student learning.

Critics

Once curriculum change had been embedded within committees, the idea had to go through a vetting process that incorporated, at least formally, faculty deliberations. Initially that spring, faculty input was gathered in the form of "focus groups" conducted in a series of meetings with small subsets of the New Delta permanent core faculty.[1] Condensing faculty feedback into meeting notes, the committees then translated these ideas into a formal proposal. This proposal was then circulated and discussed in the late fall of 2012 in the weeks prior to a final vote deadline.[2] Most notably, committee and administration leadership began speaking of it as a "framework" for a curriculum rather than a new curriculum itself. This lexical shift addressed concerns that there wouldn't be sufficient time to develop and ratify details of the program. But it also stirred up greater fears that faculty were signing off on something they could not properly see or feel.

Although this concern was shared by roughly half the faculty, they were most vocally articulated by three senior tenured professors: Oscar, Rose, and Jesús. Collectively, these three shouldered most of the burden of criticism and dissent for the rest of their colleagues. In the spirit of rigorous academic debate, they consistently spoke out in the few public meetings available. In private, however, their conduct was the subject of some disagreement. By my own observation, Oscar, Rose, and Jesús appeared respectful of differing views and freedom of thought. For example, in a private conversation with Jesús in the weeks before the vote, I expressed my own misgivings about the proposals.

"What should we do?" I asked him expecting to hear some clear indication of how he wanted to see junior colleagues vote. To my surprise, he gave no instruction.

"Just vote your conscience," he said—a look of concern lingering behind thick glasses. Perhaps he already felt I would oppose the proposals. Perhaps he would have been more partisan, more forceful if he suspected I was ambivalent. Either way, my experience did not comport with one others would report to administration weeks later. Meanwhile, the three senior colleagues voiced concerns many were feeling.

First they said the development process was happening too fast. U.S. legal education had evolved over a century, New Delta was built up and earned accreditation over half a decade, and now Law Corp was mandating a new legal education format to be ready within half a year. Asking whether passage of the proposal could be followed by at least one year of development, professors were again told "no"—the new courses would have to be operational by the following fall. Moreover, changes to substantive offerings were supposed to go through *standing* faculty committees, not ad hoc deciding bodies. In later court documents, Oscar and Rose referred to New Delta's maneuvering through hand-picked committees as violations of both the local faculty handbook and ABA standards on faculty governance.

The second concern was a stark lack of empirical evidence suggesting these specific proposal ideas would be effective. Indeed, many said, integrating bar-tested legal doctrine into single conglomerate courses would very well confuse low-indicator law students about the source or application of specific rules. Stemming from this, a third concern was over the lack of a test group. Uncertain about the long-term effects of integrated learning on outcomes like bar preparation and gainful employment, faculty again requested that the school contract with particular students to serve as a pilot group. These requests were rebuffed on more than one occasion as unnecessarily delaying the success of the new program.[3] Relatedly, the fourth concern emerged over future bar passage rates. Already New Delta had fallen from its onetime position of "market leading" bar passage—with rates higher than its in-state competitors ranked far higher by *U.S. News*—to the lowest rate in the jurisdiction.[4]

Fifth, as a few faculty realized and pointed out, the integration of first-year courses into large five-unit blocks would cause transfer admissions officers elsewhere great difficulty interpreting the completed coursework of transfer applicants from New Delta. New students, some said, would later sue the school if they were not properly informed on enrollment of this potential disadvantage.

Finally, the last major point of hesitancy was around course materials. To truly integrate subjects, conglomerate courses could not continue using extant law textbooks; they would instead need all new materials and, of course, new preparation of those. Professors would spend valuable time preparing, and students would not be able to acquire used textbooks nearly as cheaply.

As might already be clear, this list contained items that—although regrettable to student-minded faculty—could be a boon for New Delta's business office. For example, the problem of transfer attrition, as already discussed, had become a major thorn in the side of administration. Its unpredictability made budget projections difficult and revenue rate assurances risky. Although for most other institutions this was a major inconvenience, at Law Corp it undermined the very model of private equity financing. Integration of courses, to the extent it would scramble the standard first-year law transcript, would help solve this problem. If Program 2.0 made transfer more difficult, so much the better. New Delta's dean referenced this advantage during the voting period. There, sensing faculty hesitancy to pass a still incomplete curriculum "framework," she reminded the professors that this change was mandatory and that if it remained unelected by New Delta faculty it would simply be imposed on them by Law Corp. "Remember," she continued, "we are reinventing legal education. This is your chance to build a better mousetrap." Faculty in the room during this meeting understood the double entendre of this statement. As the dean herself later conceded, this precise choice of words would come back to haunt her once the 2.0 dust had finally settled on New Delta.

In the meantime, faculty would have to vote to approve the new proposal. Prior to the voting meeting, professors were anxious. Most did not understand how exactly it would affect their job duties. Would they have to teach the new courses? Would they be among the first required to do it? Would anyone volunteer for this? Would all-new preparation eliminate their research time? And would there be additional compensation for contributing extra time and energy to an essentially corporation-driven policy reform? These questions loomed as the vote approached.

Voting

In September 2012, the New Delta president called a "town hall" meeting to formally announce the coming curricular changes. There, he declared that the school had experienced the loss of sixty-eight transfer students from the finishing 2011 first-year cohort. Although that number represented only half of all transfer hopefuls (known because of the rule that all applicants must take formal steps to release their transcripts), it did represent a stunning 18 percent of that class—the largest in the school's brief history.[5] In its campaign to grow quickly and accommodate more students, New Delta was becoming a kind of "junior college" for other law programs, especially the two public universities in the state. In other contexts, some faculty suggested embracing this role, marketing to low LSAT-scoring transfer hopefuls and then budgeting for the predictable attrition that would result. Law Corp officers vehemently opposed this idea.

So, at the "town hall," the school president announced the need for a revised curriculum that would help stem the flow of 2L transfers. Another idea raised at this time was the possibility of a "pass/fail" only grading system for first years. In both cases, the message was that alterations to the students' first-year transcript would have a direct beneficial impact on the transfer epidemic and in turn on faculty job security. At the same time, the president wanted to send a clearer message to faculty regarding the need for a successful vote on the new program. Those who didn't vote for these transfer-reducing reforms, he implied according to my informants, could be easily replaced.

In November, the ad hoc committees made more efforts to seek input. They presented ideas at the regular faculty meeting and organized still more focus groups to fine-tune proposal ideas already raised throughout the summer. The Program 2.0 committee released a document including an annotated bibliography and summary of research advocating the integration of courses. Later that month, the dean circulated an email whose subject line read, "A Time for Change." In this message, the dean made an explicit argument that whereas New Delta was once on the cutting edge of legal education innovation, its offerings now appeared "conventional." The new curriculum, the email said, would help the school remain competitive in a tightening admissions market. Following this missive, the dean announced a series of "open office hours" for faculty and students to come in and discuss the proposed changes with her. Shortly thereafter, in a manner most would consider uncharacteristic of a top administrator who had heretofore been somewhat withdrawn, she sent an extensive, warm Thanksgiving holiday email message listing items to be thankful for in work and personal life. Finally, toward the end of November, in preparation for a vote a few weeks away, the Program 2.0 committee sent its final proposal to the full-time faculty distribution list.

With the vote looming after the Thanksgiving break, December was by far the busiest month in the campaign. The Faculty 2.0 committee circulated a brief survey asking for input about the new "faculty tracks" and soliciting professors' intent to move onto the "teaching track" option. Around the same time, the school announced internally an organizational change that would puzzle many faculty and staff. The admissions office, until now reporting to the dean with considerable accountability to the faculty admissions committee, was being moved. From December 2012 onward, admissions would report directly to the school president. This move effectively shifted reporting of admissions standards and practices from academic affairs to the business office. Responding to faculty pressure for more details about 2.0, draft proposals from the Law Corp "sister schools" were circulated among New Delta faculty. It was assumed the intent was to illustrate that this would be a "consortium-wide" changeover. Meanwhile, one first-semester legal writing professor circulated a plan for the proposed "criminal practice" integrated course, whereas the assistant dean of career services circulated a sample document reflecting what a first-year student would see as her transcript under the new changes. The program committee then circulated a summary of notes and suggestions culled from the previous months' meetings, and senior faculty began commenting on the proposals over email.

Oscar and Jesús grew more vocal about deficiencies in both the plans and the debates. In a regular meeting that month, the school president opened with a call for faculty to offer feedback on the proposal without "just throwing stones"—a reference to what he perceived as the overly critical nature of academics. The statement highlighted a palpable disdain between the business office and academic personnel. Oscar responded that such an opening statement had already "poisoned the well" for open discussion about the changes. In a separate meeting of committee chairs only, he also questioned the "faculty-driven" nature of the changes as described by the dean. Oscar argued, "There was insufficient evidence that this program would allow faculty members and NDSL to meet their ethical obligations to the students and the profession." In a puzzling message that day, the dean emailed the faculty saying, "We are almost home!," acknowledging that the 2.0 campaign came from Law Corp headquarters and announcing that the proposal had now—well before any faculty vote—been "approved" by the unseen 2.0 "steering committee" and the Law Corp "national policy board." Later that week, the dean announced to faculty that both Law Corp sister schools had now passed their own proposals, and she noted her own expected absence from the actual voting meeting in a few days.

As faculty reviewed the multitude of documents and emails in circulation offering conflicting views on Legal Ed 2.0 and deliberated on their individual votes, an unrelated announcement came down in an email from the associate dean of academic affairs stating that the school "may be" moving to a trimester scheduling system. This move, they later learned, would shift from allowing students to take condensed "intersession" courses in winter and summer breaks to shortening the winter holiday and offering a full summer term shortly after the conclusion of classes in May.

On Thursday, December 13, the full-time professors gathered on the nineteenth floor of the new building in a large lecture hall to conduct the final vote. As was customary and prescribed by the handbook, faculty were normally invited to discuss items set forth on the agenda before any voting could take place. In the case of a comprehensive proposal to inscribe an all-new first-year curriculum, expectations for this process were especially high. In the absence of the school dean, the associate dean for academic affairs—a retired judge who had been running the scheduling and approval of all support resources, big or small, needed by faculty—ran the meeting.[6]

After discussion of minor points of business, she came to the most anticipated item of the year. "Any discussion?" she queried.

"Yes, dean, I have a comment," said Jesús, sitting to the rear corner of the large room, one hand raised the way a student registers intention to speak.

"Okay, go ahead. You have three minutes," the associate dean replied. She clutched a handheld microphone during this meeting. The faculty, seated in chairs at long desks normally used by students, were spread throughout the rectilinear lecture hall, making it difficult for people on opposite ends to hear each other. Faculty would have had access to student microphones installed at each seat, though these devices frequently did not work. Jesús did not activate his own and did not need to. He spoke with high volume in a slightly high pitch that pierced the space of the room and could be audible to all present. Gesturing with his hands and leaning forward over the desk, he outlined the detriment of integrated courses to at-risk, particularly minority, students. He spoke about the administration and Law Corp's guidance of the proposal process and the discounting of faculty caution or requests for more time. He began to connect these issues with the school's plummeting bar passage rate but was finally cut short.

"Thirty seconds, Jesús!" the associate dean barked out over her microphone. Stunned, the other faculty in the room looked at him and then at one another. He was taken off guard. At this time, the meeting had run for only thirty minutes, so no one felt pressure to end the discussion quickly. More importantly, faculty had reportedly never experienced any time limits on their commentary in meetings.

"Uh, OK, but I think that is highly unfair, dean," Jesús responded, flustered.

"So be it, thirty seconds," she responded with the steadfastness of a bureaucrat.

In speaking to informants since, no one seems to remember much of the ensuing discussion. A few more spoke, including at least one or two lawyering process faculty in favor of the plans. Following the silencing of Jesús, other faculty became uncomfortable speaking critically about the proposal. As one professor named Miranda put it:

I found it incredibly difficult to watch how Jesús was disrespected. . . . We'd never had anything like that—academics tend to be long winded—and it hadn't really been used that day. . . It was horrible to watch this committed and talented teacher get treated like that and particularly when he was talking about diversity.

Finally, after a brief discussion, the Program 2.0 proposal, over one year in the making, was put to a vote. The feeling at the time was one of relief; "the drama would soon be over," many seemed to feel. But the 2.0 committee had no ballots to circulate; on the morning of the vote there had been some confusion among the group about who exactly was to bring the voting instrument. Quickly a pair of faculty left the room to generate hard copies of the ballot.

When the ballots finally arrived, they were complicated. In the week prior, the committee had notified their colleagues that they would get to vote on the various components of an itemized proposal. Items included an "integrated civil litigation course" combining torts and civil procedure, or an "integrated criminal practice" course integrating criminal law and legal writing. Days before the vote, Oscar wrote to New Delta's dean asking how such ballots would be interpreted, but he received no response. Finally, at the meeting, ballots were circulated on regular 8½ × 11–inch sheets of paper with multiple lines at which to select "Yes" or "No." The first line asked whether one supported Program 2.0 in its entirety. The remaining dozen lines asked whether one supported this or that specific idea articulated. Faculty eagerly completed these ballots and passed them forward to be counted. Myra described it thus:

As I recall, right, it was a ballot vote, and we were given a sheet of paper. You had to, I guess, check . . . Because the classes were presented to us, there was the substantive curriculum, and then we had some other classes. I don't remember when this came up . . . but there was a class that was proposed called "Pathways to Practice." There were a couple classes like that that were just brand-new classes, not even integrated, but brand-new. You had integrated classes, and then you had some classes that were designed, like "Pathways to Practice," to get more hands-on work and less theory and more substance. Because there were a few different ideas contained within this package, it was confusing to us if whether we could just vote yes to a couple of the integrated courses but, say, vote no to some of these other proposed new courses, or if a vote "yes" is a vote for the entire package, or a vote "no" is a vote no for the entire package.

As a participant-observer in this process, I voted "No" on everything. Although there were items in the proposal that represented respectable responses to general problems in legal education—such as offering the introductory two-week "frontmester" course to prepare students in study skills for the new environment—I was concerned any single vote in favor of any "item" could be viewed as contradictory toward any general opposition to the mandated change. Echoing this, Myra continued,

I think a lot of us felt that we might vote yes to some of these classes but vote no to some of the others. Some people maybe liked the new proposed course, but they didn't like the idea of integrated courses. It actually wasn't clear while we were voting. I think some people had their own ideas. It was clear to some people that they could split their vote, and it was clear to others that they couldn't. Everybody voted, and then it was after the vote I think that this discussion came up of, "Wait, was a vote yes . . . But I voted yes for this but no for this?" "Oh, wait, no, but you can't do that. OK, wait, what?" There was a lot of confusion over could the vote be split and how, and I think we already voted before we even realized there was confusion, because it seemed clear to everybody, but in different ways. It wasn't handled well.

A small group of faculty gathered the ballots in a pile and left the room to count them. In prior circumstances, such as in choosing new faculty candidates in batches of five or six applicants, voting seemed to take surprisingly long at New Delta. Often, meetings would run over time so faculty would be forced to vote but leave before the conclusion. This time was no exception; at least two faculty departed before the results were known.

Finally, after a thirty- or forty-minute wait, the committee members reentered the room. They looked somber. "It didn't pass," one member blurted out.

Interpretations

"Wait," another said. "It *sort of* didn't pass." Committee members whispered to one another while one explained the situation to the associate dean presiding.

"Okay," someone finally announced. "We are a faculty of forty-four. The proposal needed twenty-three votes in favor to pass. The results for general approval of the entire program were twenty in favor, twenty-two against."

The group let out a collective sigh. The "No" meant roughly one-quarter of them were out of a $30,000 raise.

"But, we don't know how to interpret this," another member continued. "We have certain items where the faculty were specifically in favor of parts of the proposal, so we have conflicting results."

"Why don't we just vote again?" another professor proposed. Whether this was even possible after voting members of the group had left remained a further question.

"No," the associate dean replied after her silence so far. "I will forward these results to the dean. *She* will decide if a new vote is necessary. We are done here today."

On her arrival back to town, the dean sent a triumphant message. She thanked the faculty for its commitment to change and work on the proposals. She described the faculty's opinion as clearly in favor of the general changes but hesitant on a few specific ideas offered. She called for new committees to "refine" the original proposals into something faculty could vote on again, but she was careful not to use words like *revote* or *reconsider*. Finally, she called a follow-up meeting to allow the president to address the faculty directly about the vote. At that gathering, the president scolded faculty for its resistance to change. Afterwards, the dean took comments, and Oscar raised complaints that the vote could not be unilaterally favorably interpreted. During this exchange the two engaged in open shouting in front of the president and attendant professors, one of whom later told me it felt like "the kids watching mom and dad in a heated fight just before the big divorce."

*   *   *

A few days later I received an ominous text message: "Did you hear about Jesús?"

"No, why?" I wrote back anxiously.

"He's been fired," the sender replied.

It was just days before Christmas. The following morning I drove in to school in part to accomplish some grading business and in part to figure out what was happening. I stumbled upon Jesús unusually on my floor—two levels up from his own office—pushing an empty mail cart toward the elevators. Typically, when New Delta fired an employee, it did so with almost no advance notice. It was not unusual for staff to learn of their dismissal one morning and be forced to empty their office under security surveillance by the afternoon. But no one had ever heard of this happening to a tenured full professor.

"Are you gonna be all right, man?" I asked him, assuming he could not speak at the time even if he had wanted to. "Give me a ring, you have my number."

"I will," he said illuminating the call button and heading downstairs.

Jesús would later file a suit against the school for wrongful termination, but it would settle for an undisclosed amount and with a confidentiality agreement. From other informants, however, I learned that he had been called in to a meeting with the dean and human resources (HR) shortly after we had all voted. By those accounts, people described it as an "ambush" of sorts. They said the school had kept a file containing documentation of several incidents and complaints from female faculty members that Jesús had noted their disagreement with an idea or opinion he held and become aggressive in trying to persuade them. They said he was informed the documents suggested a pattern of intimidation, and an apparent increase in complaints in the months leading up to the Program 2.0 faculty vote.

Thinking back on my own relations with Jesús, including an opportunity in that same semester to serve as chair of a committee he sat on—a junior faculty in effect "directing" a much more senior one—I was surprised and unconvinced by the allegations. On our committee he had been genial, and supportive. In private, as already described, he expressed advice to "vote one's conscience." And another former faculty informant told me, Jesús had at times upset her with his passionate advocacy, but, never rising to the level now alleged. Moreover, she said, he was someone you could speak to openly.

> Nevina: I had complaints about Jesús. I shared them with him directly after he was being investigated, just to let him know those women weren't crazy, 'cause he thought I was all right, and I had concerns about his tone and volume many times.
>
> RT: I didn't know.
>
> Nevina: He listened to my comments and was respectful while I told him things he did and said that had irked me. Those other women didn't need to get him fired . . . But really, I blame the dean, not the other women.

To most other observers as well, mere allegations of passionate tone and volume were insufficient to justify his termination. In important cases, it was this passion for speaking on behalf of the "underserved" students and junior colleagues the school based its business on that earned him such respect. Former faculty member Kate told me more about this:

> RT: Why was Jesús fired?
>
> Kate: I heard some stories, but the main reason, I believe, and the "corporate reason" is a pretext, is that he was the most outspoken and influenced us with his reason and research. The corporation didn't appreciate it, and I think his firing was a weapon to shut us [the faculty] up and to whip us into shape to toe the corporate line. "Do as we say or you are gone . . . no sweat off our back." I heard that he was offensive to some and they reported him; I did see him react to [two female professors on the program committee] in a harsh way, but he was making a point that they were bent on not listening to because they were so invested in getting the curriculum changes, some changes that I don't think [one] was all on board about. Again, we weren't told the reason why, only that it was an HR thing, and privacy ruled so they didn't have to tell us!

Others also doubted that this senior professor had ever harmed or threatened anyone. As Hilary put it,

It seems to me . . . There's always rumors when somebody is terminated, but it seems to me that there were stories. Like Jesús was going door-to-door trying to strong-arm people into voting against this. I don't think that happened. I never heard anybody complain that he was doing that. If he did, he certainly didn't come to me, or anybody I spoke to.

The allegations did little to minimize the damage Jesús's firing caused at New Delta. Although the Legal Ed 2.0 proposal and voting processes were irregular and disturbed organizational power arrangements established from the school's early preaccreditation days, no other incident during my observations was as emotionally impactful on professors and students. For professors it was understood, validly or not, as the most unequivocal signal that opposition to Law Corp prerogatives would not long be tolerated—not even among those with "tenure." Said Kate,

I think after Jesús was hatcheted, we became more afraid to speak up, and I think I became detached and didn't want to "play" anymore. It was a very hard time for me and many others. I remember two of my colleagues called me to tell me the news about Jesús, and we cried and cried . . . it was a sad day that has turned into a very sad year-and-a-half. Students don't feel heard either. And perhaps many know they couldn't get into any other law school and feel loyal and get along to be in the school. Many of my students are not happy with the many changes that neither they nor the faculty had any choice over . . .

I asked others directly if the dismissal of a senior colleague placed them in peril. New Delta's then-president described himself as a former hatchet man—the guy who had to fire people in his previous executive positions outside education. For some in the corporate world, these kinds of threats help prod employees to work harder, or better. In the education context—at least this one—it seemed to have an opposite influence. I asked former professor Carl about this:

RT: Did you feel in any way personally threatened or affected, or did you feel like that's what happens when you are the low-hanging fruit or something? I mean, how did it affect you in a way?

Carl: I think it was, it was very scary, you know? And it, it was very demoralizing, I think . . . to me those were probably, those were the . . . people I would identify as the people I look up to, people who I thought were just so committed, so passionate, incredibly dedicated to their jobs and their students, and the people who worked tirelessly, right? Jesús was never not in his office meeting with students.

RT: Hmm.

Carl: To me it was very, it was demoralizing. So it made me think, no matter how good I am at my job, no matter how much, how hard I work at this job, my job could disappear at any moment.

For others, dismissal of one of the most senior professors spoke clearly about the school's approach to tenure more generally. This approach, in turn, had a negative impact on students:

RT: Any sense of how the firing of professors . . . affected students or student life? Or the school generally?

Isaac: Well, certainly, when tenured or at least supposedly tenured people are being let go with no recourse, I think it affects everyone in terms of what they are and are not willing to say and do. I think after they were let go that most people there were smart enough to get the message that this was a topic that was not to be discussed. And of course it's quite unfortunate when something like that happens in an academic institution where freedom of discourse should be prized. . . . I do know I never had as many angry students in my office on any one day as I did the day the students found out that Jesús had been fired.

RT: Do you see value in faculty academic tenure even if casually employed faculty could be cheaper?

Isaac: I don't see any value in tenure if people can still be pushed out of jobs for no reason. Personally, in a school like NDSL, where the emphasis is on teaching and not as much on research, I can understand why the administration might want to change or eliminate the system. . . . It's expensive and arguably doesn't serve any core mission of the school.

As this former staff member indicates, amid the larger point about academic freedom, students were notably distressed about Jesús's dismissal. For most he was an affable older academic with an advanced law degree from Yale that lent legitimacy to the still-young, private, for-profit law school. For others, he was one of only a few Latino professors who mentored student organizations—particularly minority groups. For still others, he was one reason they justified enrolling at the school despite perhaps wanting to be elsewhere. His elimination became, for purposes of transfer attrition therefore, another significant push factor. Students who had otherwise actually liked the school viewed Jesús's firing as part of a watershed moment. As transfer student Fred explained,

I honestly enjoyed NDSL and my time there. As bad as the reviews and the blogs were, administration and the recruitment office seemed to have answers to all the bad press. They had high bar pass rates and a high job placement rate. The administrative zealousness to promote the school, coupled with a generous scholarship, are the main reasons I began law school at NDSL. Also, I sat in on a mock class with Professor Jesús and simply loved the way the classes were run. I felt as though I could do well there. Soon after I started, most of the recruitment staff was let go, as well as Professor Jesús. Then it seemed as though it was one thing after another. There were rumors that the curriculum would be changing and that some favored professors were not coming back. There was a rumor that NDSL could lose their ABA certification. The atmosphere changed from one of excitement to one of stress.

For the Latino students, Jesús' advising had been very important. Watching the school terminate a professor of color only encouraged talented diverse students to seek out transfer in greater numbers. Some, like Tomás, found attorney mentors in the outlying community also reacting negatively:

Tomás: I think the floodgates really were opened up after Professor Jesús was fired. The discussions among students led to discussions with attorneys and employers.

RT: Almost sounds like an informal boycott among local employers . . .

Tomás: I really started noticing when Professor Jesús was fired; as part of the Hispanic Law Students Association, he was our advisor, and I believe we wrote a letter to the dean as an org[anization] asking her questions, and they were all what seems to be "company lines." As far as I was concerned, they were not very honest with us.

These developments did a great deal to undermine positive images of New Delta that school marketers had created in the minds of enrolling students— particularly nontraditional ones. For them, the school styled itself as the only law program specifically designed to help *them* get back into higher education after long hiatuses in careers or raising families. Like for-profit colleges, New Delta had grown adept at courting this market niche. In the wake of terminating Jesús—also a strong supporter of nontraditional students—these claims were less tenable. For students like Emilia, who had otherwise embraced the idea of a "for-profit" law school, these events raised an alarm:

> Emilia: I read numerous blogs and critics and/or old students were not very kind about NDSL overall. I had no problem with NDSL being for-profit. If anything, after going to an orientation before signing up, I felt that the way they were structured may have been more appropriate for an adult . . . and more focused on getting practice ready, as they claimed. I actually defended NDSL under those pretenses because I was going there mostly. I changed my opinion after first semester and Professor Jesús's departure. I began to hear rumors about the dean and then more firings and then more rumors.

> RT: Jesús . . . . why did his departure affect you in that way?

> Emilia: He was the very first professor I met in the presentations . . . he put on a property class for all of us "spectators," my husband included . . . his style was very similar to that I had experienced at Ole Miss summer . . . the six weeks I did in preparation of law school . . . so I expected all professors would be that way. He seemed like a genuine person who helped a handful of students I became close to during the boot camp, where I met Maria. They spoke wonders of him, though I did not know him that closely. After he left, people speculated, and others would not say except that the school was so full of politics and that Prof Jesús did not feel that was the direction the school should be heading in . . . it was said that because he disagreed with the profit . . . business . . . approach . . . he was fired as he did not agree.

*　*　*

After Jesús's termination, the 2.0 proposal was revised by a different ad hoc committee. This time, after putting out a call for volunteers, the groups were constituted differently with the inclusion of primarily lawyering process faculty and a new cohort of academic success counselors and noninstructional staff. By at least one count, there were almost no doctrinal faculty on the remaining committees, and legal writing faculty were themselves outnumbered by staff. The groups made several de minimis changes to the proposal (such as renaming the "Frontmester" term "Introduction to Legal Studies"); filled out more details, including precise topics to be covered after course integration; and included the possibility that at least some would be taught by nonvoting academic success lecturers.

Meanwhile, over the winter holiday the dean made personal updates to the teaching faculty. In one case, a previously departed senior faculty who had left to take up office high in state government was reappointed. An email circulated announcing this as a visiting appointment, and it was made unilaterally on the part of the dean. A few weeks later, a second unilateral visiting appointment was made of a local practitioner who had served as adjunct to the school for several years prior. In her case, through involvement in several bar and city government organizations, she had developed a close relationship with the dean and already acted as a kind of community liaison. In both cases, some faculty felt on learning of the appointments that New Delta had purchased two new favorable votes for the 2.0 program.

In January 2013, the slightly revised program was put to a second vote. This time, the decision was to be made "all or nothing." By a margin of one, the vote failed again. Following this outcome, the dean ratcheted up control of the situation. She emailed voting faculty that the decision to move forward on a new curriculum was hers to make and that professor voting was simply an advisory step. In the ensuing weeks, senior faculty like Oscar and Rose proposed alternate course integration schemes that might be less burdensome on students—ideas such as reserving integration for the second and third years only. Additional meetings covered topics such as which precise "skills" to include.

Finally, on February 26, a third voting meeting was scheduled. In this case, a sample ballot was circulated in advance with only two choices: full support or nonsupport. This time around, one professor considered to be administration friendly suggested that, to discern immediate results, the voting be conducted by electronic "clickers" of the kind a few professors used in classrooms with students. Some faculty were very perturbed by this idea of using corporation-owned equipment to electronically register faculty support for a corporation-based change to something so fundamental as law school course offerings. Nonetheless, on the morning of the meeting, clickers were distributed, and professors were instructed in how to activate, configure, and register votes on them. Several had technical difficulties and grew increasingly agitated as the process started. But, when all was said and done, the Program 2.0 proposal finally passed by two votes—*exactly the number of visiting appointments made since the first vote.*

Later that day, the dean messaged the faculty reminding them that time had "already" been lost and that speedy implementation would now be key. In the ensuing months, professors were asked to form new committees to "flesh out" the course descriptions for the three standing first-year courses. Where once there had been torts, civil procedure, property, contracts, criminal law, constitutional law, and legal writing, there was now to be "Introduction to Civil Litigation," "Introduction to Transactional Practice," and "Introduction to Criminal Practice." As committees argued over which subtopics to include in the catalog descriptions for these and which to omit for purposes of squeezing into the five-unit parameters of each, all new committees were formed to go through the same process for second- and third-year courses. By November of the following year, a staff member would write, "Having attended meetings for the now merged Second and Third Year Curriculum Committee, I have seen with my own eyes the chaos that proposing changes to the curriculum has become."

By this time, permanent faculty were tired, and few served on these bodies. Many saw little point; some felt demoralized. The vertical policy mandate had been, it seemed from its inception among consultants from McKinsey & Company, a financial marketing device. Professors' opposition to it in the first vote simply led to more voting. The democratic process normally employed to decide key issues was, in this case, concluded only after NDSL administration could tell Law Corp it had obtained faculty buy-in.[7]

Governance Risk Utility: Costs and Benefits of Mandated Institutional Policy

In pushing for curricular change, Law Corp had taken a calculated risk. The admissions market was contracting, and capital investors were liable to withdraw their investments if New Delta and its sister schools appeared to act as if things were still "business as usual." At the bottom of the rankings, they were among those predicted most likely to fail. So a policy change that could be marketed as a form of inoculation to market pathologies would have definite benefits. On one hand, the standard curriculum had crystallized over at least a century in American law schools to become a hallmark of "legitimate" legal education, and this was now to be changed virtually overnight. But on the other hand, *prospective* students wouldn't typically know all this: new curriculum might sound "new and improved" to them, but its ramifications from the classroom to the bar exam and to the job market would remain beyond the prior understanding of most applicants.

Yet for *current* students and their teachers, the effect was very consequential. Legal Education 2.0's symbolic value was probably highest between these two groups of potential stakeholders. Both groups seemed to interpret the changes as not for their benefit or for the benefit of their daily work. Said one student:

> Lawrence: While the previous curriculum changes may have been gradual, the new curriculum being instituted was drastic. As I understood it, it was a vast departure from the traditional legal education. Some of the subjects I did not even recognize, to be frank. So these drastic changes happened quickly because the school was losing students and needed to make some kind of change to stand out, I suppose.

> RT: Any sense that these drastic changes were for someone other than the students? This was the same time enrollments were set to free-fall; investors were getting jittery. Could the changes have been meant to soothe the investors?

> Lawrence: There is no doubt in my mind it was for the investors. This is what companies do. If revenues fall, you must be doing something wrong. In business, doing something wrong often means you are not adapting, or you are not "state of the art," or you are not progressive enough. So the school, in an effort to appease investors, made changes.

Students watched the 2.0 process with limited access to information and reported feeling two things. First, they felt fearful that a curriculum overhaul would water down the law school experience and diminish the fledgling school's already tenuous reputation in the community. And, second, many students saw frustration among their professors and concluded in almost ethnographic fashion (through the eyes of their informants) that the parent company was primarily interested in making money off them.[8] As one put it,

> Botero: It was the fact that those decisions were made in an almost secretive manner. Students were kept out of the loop and were then given a seven-page pamphlet written by someone who was not, by any means, an individual known as a specialist in education, explaining the reasons for the change. It all seemed very suspect. Generally, when you are doing something for the right reasons, you do it openly and, if possible, with the opinion of professional educators as well as students. Here, none of that seemed to have taken place.

RT: And I gather you heard about the multiple faculty votes it took to pass that through. In the process, the most outspoken student advocate faculty were targeted and terminated. How did this affect you and the other students at the time?

Botero: All we knew is that a number of professors started to get fired, and we never got explanations as to why. I did hear from some professors that there was a voting process that was not very transparent either. However, the situation affected me a lot psychologically. For example, I went to speak with one of my professors about my concerns regarding the new curriculum changes. She knew me well from class, and I think she liked me. She then said, "Close the door." The next words out of her mouth were, "You need to get out of here." Imagine being in that situation. Where you are concerned that the school is risking its reputation for who knows what reason and then having a faculty member telling me that if I stayed, I would be making a terrible choice. I could not sleep well for weeks, maybe a month or more, thinking about all these issues and the lack of transparency surrounding them. The worst was we, as students, demanded answers and to be taken into account. We got neither. Nada.

Up until that time, New Delta had operated, with few exceptions, as a standard, ABA-accredited American law program. Many of its limitations up to that point could be easily explained as the result of being new or remaining freestanding rather than tied to a university. For some, these qualities even brought concomitant advantages, such as in the days when financial resources could be committed to problem solving on relatively short notice. In a faculty meeting just weeks after my arrival, for instance, the associate dean had announced that a new budget had not been approved and that funding for teaching assistants was not available. The timing was inopportune for new professors teaching class sizes larger than anything the school had seen before in a new building that lacked full resources. Standing for the new teachers, Jesús spoke up at the time. "Dean," he said, "this is why I agreed to join private equity education. They told us with this model money could be moved around more quickly to help faculty serve students. We promised these guys . . ."

By the end of the 2012–2013 academic year, illusions about the priorities of this model were clarified. More important were the distinct roles of faculty and upper-level administration. As Sonia told me,

You know that ... if you look at it this way, those of us or those faculty members who were brave enough to speak out against it, those are the people they got rid of because these faculty members were able to stand up and say, "Changing the curriculum like this, mixing torts and civil procedure together, all of this, it's not going to work." The people who were against it were, of course, fired in order to symbolize to those of us who remained, "If you speak up against this, if you don't go for this, you're going to follow the same path; you're going to be fired."

Faculty saw this marginalization as one step in a larger process harming students. Their self-awareness about agency under conditions of moral hazard was now, if it hadn't been already, heightened. Sonia continued,

Those of us who remained certainly have no choice but to go along with it, even if we know it wasn't going to work. And so that goes back to if you were servicing a different demographic of students who came from a family of lawyers, right, like the kind of people who probably go to Big State and U of S, a family of lawyers and judges and all of that, who know exactly what they need in order to succeed, would you be allowed to mess with this curriculum in such a drastic way? *Or did you feel comfortable doing it because you know that, you view your population as so desperate, as so powerless to stop you?*

Conclusion

Institutions of higher education, whether public or private, nonprofit or for profit, are bound by basic norms that define them as "academic." Chief among those is an expectation that academics, including professional teachers, scholars, or both, are responsible for and invested in the material they are teaching. This expectation is usually met by securing faculty buy-in through a governance structure placing professors at the center of decisions on academic standards and curriculum. But this expectation is a custom, not a law. Organizations may disregard it, at least to the extent they can secure accreditation without it. Nevertheless, when a school flouts this expectation, as is frequently the case among for-profit colleges, it tends to suffer reputational consequences in the wider academic community.

Whether or not a formal goal of the Law Corp schools, achievement of professor fungibility clearly added to the investment value of the organization and its parent company. In publicly held corporations, executive decisions are made by boards of directors, executives, and sometimes shareholders. The very purpose of the corporate form is to formalize this decision making and organize what are otherwise conflicting interests among executives, managers, and workers. Managers, most would say, just like regular workers, are employees. The dilemma of Law Corp was that to remain legitimate—indeed to remain ABA accredited—its faculty had to share in a large degree of corporate decision making. Yet to maintain its financial structure, this same group had to be circumscribed as "mere" employees. This single contradiction, between faculty as decision-making managers and faculty as employees, lay at the heart of new traumas New Delta would experience over the next year of its life as a reinvented law school.

Chapter 6

"They Want the Rebels Gone"

Contract Relations in a Fiscal State of Exception

I N late May 2013, at a scheduled meeting on the seventeenth floor of New Delta School of Law, the dean called for "good news reports," asking faculty to announce any recent publications or conference talks. A female colleague raised her hand.

"I just wanted to take a moment to recognize Oscar and Rose," she said gently, her voice beginning to tremble. "They have been great leaders and mentors to many of us, and we will miss them dearly," she continued. The entire group burst into applause. A second professor leapt up from her seat, still clapping. The rest of the room—all except two with disabilities unable to rise—followed suit with a standing ovation. Oscar and Rose, married partners, rarely sat near each other in these meetings, possibly to avoid the appearance of cliquishness or of voting as a block. Oscar turned around more than 90 degrees in his seat to see the look on his wife's face. The two made eye contact, and glanced around the room. Both, along with others present, had tears in their eyes. This was to be their final faculty meeting.

Despite holding tenured positions, they too had just been terminated. After carrying significant workloads through the school's first ABA accreditation process and expansion, they were now not to return. To understand how this occurred, a closer look at the role they played in policy and governance at the law school is necessary. In offering that account, this chapter highlights the role of contracts in the for-profit law school context. Whereas faculty employment contracts had heretofore served only to memorialize otherwise mutually understood academic commitments to the tenure system, New Delta leadership moved in the wake of Legal Ed 2.0 to reinterpret this underlying system altogether. No longer about memorializing long-standing commitments, the new vision would be that faculty contracts were themselves the only commitments enforceable against the company.

This shift, I claim here, from *customary* to *contractual* security of position, places this story well within the larger framework of neoliberal governance and legal culture pervasive in this period. As articulated in the following discussion, although Oscar and Rose would later argue that their termination was a direct response to vocal criticisms of 2.0, I suggest that this itself was one indicator of the larger shift toward academic casualization within Law Corp. In business the interests of directors, managers, and employees often tend not to be aligned, and the former two tend to harbor suspicion toward the latter when they view them as obstructionist. But what allows for termination is the absence of governing norms that are either supercontractual (for example, tenure) or explicitly contractual in nature. In the case of Rose and Oscar, their firings—regardless of alleged causes—depended on a subtler transformation of tenured and tenure-track faculty into more casual contractual workers.

Oscar and Rose

Both in their early to mid-fifties, Oscar and Rose were married without children. This gave them extraordinary time and energy to devote to school business. They each had significant legal practice experience and substantial teaching experience from several other ABA law schools. Proud of their Irish Catholic heritage, the pair had lived and taught law in Ireland. In their most recent law practice, they had represented the Mexican government. Some thought it curious that Oscar, holding a primary law degree from Yale, had wound up at the fledgling New Delta. He explained it to me as follows:

> RT: Going back to the beginning, what made you come on board to a for-profit law school?

> Oscar: A number of things. I was representing the government of Mexico in the two years immediately preceding my accepting a position at NDSL. I was not teaching during those two years. In the spring of 2007, I was invited to guest lecture in a human rights class at Northwestern University School of Law and to speak in a conference regarding torture. I realized how much I missed teaching, so I sent out letters to the only two schools in the . . . area, Big State (where I used to teach) and NDSL. We were limited geographically for familial reasons. It was April and not the hiring season for law schools. I was very surprised to hear back from NDSL almost immediately. I interviewed and was offered a position within the week. I had some questions for them about the for-profit nature of the school. They gave me the right

answers, i.e., that they were in this for the long term, that they would never compromise admissions standards for profit, and that a for-profit was not really any different from a university that seeks to obtain revenue from its law school. I sought advice from a number of former colleagues who had been teaching for decades, and some agreed that all schools are "for profit" on some level (in that they seek to bring in more revenue than they expend). Initially, New Delta/Law Corp behaved somewhat in accordance with what they promised. That all changed once they obtained accreditation and access to Title IV funds.

Oscar was hired as an untenured associate professor in 2007. Rose was then also hired at that rank the following year. Both achieved tenure within three years of their arrival. When I arrived at the school in 2011, both were chairing faculty committees. In Oscar's case, he was head of faculty retention, promotion, and tenure—a strenuous and integral committee responsible for reviewing all internal applications for promotion in rank or tenure status.

In Rose's case, she had chaired the faculty appointments (in other words recruitment) committee the year I was hired. The following term, on my arrival, she was appointed chair of international program development (IPD). Drawing ostensibly on her experience in Ireland, Mexico, and beyond, Rose was charged with expanding the international horizons and profile of the law school. In that role, she was a dogged advocate for student opportunities; the committee sent a delegation of students to the International Law Students Association conference in New York and began researching prospects for an LLM or concentration in international law. But, as became common in that year of falling applications, New Delta's budget for program enrichment appeared to grow thinner. Following a meeting with the dean, Rose reported back that her request for a meager $5,000 budget had been denied, and that the committee would retain only $3,000 for planning that year. In subsequent years, this amount would be further cut. What made these spending choices particularly frustrating, Rose said at the time, was Law Corp's own proclamations that it hosted "student outcome–centered" programming. In cutting the budget for international development, the committee surmised, Law Corp had come to the realization that it would not see monetary benefits from investing in "bells and whistles" like transnationalism. Its students, leadership seemed to feel, did not choose New Delta for these high-flying academic opportunities; they did so to get a required degree, sit for the bar, and take on small casework.

Not only was investment in international programs treated as inefficient, Law Corp in fact looked to the international program development committee, among others, for ideas to expand and internationalize its revenue streams. Perhaps the greatest example of this was in an abrupt attempt by the corporation—using Oscar and Rose as key agents—to globalize its reach into southern Africa.

Botswana

It all began when executives of Law Corp received contact from officials in the southern African nation of Botswana. As conveyed to the international program development committee, Botswana was interested in making its judicial system more like the American one. To help do this, its bar association wanted to partner with an American law school to begin training judges and attorneys in American-style procedures and institutional reforms. Thanks to an abundance of wealth generated by its active diamond industry, Botswana, Law Corp felt, was in a position to pay for professors to travel from the United States and for its own attorneys to travel to the United States to acquire an LLM degree.

The company decided to pass this opportunity down to New Delta. Although it held other law schools, one of those already offered an LLM program and the other, only recently accredited by the ABA, was less at risk of violating the so-called 90/10 rule. The "90/10 rule" is the informal name for section 487(a)(24) of the Higher Education Act of 1965 [20 USC 1094(a)(24)] passed by Congress in 1998. It holds that for-profit colleges and vocational schools must generate at least 10 percent of their revenue from nonfederal public sources.[1] If New Delta could capitalize on the new opportunity for relatively easy foreign business, this could make a significant contribution to the 10 percent it needed from non–Title IV sources.

For the first step in this process, the dean hand-selected Oscar and Rose prior to their departures to be the first to travel to Botswana on behalf of the school to learn more of the country's needs. As Rose told me,

We were approached to be NDSL delegates on the educational mission in Botswana. Faculty from all three schools were going on behalf of Law Corp to explore whether there were opportunities there to either partner with schools or establish schools there. In Botswana there is a shortage of lawyers. I know that the dean did not want to send us—but the associate dean urged her to send us. We had both been trying to develop international opportunities for our students, for example by bringing the Chinese judges to speak, and we had both been to Africa before doing some volunteer work on a human rights project, so the associate dean urged the dean to send us. In any event, the trip was planned for a few weeks after they first asked us to go—and, to be honest, we were unsure of the objectives before we went. We landed, and frankly the Botswanans were kind of surprised we were there. In any event, in speaking with our faculty counterparts from the other schools, we got a sense of what was going on and tried to learn as much as we could to see if there were needs there that might provide the corporation with opportunities that might be lucrative in the future if pursued and tried to discover any possible opportunities for our students to gain international training/experience/contacts. Ultimately, we were able to arrange for student externships in Botswana for NDSL students. We were also able to arrange to have professors from NDSL participate in judicial training programs in Botswana.

Following the trip, the pair made a detailed report to faculty explaining that the nation's ministry of justice wanted to reform its "law society" (bar) and industrial courts. Initially the hope was to use New Delta faculty to "train" industrial court judges in U.S. legal doctrine. Later, Rose, the dean, and the Center for Professional Development determined it would be feasible to begin by placing only a few NDSL students under a "remote" externship program whereby they would take assignments and conduct research for the industrial court judges online. The students, two initially chosen for the first round that summer, "met" with judges via Skype, submitted memos, and offered advice on discrete issues in their cases. In spring 2013, New Delta's dean traveled to Botswana herself along with a professor with local contacts, and they returned with more remote student externship opportunities for which five students were promptly selected. In each case, students were told this could be the first part of an ultimate international clinical experience, and it was promoted as one of the only opportunities for transnational work/study offered directly by New Delta. The dean described this as part of an effort to become a "regional center of excellence," a term thrown around in discussions about meeting the 90/10 rule and, some felt, effectively code language for "alternative income stream."

For Law Corp, a prospective partnership between NDSL and Botswana seemed natural. Its parent company, Venture Partners Group, held as one of its portfolio companies another firm, Prometheus Group, whose entire business had been private education in Europe, North and South America, East and South Asia, the Middle East, and parts of Africa. Some even wondered if VPG would simply pair NDSL with one of its Prometheus schools already in the region. But Prometheus certainly had no prior contacts with Botswana, and hopes ran high that New Delta could treat this project as its own to comply with the 90/10 rule.

Despite those hopes, however, little more came of the collaboration besides those remote externships and occasional faculty travels:

> Rose: There were so many other possibilities and programs that could have been mutually beneficial to both Botswana and the students in the Law Corp schools—as well as their financial bottom line—but, ultimately, I believe there really was no long-term commitment on the part of Law Corp to develop these. They were most concerned with short-term financial goals. Oscar and I were both removed from the program and replaced with people the dean favored more.

> RT: What was in it for the corporation (in terms of income streams) to expand to Africa in that way? . . .

> Rose: Yes—they were motivated by any revenue streams that could come from it—but 90/10 was definitely a consideration. In Botswana, the government pays for the education of all students—so there would be money coming in from a source that would help with 90/10. When we were there, we learned that Botswana did not want to send their students abroad because, when students leave, they often do not return—so then the idea was to partner with schools there or explore opening one there. As you may remember, all along at NDSL we had to learn to present proposals in a way that the corporation could envision profit from them. It was not enough to have a good idea that would be fabulous for students—it had to be couched in the language of profit if it was going to get any traction.

Oscar and Rose's involvement in the Botswana project illustrates several important tensions within life at New Delta under the distinct for-profit status the school occupied. First, although declaring at the heart of its charter to be "student outcome-centered," the school was required to find at least 10 percent of its income from nonfederal funding. For reasons that are beyond the scope of this discussion—and that implicate all for-profit colleges and universities—New Delta had a difficult time meeting this threshold amount, already reduced from a one-time statutory level of 15 percent. Because of this, school officials came under pressure at about the same time I began this fieldwork to draw income from other programs and sources. Several faculty meetings turned into brainstorming sessions to harvest ideas for such sources, and frequent proposals included more continuing legal education (CLE) offerings, paid legal services offered in the community, bar preparation courses, and even renting out the school's covered parking to the public.[2] Ultimately, the bar preparation program rose to the fore. Meanwhile, a project such as partnering with a wealthy African nation seemed like a surprise gift from the 90/10 deities, but this would ultimately fizzle out for politico-cultural reasons: Botwsana did not want to risk losing its precious human resources by sending them out to earn LLMs in the United States.

Second, this example shows the tension within New Delta leadership when it came to dealing with dissident senior professors like Oscar and Rose. The two were showing themselves to be highly passionate advocates for students and critics of administrative and fiscal austerity choices. And yet, as senior faculty, they were relied on as leaders and representatives to seek out new income streams. In regards to their dispatch to Botswana, Oscar and Rose were among the only professors with international work and teaching experience qualifying them for this role.

And, finally, the Botswana example illustrates the need for New Delta administration to rely at least initially on faculty to help solve its 90/10 dilemma. In this case, the very idea for the project emerged from the top. In others, faculty were asked to brainstorm new possibilities from scratch. But in either event, professors and staff were needed to execute any proposed solutions. What this meant was that, unlike in other academic environments where business development and teaching responsibilities are finely divided, here they could be blurred. If at ordinary universities interests could be sustainably antagonistic, at New Delta they would, for the purposes of survival, have to be aligned. For them to be aligned, dissident voices would have to be neutralized. In the remainder of this chapter, I want to resist the notion that institutional measures to accomplish this were somehow part of an "understandable logic" pervading business management of legal education in this period. Although survivability of the legal education market downturn was indeed understandable (and a goal shared by administration and faculty), its pursuit at the cost of key academic institutional precepts such as "security of position" was not. Here, the collision between marketization and education is at its most apparent.

"Any Fewer Protections"

New Delta's collaboration with Botswana continued beyond the timeline of my research, but Oscar and Rose's integral involvement in it did not. Following their first envoy to the southern African nation, and after several more months of service to the project, both were summarily removed.

In a similar subsequent example, both Oscar and Rose as senior professors had volunteered to serve as "mentors" to incoming junior faculty. Thus, during my own first year at the law school, Oscar was my mentor. From the beginning, he made it clear that I should check in with him regularly and let him know of any problems. He scheduled bimonthly meetings with me, and, even in the early days when faculty of the school were split between two campuses, we alternated meeting sites, and he traveled by bike or light rail to my location half the time to ensure that we had time to talk about any difficulties I was facing. And, as I have already described, there were quite a few such difficulties related not to teaching or to research activities but to basic requests for and navigation of institutional support. In a school being run as a business, faculty monetary requests for support needs were often met with suspicion and refusal. Senior colleagues like Oscar and Rose, by their insistence on bureaucratic transparency and promise keeping, became to my entire cohort of junior law faculty guardians of accountability. The pair often described their approach as "speaking truth to power." Perhaps for this reason, even after an administrative survey at the end of my first year queried whether faculty wished to retain their mentors and mentees, and even after most including myself elected to do so, a committee in charge of the matter separated Oscar from both of his first-year mentees—a sign that administration perhaps did not want him influencing junior colleagues as much as he had been. Moreover, although Oscar and Rose had possessed the institutional savoir faire and cultural capital to "speak truth to power" on behalf of colleagues, the latter were unable to return the favor when Oscar and Rose would need them most.

* * *

In early May 2013, the school's human resources department emailed faculty with a statement that all professors would be issued "letters of reappointment" in lieu of what it called "lengthy" contracts. Prior to this, New Delta had been issuing full employment contracts every academic year. These documents contained basic information such as academic year salary, fringe benefit amounts, termination and choice of venue[3] clauses, and, perhaps most important, a clause incorporating one chapter of the school's faculty handbook governing faculty duties and responsibilities. Despite New Delta's description of extant contracts as too lengthy, they had amounted to only two pages of text.

The new appointment letters, issued on May 3, were one page in length. In these documents, New Delta described reappointment of faculty to a full-time position as either *teaching track*, *tenure track*, or *tenured* full-time faculty. The letters again referenced handbook Chapter II and assured recipients that "the appointment letter does not contain any fewer protections, rights, and responsibilities than the previous contract issued to returning faculty." Faculty were given exactly two full weeks to return signed copies of the appointment letter to New Delta human resources.

By describing the new letters as "simpler," less "redundant," and equally protective of faculty employees, the school sought to establish the new practice of appointment letters as a *greater* realization of existing commitments. But several items were different. First, the issuance and due dates came far earlier than in previous years when New Delta had usually waited beyond August or September of the *next* academic year—one month into the next contractual cycle—to issue agreements. Second, the documents omitted "material terms" for individual professors—items such as specific salary and benefits, which would make them most instrumentally enforceable against the company. And finally, in their overall form, the letters seemed to contradict provisions of the very faculty handbook they claimed to partially incorporate. Under one particular subsection, Chapter II of the handbook spelled out in clear terms the form every faculty contract was supposed to take, leaving open discrete blanks for key terms such as salary. This form, presumably, was designed and agreed on by founding faculty so that all would be governed by the same terms. Making little effort to fill out those terms, the new letters could have effectively created agreements that were formally different for each individual professor.

In early April, I was talking with Rose about matters related to the IPD committee's work establishing a new international certificate program. As former committee chair she would have valuable insights about navigating the various institutional hurdles—most notably a visible lack of resource commitment to program development. In this meeting, I asked Rose about rumors that the school was about to unilaterally alter our contracts. "Well," she told me, "if they do, Oscar and I are prepared to lawyer up."[4]

Following the issuance of appointment letters on May 3, they did "lawyer up" and decided not to return the signed letters. Doing so, they felt, would invalidate the faculty-crafted handbook provisions. In addition, this was not necessary in their case; because they were "tenured" faculty, Rose said she and Oscar were already governed by a longer-term contract. Under the same handbook section, tenured faculty could be subject to termination only on completion of "posttenure" reviews at regular five-year intervals:

Once a faculty member has attained tenure, the faculty member shall be presumed to continue in that position. In order to assure that the tenured faculty member continues to contribute to the School, the tenured faculty member's record shall be reviewed in the fifth full academic year after grant of tenure and every five years after each extension of tenure.[5]

At worst, they felt, their failure to return the signed letters would entitle them to negotiations on the material terms left unanswered in the new format. But, rather than simply waiting for the May 17 return date to lapse, on May 10 Oscar and Rose took the affirmative step of returning not the new letters but rather updated versions of the existing form contract to which they had been accustomed for the previous five years. Most faculty, meanwhile, returned signed letters. Even though many objected to the unilateral change, few were willing to contest the school's claims about sustained protections under the new agreements. Meanwhile, a few junior faculty, some already searching for positions outside the school after it had fired Jesús, themselves lapsed in returning the new forms by a day or more beyond their due date.

For Oscar and Rose, this began a tense waiting period during which they did not receive any communications. Despite their follow-up inquiries, New Delta human resources, they said, never acknowledged receiving their reply contracts. On May 17 the deadline came and went. On May 18 the school held its spring graduation ceremony. Attending that event, the pair received no updates from the president or dean on their status. On May 20, the couple met with the dean to discuss "long-term planned projects" on which they had been working for revenue creation at the school. Here, the couple asked whether the dean had received word of their contracts to which she responded the matter was then "with legal."

Finally, just before the 5 p.m. close of business on May 20, the dean sent each a letter, saying in part :

The deadline for you to accept the offer of continued employment for the upcoming academic year was Friday, May 17, 2013. We received your written communication indicating that you do not accept the offer of employment made to you. For this reason, the offer of a position for the 2013–2014 academic year is withdrawn.

Your current contract runs through May 31, 2013. In light of your rejection of our offer of continued employment for the 2013–2014 academic year, your employment at New Delta School of Law will end on May 31, 2013 as that is the last day of the term of your contract.

On or before May 31, 2013 you will need to have completed the following:

· Cleaned out your office of all personal belongings.

· Anything that is company property, proprietary and/or confidential must remain.

· Return your ID badge, keys, laptop, company credit card and cell phone (if applicable) to . . . Human Resources.

· Ensure any personal emails or documents are retrieved from your computer.[6]

On the same day their extant contracts expired, Oscar and Rose, through a local law firm that had represented their friend and colleague Jesús, filed suit in U.S. District Court. Unlike Jesús' claim, which disappeared quietly under a quick settlement and likely confidentiality agreement, this dispute—for both the couple and New Delta—would prove more noisy.

Oscar and Rose v. New Delta and Law Corp

In their federal complaint, the pair asserted claims for *breach of contract* and *breach of implied covenant of good faith and fair dealing.* But, from almost the moment it became public, Oscar and Rose's case against the school was much more than a legal grievance. The introductory framework, setting out the timeline and series of facts, painted in minute detail many of the events and conversations from the preceding one year at NDSL. For five pages, it described the organizational structure, hiring timeline, tenure status, and contractual terms Oscar and Rose experienced prior to the unilateral changes in 2013. This section alleged that the school itself was institutionally opposed to the very idea of "tenure." They also alleged the defendants' conduct directly contravened ABA Standard 205(b) on faculty governance, stating:

The dean and faculty shall formulate and administer the educational program of the law school, including curriculum; methods of instruction; admissions; and academic standards for retention, advancement, and graduation of students; and shall recommend the selection, retention, promotion, and tenure (or granting of security of position) of the faculty.

Oscar and Rose's overarching argument was that NDSL had maintained the appearances of faculty governance until roughly the moment it had secured ABA full accreditation in 2010. From then on, they argued, the school began dismantling faculty oversight.

From there, the complaint continued for thirteen pages in an elaborate, chronological description of events surrounding the Program 2.0 and Faculty 2.0 initiatives. It underscored the dean's call to "build a better mousetrap"[7] and the associate dean's personal policy of denying letters of recommendation for transfer and asserted that the recent policy changes were above all an effort to restrain students from transferring. It described the multiple mandatory votes expected from faculty and the disorganized manner in which these were conducted. And it set forth the very short timeline along which Oscar and Rose received altered contracts, returned unaltered ones, and were informed that they had thereby elected not to return. Finally, the complaint articulated the couple's expressed objections to policy and contractual changes and concluded that these objections were the only real basis for their dismissal and thus invalid.

From the perspectives of other faculty who had witnessed all this, the allegations were probably fair. However, some said, many included details were not necessarily essential to the couple's legal claims. If all they had wanted was their jobs back, some said, they could have filed for an injunction from the moment of termination, preventing NDSL from acting on its own decisions. Then, if what they claimed was a breach of contract, the couple could have filed a shorter complaint arguing only their points that they had opened negotiations with the school rather than refused its initial offer.

The complaint filed was more expansive than those documents would have been—and this was probably for a reason. Without saying so explicitly, Oscar and Rose appeared to use the occasion of their legal grievance to document publicly—and legally—dubious internal matters that had been transpiring quietly in a for-profit institution for several years. Because NDSL was privately owned and controlled, it could maintain near secrecy over its organizational policy. Although such a policy was not in place during the duration of this fieldwork, the school eventually required all employees to sign a confidentiality agreement—something rarely seen in educational environments. But Oscar and Rose knew that allegations made in a court filing are privileged from liability and can also become public.[8]

And public they became, almost overnight—indicating someone near the case had leaked the complaint. Together, the online media attention surrounding the case fixated on the allegations about governance tampering and student entrapment. On June 3, just three days after being filed, the suit was reported by the *National Law Journal* online with the leading statement, "Two former tenured professors have sued [their] School of Law and the company that owns it, claiming that they were improperly fired after raising concerns about what they called a drive for profits at the expense of students and faculty." The next day, a courtroom news website reposted and summarized the complaint in a lengthy online article. Although it only restated most of the alleged facts, including the "build a better mousetrap" sound bite, the post immediately lent credence to the allegations and allowed the narrative to congeal. Meanwhile, that same day *ABA Journal* online, a trade newsletter for the American Bar Association, repeated the same narrative to a far wider audience. It later updated that piece to include a response statement from NDSL. On June 10, another small blurb appeared in the *National Jurist*, another major trade magazine, again reiterating the narrative that this was retaliation for objections to antitransfer policies couched as curricular reform.

If Oscar and Rose had made a calculated choice to include extracontractual details as a way of garnering media attention, the plan seemed to have worked— but only up to a point. Typically in legal strategy, such moves are designed to increase the bargaining position of the aggrieved party. When levied against large publicly visible corporations, this strategy takes advantage of the intense organizational drive to control public relations and perceptions. A normal institutional response, therefore, might be a settlement to make the claim "go away." In some areas of law, such disputes are common and have what some describe as "nuisance value"—a monetary value equivalent to an amount *less than* the loss of business resulting from the nuisance (to public relations, daily operations) they create.[9] But this case did not unfold that way. New Delta seemed surprised that the information could become public so quickly. As things were unfolding fast, the organization was slow to respond. A former employee told me about the public relations officer's role in this,

She came in that Monday and [got] a request for comment from a national online publication—I believe it was the *National* or *U.S. Law Review*. She desperately tried to get the administration to provide a short response (i.e., "We can't comment as we've not seen the lawsuit, but we treat our professors/employees with respect" . . . etc.). It would be an entire week before they provided a response, and, by then, the social media had overwhelmed any message the school could do to respond.

She was well aware of what the "silence" could mean to the reputation of the school. She had many sleepless nights during that week and felt frustrated that she was to be the only one (at the school or at Law Corp) that realized that for every hour that went by the Internet was going crazy with negative comments about the school.

The social media frenzy around the case grew rapidly. From approximately June 4 onward, students began first learning about the story online and then about the allegations that their dean may have referred to them as "mice."[10] Just as the national legal trade press had reproduced the narrative, so too—and in some cases with much stronger vitriol amid a rising "don't go to law school" sentiment among millennials—did new law school blogs like *Above the Law* and *Inside the Law School Scam*. Then-current students of New Delta, most well connected via Facebook, began chattering about the terminations, suit, and governance problems. In the month of June that year, typically late in the transfer admissions cycle, I received messages from roughly a dozen concerned students asking for letters of reference, worried that this would be their last chance to obtain one. Other faculty reported similar developments.

Student reactions to the publicity and its underlying narrative were severe. Among former students, it stirred up feelings of anger and vindication for having left. As Melanie, the former student who had already transferred to Big State by this time, explained,

The whole "build a better mousetrap" complaint really fired everyone up here. That the administration was viewing students like dollar signs and preventing them from bettering their positions by blocking transfers in any way possible was offensive. We heard about so many professors (like you) leaving and had heard a lot of rumors circulating even before your decision that the administration didn't value faculty opinion and really shut down the ones that stood up for the students.

For current students, the publicity reinforced suspicions already developing that NDSL was only interested in them for their tuition dollars. Stevie, another of NDSL's "underserved" minority students, was particularly worried about how the publicity reflected on the long-term life of the school and his own life chances:

Yes, I know about the two professors' complaint and the "mousetrap". I even spoke to a professor [who] said that if professors do not get in line they will be [shown] out. It is so rare for tenured professors to be kicked out. Students are locked in, and I am locked in. I owe the federal government so much money, and the legal job market is not good.

For other students observing the dispute, the connection between Oscar and Rose's terminations and the antecedent curriculum debates was increasingly apparent. Student Botero described his epiphany on this issue:

Of course, then came the news of the professors suing the school, and the dean making references to making the school "a better mousetrap" that would keep students from going to other schools. My concerns became a reality. I do not know if that worked or not; I do not know if other schools kept some of our students from being able to transfer out. However, at the moment it all seemed to make sense.

For still others such as Terrence, the court filings themselves shaped such conclusions:

Terrence: My guess from reading the court documents and the news is that they appeared to be forced out because they spoke out against policies. Oscar and Rose were favorites of the students.

RT: In your view, should it be the place of faculty to speak up in that way, or should decisions be left to administrators and business officers?

Terrence: In this instance, I do not feel that the administration listened to us. I feel as if some of the faculty were advocating for the students' interests. The administration only seemed to care about marketing and the profit of the school. At New Delta, it seemed like the professors were the ones who advocated for the students' best interest.

Another student, Lawrence, had studied under Oscar and felt attached to his approach and leadership. According to emails I received from Lawrence at the time, he was particularly distraught over the loss of his favorite professor. Making sense of this loss in the hagiography of his own progressive, Catholic formation, Lawrence described the terminations of Oscar and Rose as a kind of "martyrdom":

RT: And you mentioned faculty martyrs; can you describe some of those and how they made you feel at the time?

Lawrence: Rose and Oscar [are] the first that come to mind. I was in a class with Oscar right before he was terminated. The man was a sage. He loved the law and loved teaching it. His resumé was unparalleled in his field. And he was a scholar. This was a rare trait among teachers at our school. In any case, I understand that he fought the curriculum changes and was punished for it. They were supposed to receive a tenured contract and received an inadequate agreement instead. When they protested, the school said, "That's a counteroffer and a rejection, and we opt not to make you another offer. See yourselves out." They wanted the rebels gone, and they orchestrated a way to do it.

The experience of spring semester 2013 was traumatic for many current students and angering for many recent transfers. But, in a way perhaps already included in New Delta's calculations on this matter, this trauma was circumscribed by the temporal limits of any one student's legal education. At only three years in duration, the law school matriculation of all those who witnessed the public dispute between NDSL and some of its most valued senior professors was relatively short. Within another year or two, all those who had studied with these professors would be graduated, and few current students would recognize their names. In that same amount of time, the full tuition sum represented by each student enrolled at that time would have been collected, recirculated, and divided for operations and investor returns.

But for faculty, many of whom remained close with Oscar and Rose beyond their terminations, the trauma would be more enduring. Even for those not closely associated with the pair, the impact on their role within the organization had been permanently altered by the manner of their dismissal. Some made the connection between the oppositional style of Jesús and the rigorous challenges Oscar and Rose each posed for the imposition of corporate policy. These three tenured colleagues, other faculty clearly felt, had been targeted for vocal advocacy in general. The 2.0 debates, some said, may have only been one example of this:

> Carl: I think with respect to Jesús, Rose, and Oscar, they were very outspoken and vocal about many, many things; to me it just seems [sigh], I don't know. I, I thought that was just the dean wanting to get rid of them in general.
>
> RT: Hmm.
>
> Carl: I don't know if I would tie it specifically to, to the curriculum 2.0 and the teaching-track discussion. I mean, and that may be, maybe that's naïve of me, but it seemed to me that those were some of the individuals whom she disliked the most and really felt somewhat threatened by or challenged

by, and so I'm sure their speaking out on that was part of it, but it also seemed to me that they were just, you know, they were kind of the "squeaky wheels," right?

Despite this feeling of inevitability, the loss dealt a blow to the many junior colleagues they left behind. Most of all, professors felt disheartened that the most vocal among them could be removed for standing up for students. Kate put it this way:

Oscar and Rose were another "shock"; yes and no, they too were incredible leaders and spoke out when they saw something that wasn't going to be good for the school or for the students. I think they were let go because they didn't just lie down or jump when the school said jump. So, it was a shock that they were let go in the way they did, but, again, they stood up when no one else did. I signed that bogus contract that year, but they saw that it was their only chance to ask for what the faculty handbook gave the faculty, but, in essence, that "contract" wasn't as clear as previous ones had been.

For many faculty thinking over this contract dispute, if tenured faculty could be dismissed for failure to sign a yearly agreement, the very concept of tenure had been redefined at NDSL. More gravely, however, this meant that the security to write or speak out against popular or executive decisions—even in *designated* spaces for faculty deliberation—was attenuated for all others. As my informant Hilary explained,

In this instance, where the faculty is supposed to be a part of the process and you've got this EQ that we're supposed to be able to speak out, I don't think in that . . . Because of the situation we were in, they should not have been terminated for speaking out. That was the forum designated for us to speak out.

While weakening the security of position represented by tenure, NDSL administration also made steps toward blurring the lines between permanent faculty and other instructional and noninstructional staff. As explained in Chapter 1, the school encouraged students to address all instructors as "professor." Soon after, it took the added step of applying this title to academic skills counselors. Next the dean announced that faculty ranks, such as assistant or associate professor, would have to be eliminated from business cards and email signatures. Finally, and by that time with no objection from remaining professors, administration unilaterally incorporated staff as voting members of "faculty meetings." Although framed as steps of antielitism and inclusionism, the direct effect of these consecutive steps, many understood, was to dilute the remaining voices of faculty oversight.

Oscar and Rose were aware of these shifts in the wake of their termination. During one of our conversations, I mentioned the absence of dissent, and Oscar had this to say:

The destruction of the faculty is complete. And the existing faculty has been so cowed by their behavior (and often complicit) that nobody will say a word. I am reminded of the [paraphrased] saying: "First, they came for the gypsies, but I wasn't a gypsy so I said nothing. Then, they came for the trade unionists, but I wasn't a trade unionist . . ." You know how it goes.

Conclusion

Oscar and Rose were valued members and leaders of the faculty and of the wider community at New Delta School of Law. Part of their value to both colleagues and students came from speaking out unhesitatingly against corporate or administrative policies that seemed to undermine faculty governance or risk harm to student learning.

The new Law Corp initiative to revamp the curricula of member schools for the 2013–2014 school year was, for this pair, an example of such policy. Whereas its underlying basis in legal education reform research—in documents such as the Carnegie Report—was appreciated by most, its corporate origins, implicit goals for investor marketing and student retention, and rapid implementation in the absence of sound development all raised red flags about the substance of the new Program 2.0 proposal. On top of this, the manner in which ad hoc committees designing the program were constituted, and in which faculty voting was influenced by substantial salary increases for some, threats about job security to all, and multiple mandated votes on the matter all contributed to feelings that the 2.0 process was destroying faculty governance over curricular matters. Although Oscar and Rose spoke clearly about these problems in real time, it was initially only Jesús who was immediately terminated, albeit under other pretenses.

Any sense of security for the pair was short lived. As if to underscore the new limits on faculty governance, New Delta's issuance of appointment letters unilaterally altered the form of contract stipulated in the school's faculty handbook since its foundation. Oscar and Rose recognized this increasing withdrawal from customary commitments to faculty and protested NDSL's unilateral move away from standard form contracts. Choosing to interpret this protest as a rejection of their offer of employment, NDSL and its legal advisors declared a withdrawal of any offer and thus termination of their most vocal critics.

The move away from full contracts toward the more casual appointment letters rendered the school *less* rather than *more* bound by past commitments to the institution's full-time academics. NDSL decidedly began to interpret its own tenure system to mean a presumed series of future contract offers capable of retraction and subject to expiration limits.[11] In pursuing their legal claim for harms resulting from this conduct, Oscar and Rose submitted an expansive complaint alleging the root motivation to be institutional hostility toward them for speaking against the 2.0 programs. For them, the conditions of academic freedom and service to students embraced by the law school were the most salient norms. The school's obligation toward them, represented most in the "breach of implied covenant of good faith and fair dealing," arose from professional social norms that characterize academic tenure and exceeded any details about individual contracts. For New Delta officers, the relationship with these two faculty critics was more properly reducible to individual contracts, which, it argued, they themselves did not accept in a timely manner. At the district court level, the pair's suit would be dismissed, setting off a long appeals process.

The casualization of workforce is certainly not unique to this setting. Across the United States, tenure-track positions for college and university teaching and research have dwindled to historic lows while unprecedented numbers of adjuncts, lecturers, and visiting appointees teach core subjects in almost every major academic discipline. And outside these environments, "right to work" laws prohibiting union activities and bans on "fair share" rules collecting fees from nonunion workers benefiting from collective bargaining both exemplify a wider movement toward worker casualization and managed precarity. But what was most striking about the 2.0 episode and resulting terminations at New Delta was the divergence of interests between academic administration and faculty. Here again, it must be repeated that resulting measures were not just part of an "understandable logic" that says institutional survival in higher education requires casualization. To treat these approaches as understandable is to forestall moral judgment of the kind this study hopes to provoke—the kind that distinguishes education in its social embeddedness from pure commercial or industrial activity. In commerce, complicity with bad policy may result in lost revenue. In education, such losses, measured in knowledge, skills, and life chances, can be more far reaching.

At New Delta, the freedom protected by respect for tenure was precisely the kind of freedom necessary to point out weaknesses in sweeping new policy changes such as Program 2.0. Because the new curriculum would have immediate impacts on student learning, retention, and bar passage rates, one might expect school administration and business officials to retain and incorporate critical perspectives in an effort to assure that major flaws—ones that could harm the company's own mission—would be identified and corrected. Dissent would not be pretty but it would at least help assure quality. Protecting it would foster this quality assurance in a way that consensus, organic or artificial, simply would not. Elimination of Jesús, Oscar, and Rose was, at this level, bad for business.

But it was also damaging in the more obvious sense that it further disturbed increasingly skittish students. As if membership in a new low-ranked law school in an industry obsessed with tradition and institutional prestige was not precarious enough, more students than ever contemplated departure in the wake of these very public terminations. In the immediate aftermath of these events, the school suffered extended public relations harm. Over the next few years, as students from the first high-volume classes began to graduate, bar passage rates continued to decline steadily. In 2014, four junior professors, myself included, left New Delta for other academic employment or advanced degree study. And, by spring 2015, after revisiting the success of student learning in the new integrated courses foisted on all-new 1Ls and at least half the professors, administration announced a bold reversal: it would be uncoupling at least two first-year subject areas in addition to finally reverting back to a semester scheduling system. Rather than admit this as a partial failure of the Program 2.0 policies, and thus an outcome of its feverish campaign that left three tenured faculty careers nearly destroyed, leaders described it as another step in the school's march toward "continuous improvement."

Chapter 7

The Policy Cascade

Deregulation and Moral Hazard

JUST a year after three tenured professors were dismissed for what many felt was dissent from academic policies driven by business need, New Delta School of Law became due for reaccreditation by the American Bar Association's Council of the Section of Legal Education and Admissions to the Bar. This process would include a lengthy self-study report, a site visit from a delegation of the Section's separate Accreditation Committee (including meetings with current faculty), and production and review of documents such as syllabi and final exams. In the months leading up to this heightened scrutiny some felt the school—having just recently reconfigured its commitments to security of position and academic freedom—was bound for reprimand.

Meanwhile, students began to take greater note of declining bar passage rates and, as the large class that began in 2011 came into its third year and began to actively seek postgraduate employment, more students ran up against growing skepticism among members of the local bench and bar. The local community—initially indifferent to the new school turning out more lawyers in the area—was now more sensitive to saturation of the local job market and the primary role revenue played in the school's operations. As student Tomás learned, this had direct impact on employment opportunities for himself and other students. "One example I can think of," he told me, "was at a Los Abogados (Hispanic Bar Association) function":

I was speaking to an attorney there about where I went to school, etc., and he was brutally honest with me about how my road would be harder to land some of the opportunities out there because he knew specifically of various firms that did not even entertain applications from NDSL. He even gave me examples of the bigger firms and for clerkships [where school rankings and the like are looked at] that would not entertain our applications. When I inquired more as to why, they mentioned the school's model, the sense that they were more worried about generating income than giving the students more value. I remember someone else mentioning to me that he once read that the dean said specifically that the school was not worried about generating a higher ranking, that they were more focused on diversity—good for me, but I think something like that didn't sit well with some employers.

Walt, a first-year student educated under the newly integrated curriculum, experienced similar resistance. For him this was due to growing suspicions about the quality of students after the school lowered standards to increase or maintain class sizes. "[Employers] blatantly . . . came out and said, 'Hey, if you have a need for some work in here, I would highly suggest graduating from somewhere else.'" These experiences directly contradicted statements by administration that reputation was unimportant.

Prestige and hierarchy have long played a role in law school employment outcomes.[1] But reputation in this case was limited not simply by the youth of NDSL as an institution or the shallow depth of its alumni network. It stemmed in large part from the ways in which the business model had an impact on graduate life chances. By recruiting increasingly diverse students at high rates of federally loaned tuition, and by offering those students an increasingly austere legal education package, the school seemed to be branding its students with the mark of lower quality.[2] Though it gave more minority and nontraditional students the chance at becoming lawyers, it did little to benefit those students culturally within the status-preoccupied world of local professional law. This emphasis, on *becoming* versus *being* a legal professional, was at the center of Law Corp's use of "access" as both a marketing and deregulatory argument.

Regulatory frameworks governing schools like New Delta have been greatly influenced by the rhetoric of access. Accepting school officials' narrative that the main hurdle to professional diversity is *becoming* a lawyer, the key regulatory actors—here the ED and the ABA—have until very recently failed to properly grasp the potential harm for-profit law schools are liable to generate.[3]

This chapter first organizes and presents key regulatory policies and their institutional guardians. It then offers examples of the sometimes creative ways in which New Delta leadership sought to comply with such policies. And, finally, the chapter offers interpretive evidence culled from student and faculty informants suggesting how the moral hazard generated through Law Corps' conversion of public loan dollars into private revenue streams may be transmitted to and absorbed by graduates of its law schools.

Whither Regulation

All law schools are governed by a regulatory apparatus that combines policy expectations from both the Department of Education and the American Bar Association's Council of the Section of Legal Education and Admissions to the Bar.[4] The Council has been delegated the responsibility of accrediting law programs seeking to benefit from student access to federal loan moneys. Meanwhile, to obtain ABA accreditation and to receive those funds, a school must comply with the *ABA Standards and Rules of Procedure for Approval of Law Schools*, a 200-page rule book promulgated by the Council covering topics from the basic requirements of accreditation to the acceptance of academic credits from foreign institutions.[5]

In addition to these, for-profit law schools, like their proprietary trade school, college, and university kin, must also comply with additional policies governing for-profit higher education specifically. There is some overlap between these and the new ABA requirements following a series of recent anti-fraud lawsuits against U.S. law programs, and there are now also new gainful employment (GE) rules for for-profits despite recent intense lobbying and litigation against them by groups like the Association of Private Sector Colleges and Universities (APSCU).[6]

Different aspects of this framework have been targeted by some legal education experts as having increased rather than reduced the conditions that led to the crisis of the late 2000s. Chief among these targets have been the ABA Standards on tenure, scholarship, and law library resources.[7] These Standards, critics said, had created a problematic expectation that all law schools, from top Ivy League programs to bottom freestanding and startup schools, must behave in the same way.[8] For Brian Tamanaha and others, this rule has precluded the important development of "differentiation" among schools that could otherwise specialize in training large-firm corporate attorneys or small-firm and solo practitioners.[9] Graduates in the first category, Tamanaha rightly points out, are the only ones truly able to "afford" the high price of contemporary law school tuitions; they are the only graduates for whom current legal education is worth the cost.[10] The problem is that most students entering law school cannot know in advance whether they will fall into this group, and, even if they could, this creates incentives for legal advocacy for moneyed interests over social justice.[11] Tamanaha labels the dominant paradigm the "Ritz-Carlton" model, whereas similar critics describe the ABA Council's unitary model as promoting "Cadillac" law schools.[12] For him and others, this homogenizing policy runs counter to the operations of a free market in law school offerings. Bryan Garth, meanwhile, told me that such critiques set up a kind of "apartheid model" of bifurcated legal education and, in turn, professional citizenship.

Some of these same critics also point out that easy access to Title IV moneys is a further distortion of a "properly functioning market."[13] Because students have access to almost unlimited federal funding and are generally oblivious to long-term interest-added costs of attendance, law schools from top to bottom have priced their tuition at nearly identical rates with the very top two or three schools establishing the ceiling for everything below.[14] In a properly function- ing market, they say, where consumers are otherwise sensitive to differences in pricing, there is little reason to justify a school like New Delta charging the same or greater tuition than law schools at Yale or Stanford. In recent years, at least one major credit rating agency has begun ranking law programs based on a ratio between cost of attendance and gainful employment rates to better assess the creditworthiness of student borrowers.[15] Most recently, the Department of Education has sanctioned several for-profit law schools for failing or nearly fail- ing to meet its new gainful employment rules.[16] Such responses are a significant step toward making legal education operate as a "true" market.[17]

But few commentators have interrogated this underlying faith in the mar- ket as such to sort out problems in legal education offerings. A functioning market could potentially solve the specific problem of differentiation in cost and practice area. But how might this very framing of problem and solution exacerbate other existing issues? Trained almost exclusively in the discipline of academic law, most key commentators seem to take for granted the wis- dom of economics over the role played by society and culture in this debate. In doing so, they often describe law school offerings as "products" among which there should rightly be differentiation in quality and pricing. What this forgets is that lawyers and the expertise they wield are not fungible goods but rather human agents of an imperfect justice system dependent on their own value judgments and political and economic allegiances. Much like the politics of "access" in Law Corp's own mission rhetoric, this emphasizes economic trans- actions for *becoming* a lawyer over the social realities of being one. The fram- ing of this problem as an economic one to the exclusion of its more moral implications further omits the role that ethical judgment—and teaching and learning therein—will play in the life of legal professionals as "officers of the court." If the contribution of this book has been to explore this omission at the level of business model, a similar omission at the level of teaching has already been well documented by Elizabeth Mertz in her important study of law school language.[18]

This critique of extant law school reform discourses flows from the theoretical awareness of my informants—themselves educators and students close to the ground of law teaching and learning outside the "elite" policy and research schools. One of these individuals, Suzette, reflecting on Law Corp's approach to the financialization of academic life, was prompted to make an important distinction:

While I believe that education can be profitable, education is not a car or a widget. It is much more complicated, and the success of the student should be what drives the profit. However, at NDSL, the profit drove the education . . . Because widgets and cars aren't complicated like people. Every car or widget can be molded and manufactured to be nearly identical. You don't have to change the mold; in fact, you want every car or widget to be standard . . . People aren't like that. Everyone learns differently. In education, you want creativity, critical thinkers, diversity of thought and expression. This is what promotes growth and innovation. You cannot create or foster this by creating an assembly line.

Arguments for differentiation in a more properly "functioning market" have tended to view ABA Council regulations as too rigid and uniform compliance with them too costly. Removal of these regulations, some believe, would subject weak or underperforming law schools—measured in terms of bar passage, employment rates, and graduate income rates, among other things—to the purported "cleansing" power of the market. Legal academics, until now heavily shielded from such so-called cleansing, seem taken by this logic. In her groundbreaking ethnography of Wall Street investment banks, Karen Ho shows the historical uptake of this reasoning in support of a much wider marketization of U.S. corporate ownership in the 1980s and 1990s.[19] Companies, whether privately or publicly held, had heretofore been conceptualized and managed as "social entities" whose success was measured in terms of product quality, market share, and employee satisfaction. During the 1980s, with the conflux of financial technologies such as private equity firms, leveraged buyouts, junk bonds, and hostile takeovers, company health came to be measured strictly in terms of one metric: shareholder value.[20] When a company was taken over, its new owners sought to raise this value by "trimming the fat," that is, by identifying and reducing so-called wasteful, bloated spending. As Ho points out, many on Wall Street narrated this as targeting precisely the kind of corporate spending that characterized the age of business as a "social entity." The all-out shift toward shareholder value for these banks represented a purification of spending practices by subjection to the market and a final retreat from corporate loyalty to stakeholders (for example, consumers, workers) other than its shareholders. Perhaps most importantly, bankers responsible for the substantial downsizing and layoffs that resulted from this period also argued that their fat-trimming efforts, to the extent they were increasing operational efficiencies, were actually a service to the public.[21]

When legal academics romantically assert the virtues of a legal education free market, they likely do not envision a world in which schools behave like companies under Wall Street control. And yet, this is what makes the story of New Delta and Law Corp compelling: It is a logical result of market-based thinking absorbed into legal education. The marketization of law school ownership and management—a move that many say calls initially for deregulation— pursues a path much of American business has already ventured down. To the extent it is one of the first law programs run by a private equity–held company, New Delta, may thus be a bellwether.

Mapping Regulation

ABA Standards

The ABA Council of the Section of Legal Education and Admissions to the Bar has been designated by the ED as the sole accreditor for American law schools for federal funding purposes. The ABA, a national organization for professional self-regulation comprising attorneys, judges, and legal educators, has long had its interests aligned with the legal academy and therefore sparked accusations of monopolistic behavior. For this reason, and to comply with the ED's expectation of an independent accrediting body, accreditation is placed under the separate oversight of the Council. The Council answers to no other agency, and it alone is responsible for promulgating and enforcing its Standards and Rules of Procedure for Approval of Law Schools. For purposes of the New Delta case study, one of the most salient of these has been Standard 405 on the maintenance of a permanent faculty with a combination of tenure and "security of position."[22] This rule had been interpreted to mean all ABA schools would be required to observe some form of tenure system whereby faculty could, through the production of teaching, research, and service, achieve a secure status within the organization unimpeachable for controversial statements or critical positions. But the Council has discussed altering this rule to require other contractual security of position and therefore a proportion of law faculty to be hired off the tenure system. What this would mean precisely for long-term security under either arrangement is unclear. Early indications such as the dismissals of Jesús, Rose, and Oscar—all tenured faculty—suggests already an immediate attenuation of security almost as soon as the Council began reconsidering interpretations of this Standard.[23]

The ABA accreditation Standards also require that schools properly vet students before admission. Ostensibly, this provision reflects an aspect of the ABA's own history as a standardizing force in not only legal education but also the legal profession. Prior to the ABA's direct involvement in overseeing legal education, the study and practice of law in the United States had been viewed as highly variable and in many circles unethical.[24] Part of the ABA's original charge, then, was to clean up the profession by applying ethical standards at the very gates of admission. Today, its accreditation Standard 501 on admissions reads in part:

A law school shall not admit an applicant who does not appear capable of satisfactorily completing its program of legal education and being admitted to the bar.[25]

In its efforts to expand in 2011, New Delta grew its first-year cohort to roughly 450 students. Already at that time, prior to the slump in applications in the subsequent years, the school began drawing more on students it earlier had deemed presumptively inadmissible. The AAMPLE program, described in Chapter 1, was a perfectly legal, institutional workaround on admissions standards whereby rejected students could "test in" to the program with lower incoming indicators than were usually admitted.[26] Over the years leading to 2011, New Delta drew increasingly on this pool. The school also lowered its own admissions indices, considering LSAT scores around 146 to be in its bottom quartile in 2011 and then scores around 140 as its bottom end in 2014. Between these two moves, arguments on compliance with Standard 501 could be increasingly difficult to sustain, particularly in light of the school's 2015 first-time bar passage rate, which fell to just above 30 percent. One possibility, going back to the very mission of the school, was to respond that NDSL and the Law Corp schools generally were more capable of turning low-performing students into success stories than most other programs. In the early days, when student–faculty ratios were low and bar passage was beyond 90 percent, this appeared true. But, on the heels of its higher AAMPLE draws, lowered admissions standards, and lower bar passage rates, this could no longer be sustained.[27] New Delta's compliance with Standard 501 therefore seemed open to skepticism.

A final ABA Standard implicated in all of this was Standard 509 on Required Disclosures.[28] This new rule does not specify any particular GE numbers to maintain accreditation but only that each school post conspicuously its employment number for prospective and current students—as well perhaps as student creditors—to see. New Delta observed this rule as soon as it was promulgated. But the precise methodology for calculating this number was open to interpretation. Did gainful employment require measurement at graduation, nine months after, or several years after? Did it include all types of employment or only those in which the law degree was essential? Moving further toward answering these questions, and indeed specifying an actual formula for this calculation, the GE rules promulgated by the Department of Education in 2014 for proprietary colleges and universities went further.[29] Indeed, by early 2017 several for-profit law schools had already run afoul of those.[30]

Higher Education Act

Beyond these key standards established by the ABA Council, regulations established by the Department of Education under the Higher Education Act are a second critical layer to the for-profit law school policy landscape. The first important ED policy pertains simply to accreditation and requires that all schools receiving federal loan moneys be accredited by a designated regional or national body. Meanwhile, beyond accreditation, Title IV of the HEA offers special provisions related specifically to proprietary higher learning. For this story, the two prominent features of this have been the so-called 90/10 rule and, although still in their early stages of enforcement, the new provisions on gainful employment.[31] Separate from the ABA's requirements of employment disclosures, the ED's new GE rules condition Title IV moneys on compliance with a clear, stricter formula for postgraduate employment.[32] Like the 90/10 policy, gainful employment rules have been the object of considerable litigation arguing them to be "arbitrary," but they have been upheld in federal court.[33]

Compliance: The Policy Cascade

Viewed substantively, NDSL leadership had to contend with policies governing *accreditation* and policies governing federally backed *student loans*. These rules combined with internal responses to form what I will call a "policy cascade." This describes the top-to-bottom flow of normative principles from high-level state regulations to midlevel professional oversight and finally to low-level organizational compliance efforts. But despite the unidirectionality of this movement, its significance cannot properly be understood solely by what those in public policy studies call "top-down" or "bottom-up" approaches; it calls for a holistic approach combining expert doctrinal knowledge of policy itself with the ethnographic constructivist awareness of ground-level anthropology.[34] The metaphor of a cascade captures the way in which policy "flows" from one level to the next ultimately shaping behavior both organizationally and individually. The gradient of this flow appears to also track descending levels of institutional power. Proceeding through this discussion, critical questions about the aptitude of this metaphor might include the following: Is it really unidirectional? Is it truly a "flow" or rather a "disturbance"? Is it structural, or do agents play a role? And are meanings transfigured along the way?

Keeping these questions in mind, an ethnographic account of local efforts to comply with ABA and federal policy developments begins with accreditation. If NDSL's access to federal Title IV moneys depended on ABA accreditation, then the school's entire business plan—requiring also eligibility of students to sit for the state bar exam—depended on this as well. For this reason, little effort was spared in securing ABA accreditation. In its setup of a "mock site visit"—including a hired team of outside experts and administrators—the school was not that unusual. But, in its practice of hiring former regulators to serve on its executive board, it perhaps was. Although not illegal, this practice created a significant overlap between Law Corp's own policy decisions and the community of lawyers, judges, and educators making up the ABA Council. As Rose put it,

Law Corp hires all the ABA players as consultants. . . . This is not illegal—and is probably SOP [standard operating procedure] for the corporate world—where the watchdogs and those they are supposed to watch slide back and forth with ease—but it sure smells bad when we are talking about the future of education in this country.

The actual site visit team, an ad hoc group organized by the Accreditation Committee and responsible for making recommendations on accreditation, is different. That body, a group of approximately seven legal educators and administrators from other law schools, makes an independent investigation of new law programs on initial application and in each of the subsequent three years, at which time the school may apply for full accreditation. For fully accredited schools, reaccreditation site visits are required every seven years.

The investigative rigor of site visit teams may be open for debate. At New Delta during this research, the school was visited by a full team shortly after the firing of Oscar, Rose, and Jesús—all of whom were highly critical of corporate policy reforms foisted on faculty. Although supported only by circumstantial evidence, my informants considered those terminations as peremptory silencing of criticism that would have otherwise emerged during the site visit months later. Had those faculty been present, they almost undoubtedly would have raised an alarm to the ABA that New Delta was neutralizing its faculty for business purposes. But, with them fired and embroiled in litigation (or a settlement with nondisclosure clause in one case), the school depicted these former faculty and any criticisms lingering behind them as a few disgruntled employees and their noisy aftermath. In any event, the ABA's team did not, on visiting the school in late 2013, raise serious questions about the terminations, governance, or morale. Former faculty member Carl was disappointed by this:

I would love to have the ABA doing more. I think it's probably too hands-off, and, for example, with respect to faculty governance, I think we've had so many different examples here of failures in that area, and yet the ABA did a site visit here and didn't really pick up on that, I thought, didn't come down strongly on the school with respect to faculty governance.

The elimination of Jesús, Rose, and Oscar could be viewed as part of a strategy of "compliance" with accreditation policies through informational management. But whereas true compliance might mean observance of governance and security of position, here it just reduced vigorous commentary about these. Taking this example, its cascadelike qualities are further spelled out in Figure 7.1. High-level rules about Title IV access required accreditation, and this was placed with the ABA Council in charge of administering this; the ABA Council one level down has promulgated and overseen rules about accreditation, including Standards on governance and security of position; Law Corp sought to mandate policy change from its headquarters, in turn eroding shared governance; New Delta quashed faculty resistance to implement Law Corp pol-

Figure 7.1.   Sample heuristic of NDSL "policy cascade."

icy; and, finally, perhaps to accomplish the latter without raising flags to the site visit team, it eliminated its three most vocal tenured faculty critics. With reaccreditation secured by 2014, this cascade appeared to have worked out in the school's favor.

After accreditation opened the door to Title IV funding, as it did for all U.S. law programs, New Delta still had to comply with specific HEA rules on proprietary education. The most salient of these, the 90/10 referenced in Chapter 6, demanded that at least 10 percent of school revenues would come from nonfederal sources. Despite the apparent leniency of this rule, allowing that a vast majority of private income could be derived from public financing, for-profits often struggled to meet its requirements.[35] One strategy they embraced was to recruit from among military and law enforcement personnel. Under 1992 amendments to the HEA, tuition moneys paid through the GI Bill were excluded from the public funds counted in the 90 percent amount.[36] And, for law enforcement, tuition benefits were paid from state rather than federal sources and therefore also discounted from the 90 percent tabulation.[37] Despite all of this, the school, like many of its counterparts, still had difficulty meeting the income ratio expectations of the ED. Its efforts to address this led New Delta to ask its faculty for solutions and to seek out creative partnerships that might generate new income streams.[38] Notwithstanding even those efforts, compounding pressures on the school to satisfy 90/10 caused it to develop internal programs such as the controversial "myBAR" program.

First announced to faculty in 2012, the myBAR (Multi-Year Bar Accelerated Review), program was an in-house bar exam preparation course students could sign up for early in their studies and then use after graduation when preparing to take the state bar. The state bar is a two to three day examination consisting of legal essay exams, multiple-choice questions, and in many cases a simulated problem-solving exercise. Students sit for each of these in three-hour blocks for two sessions per day. Like the essay examinations of law school doctrinal courses, the essay questions expect structured analysis with finely tailored application of key legal doctrine. Unlike those exams, however, students in myBAR were typically required to delve into somewhat shallow legal analysis to show mere "competence" rather than mastery. For this reason, the test was largely a matter of extreme memorization and mental endurance. Until that time, students of New Delta had the choice of either studying on their own with the use of various guidebooks and practice materials or taking a paid summer review course offered by professional agencies such as BarBri or Kaplan. In the latter courses, with few exceptions, students learned largely from watching prerecorded lectures by eminent professors in each field and then drilled themselves in multiple-choice questions and practice essays that could be submitted for grading to local instructors. This modular approach allowed BarBri and Kaplan to operate in most major cities at relatively low cost and to charge considerable sums for their courses and materials. Security controls on these were high, as for example at the BarBri West Los Angeles headquarters where lectures were recorded live in front of student audiences whose identification credentials were closely monitored on entry and departure. Similarly, BarBri stipulates ongoing ownership of its study materials and holds a significant portion of its materials cost as a deposit redeemable on return of their books.

Understanding the large sums of money to be made in this effort and understanding the implications of that money for the school's 90/10 obligations, New Delta began in 2012 to develop myBAR to consist of materials and lectures licensed from *both* BarBri and Kaplan and making use of local instructors as coaches and essay graders. Drawing these local instructors from New Delta's own recent graduate pool—a move that then helped controversially with gainful employment statistics described in the following pages—officials could keep the cost of this program relatively low while charging close to the same amounts as these other established programs.

"But," some professors asked when the program was announced, "wouldn't students simply take out more loans to pay for these?" "No," they were told. Students could not pay for nondegree study such as bar preparation with federal loan moneys. Even if diligent students saved their loan disbursement living amounts month after month to pay for bar preparation when the time came, that money would not be counted against the 90 percent portion for Title IV purposes.

Former student Ford had taken the school's myBAR program and then failed the state bar on his first sitting. I asked him how he felt about the course and whether he felt it was a reason behind his results:

I am doing it for a second time only because it's free, but I am studying on my own this time. My problem with myBAR is that the school has advertised that it's such a better program than regular BarBri. I know a student that did both, and there was no difference in the instruction. The only difference was that the school offered a classroom to come watch the instruction. They did add some myBAR coaches in the middle of the program last summer, and these coaches were just former students who passed the bar but have no credentials in instruction. My coach was not bad—I will give her that. My problem is I would expect with a school-based bar prep program that they prepare you before the program starts on what to expect . . . I asked several times beforehand what to expect and never received a response.

Other employees familiar with the program told me it was primarily a 90/10 strategy and therefore not strictly geared for student success:

Employee: myBAR was created to generate 10 money when the 90/10 rule came in effect. It was just BarBri and components of Kaplan. . . .

RT: Were they that explicit that the intent was to balance out 90/10? Do you happen to know to what extent, in what fraction, or in what amount the program succeeded in shifting that ratio for the school?

Employee: Yes, [people were] told that was the purpose and [they] needed to market as much as possible. They pay BarBri a lot to use the materials. I am not sure if it was ever considered a success. I do recall [some] at the other schools referring to it as "our 90/10 problem" so I assume it was NDSL that was in danger of violating it. Since it started the school has added a lot of unnecessary programming to it.

Within the first year of its existence, the myBAR program led to no increases in the school's bar passage rates. On the contrary, either because of the uncertain quality of this program or because of the dropping admissions standards over time, newer graduates were passing the bar at rates around 50 to 60 percent. In response to these falling numbers, the school began to more closely scrutinize the preparedness of students signed up to take the bar exam. The school then began to actively discourage students whom it determined to be at risk of failure—either because they opted out of the myBAR course or because they appeared to perform poorly in it—from sitting for the exam. In at least one case, this fact became one of several allegations listed in a lawsuit by a former student employee of the school followed by substantial social and trade media backlash. In another case, three of my own former students wrote to me after I had left the school to ask my advice as they felt the school was pressuring them to defer the bar:

Dr. T,

... Not sure if you have heard, but the school is being sued once again because of their "alleged" practice of asking students to defer. Now while Orrin and I are confident in our ability to pass, it is clear that the school is desperately finding out where we stand. What seems to us is that not only are they trying to save their accreditation, but get into students' heads that they should defer from taking the Bar Exam.

After all this, we received a[n] e-mail from a professor first asking us if we are taking the second mock Bar and finally asked us to meet with her prior to discuss our thoughts about the mock Bar. The e-mail was only sent to [our study group] from what we can tell, but we find it a coincidence that this e-mail was sent after both Orrin and I spoke up. Paul did respond, but told the professor that he would have to get with us before making a commitment. Orrin and I have decided not to respond at this time.

In light of the research you are currently doing, we were wondering with your experience, what would you advise in handling this situation?

Thank you for your time.

Gil, Orrin, and Paul

In response, I told this group that I was sorry to hear about this discouragement. I said that they had worked really hard and supported each other through the process and that if they felt confident they shouldn't let the school talk them out of sitting for the exam. Lastly, I said the only party who would benefit from their deferral of the test would be NDSL itself.

Discouragement of bar sitters initially began as a practice aimed at students who had experienced life challenges such as a death in the family. "[They] had done it in emergency situations," one informant told me, "something like a girl's father dies a week before the exam. [They] did it out of kindness." Soon, this practice developed into an organized program known as the "UP Program"—*UP* meant as an acronym for "unlock potential." Through this program, certain students were offered an iPad and living stipend to defer sitting for the bar exam while studying for it more rigorously under the eyes of myBAR course instructors. When this program was first implemented, it was done quietly, but, as students not asked to participate became aware of it, many became very upset. Terrence, a student who chose not to take the myBAR course, was among the first to tell me about reactions to the practice:

> Terrence: Two people who I knew who received the letters were very offended by it. First, the timing of the letters was absolutely horrible. Two weeks before the bar! Two weeks before the bar your school tells you that it does not believe you will pass and you should drop out.
>
> RT: Awful.
>
> Terrence: They felt like they were punched in the gut by the school. It messed with their heads too.

As examinees know, success on the bar exam is very much dependent on memory and mental endurance. For these two skills to operate at their best, the individual student must not only study hard and maintain a healthy lifestyle prior to the exam but must also build his or her own confidence up to confront the otherwise intimidating volume of material covered in the two- or three-day test. For many failed students, a personal drama or life event in the weeks leading up to the exam had disturbed this confidence and therefore their chances of success.[39] At New Delta, some felt the ability to opt out of the exam and receive compensation for lost registration fees could be a welcome offer.

But the school's proactive discouragement of some to sit out the exam for its own reasons also had apparent adverse psychological effects on students—both on those contacted and those not—trying to bolster their own confidence. For some, it felt like a perverse incentive. As student Walt told me,

> That's a little frustrating for some people who are prepared like, "Hey, one, obviously the student's money for tuition that you're going to pay these people and why are

these people getting rewarded for not doing well?" If you want to call it that. I'd love an extra $5,000 in scholarship money for doing well. You're almost being rewarded for not doing well.

Gainful Employment

Gainful employment refers to the rate at which a college or university's graduates are not only employed but also employed in a manner that supports the graduate's cost of living, including student loan debt repayments. It is widely believed that calculation of such rates should include a requirement that this employment require possession of the same degree the student just completed in the reporting college or university program. Work at a coffee shop on completion of law school, in other words, should not count toward a law program's gainful employment numbers.

Law schools have disclosed employment and salary information to *U.S. News and World Report* for its hegemonic rankings system that date back to 1987. In more recent years, they have also reported this information to the ABA itself.[40] But critics have pointed to the many flaws in this self-reporting for ranking purposes. Foremost of these is the observation that law schools themselves are beholden to data volunteered by recent graduates.[41] Graduates most likely to self-report—that is, to complete and send back any survey instrument—are those well positioned in high-paying corporate law firms, the kind that make possible repayment of the currently high law school tuition rates. Graduates near the lower end of the earning spectrum, or those without employment at all, were most likely not to respond. Under this self-reporting system, however, schools were not required to disclose their survey response rates, and therefore their numbers were not scrutinized for validity. As recent writers have said, this created the false impression that most upper tier alumni were gainfully employed and earning more than $125,000 per year.[42]

Spurred in part by a burgeoning reform "movement" led by activists like Kyle McEntee and his group Law School Transparency, the development of new ABA rules on gainful employment disclosures was a step toward better informational openness. The new policy demanded that all ABA-accredited schools place clear disclosures in their marketing materials about the rates at which graduates were finding jobs. This requirement implemented wider reasoning that law admissions should operate as a "well functioning market," a major premise of which was free flow of accurate consumer-relevant information. But the ABA policy did not itself specify how employment should be formulated for reporting purposes.

During the recent legal services employment bust, therefore, some law schools started actively hiring their own graduates in a variety of casual positions. For both *U.S. News* ranking and ABA purposes, this practice was reportable as employment in "academia," even if the students were not immediately tasked with academic labor. In all, they represented some 3 percent of reported employment.[43] In some instances, such jobs include valuable public interest work that would otherwise be done on a voluntary basis.[44] Schools reporting these self-funded positions as full-time employment have since earned substantial criticism and sparked a new ABA reporting rule requiring that such positions be excluded from employment data after 2015.[45]

At New Delta, the practice of hiring recent graduates had begun well before I began this research. On my arrival, in my first week in 2011, I was surprised to learn that many of the school's Academic Success Program (ASP) instructors—those responsible for study skills and analytical tutoring for at-risk and low-performing students—were recent alumni. In some cases, these graduates had been some of the top-scoring students in their graduating classes. In others, a few professors told me, they were very much not. This use of NDSL graduates as study skills instructors, alongside others graduated from high-ranked programs such as North Carolina and Columbia, continued unchanged for several years until approximately 2013. That year, a few more high-performing graduates were brought on as "writing fellows"—a practice not in itself unusual among ABA-accredited programs.

The next year, after a series of painfully low bar passage results arrived, New Delta reorganized its myBAR program and hired a number of its own students as "bar coaches." In several instances these were students who had recently taken and passed the state bar exam. But, curiously, as reported to me by summer 2015 bar sitters, several of these in-house coaches were still current students who had not yet even seen a bar exam.

Finally, the UP Program became still another means by which NDSL could comply with gainful employment rules. The school paid certain students to sit out the bar exam cycle for several months while completing a study regimen that they monitored closely. Meanwhile, because these students were on the school's payroll, they could at the time be classified as employees and therefore contributing to New Delta's own employment numbers.

So, to recap, two main categories of external policy applied directly to New Delta: those pertaining to accreditation and those pertaining to Title IV federal loans. Compliance with each required an amount of local institutional ingenuity. In each of these cases, high-level national policy had to be consulted, interpreted, and implemented favorably at the local institutional level. This process, which I term a *policy cascade*, is significant for its institutional rather than individual agentive mechanisms. It must be viewed separately from the interpretive work of individuals who, faced with state policy in any number of fields, assimilate and implement new norms into their everyday lives and conduct. That aspect of policy—the interpretive one—is a subset of the larger processes of meaning and world making identified by contemporary anthropologies of law and policy. In our contemporary globalized world of economic citizenship and universal human rights, individual interpretive work is a key component of all law and policy development. It is the final mechanism by which new norms become "real." People must live them.

The policy cascade, however, is different. It captures the movement of norms down a power gradient—a kind of chain reaction in lawmaking where a rule change at one center of power begets rule developments in a wide array of lower state bodies, nonstate organizations, institutions, and corporate actors. The policy cascade is still about meaning and world making; however, it captures these efforts at the intermediate levels between the state and the individual. It connects all intermediary actors in a continuum of policy vectors, carrying and transmitting a version of new norms from one level to the next and from higher layers of abstraction to lower ones.

Most importantly, the policy cascade puts state policy into a more heuristically palpable form and therefore supports what Susan Reinhold, Cris Shore, and Susan Wright have previously described as "studying through."[46] Studying through, an update on Laura Nader's onetime description of expert anthropology as "studying up," refers to the study of connections among state power, rule making, and everyday life. This idea further resembles the now familiar notion of *governmentality*, the idea that technologies of governance in our modern age are far distributed beyond the limits of official government and that civil society and individuals become complicit in the exercise of state power. But whereas governmentality captures the practices and beliefs of governing middlemen, studying through asks us to look closer beneath this layer to what it reflects about norms and norm systems. Culture, it then seems to suggest, is not simply the everyday Other to state rule making; it is rather the net sum of those governing rules interpreted through everyday meanings. Studying through finds culture and policy in the same normative space between the state and the street.

As a heuristic for studying through, the policy cascade captures the flow of norms themselves into this middle space. Emanating from a lawgiver, in most cases in the United States, the federal government regulations about higher education are proposed and commented on at the national level. But then, once adopted, they typically do not govern the conduct of individuals at street level but rather implore subsidiary institutions, such as accrediting bodies like the ABA Council or the educational bodies like Law Corp directly, to cultivate more policy. At each level of transfer, the governing norm is read, interpreted, and implemented. And although it is true that these activities are conducted by individuals themselves, under most conditions none is acting as an autonomous policy agent. Instead, officers must implement policy in accordance with the institutional norms and culture of their own organization. How the new norms enter through a policy cascade and interact with local institutional culture is thus an important lesson produced by studying through.

Student Outcomes and Moral Hazard

Moral hazard is the condition of being or feeling shielded from the consequences of one's own risk-generating practices. In today's world, we are relatively familiar with the concept as applied to the economic collapse of the late 2000s—the very same ones that would lead to a decline in Big Law, law graduate salaries, and thus law school enrollments. From the late 1990s to mid-2000s, federal regulations applied to financial institutions were relaxed in ways that permitted banks to lend to individuals and families previously considered high-risk debtors.[47] Those people, disproportionately poor and racial minorities, came through these changes with the ability to secure credit to buy homes, vehicles, and other hallmarks of American and increasingly Western upward mobility.[48] Banks such as Wachovia and Wells Fargo, aware that these transactions were generating high-risk debt, justified their practices on the basis of increasing minority "access" to the American Dream.[49] But, whereas historically these institutions would have shouldered the burden of any loss resulting from their risks, contemporary banks were able to resell this debt as a kind of security on the open market. "Credit default swaps," as these transactions became known, were at the heart of the financial collapse.[50] As housing prices inevitably fell, subprime mortgage rates increased, payment obligations ballooned, and many home owners defaulted, losing their property and leaving the final creditor unpaid.

So, while animated at least nominally by the impulse to open access to housing (and other) markets, banking practices—and this is only one example—created substantially more moral hazard in the U.S. economy. By separating the originating party of a high-risk transaction from the ultimate bearer of the risk, deregulation in this instance allowed market separation of practices and consequences. This illustration comports with original nineteenth-century definitions of moral hazard in the insurance industry.[51] There, actuaries and adjusters considered moral hazard to be the natural by-product of a system in which the risk of casualty losses was newly separated from individual insureds.[52] According to those experts, responsibility to take great care in personal and industrial behavior was perversely reduced by the advent of liability and health insurance. Normally bearing the risk of their own loss, actors had a natural incentive to be careful. But, by spreading their potential losses across wider populations, such incentives were, supposedly, reduced. Throughout the twentieth century, economists and public health and policy experts have looked at this problem again and again, expanding it far and away from the early insurance context to apply to social welfare more generally.[53] There, some experts have proposed that all forms of social welfare lessen the incentive for risk-minimizing or value-adding behavior because they encourage people to rely on the state or other providers.[54] The overarching theme in this debate has been the supposed correlation between greater social protections and increased moral hazard.

But, in light of the recent economic crisis, and in light of the evidence presented about New Delta and Law Corp, I wish to highlight the opposite. Under today's dominant culture of neoliberal governmentality, the increasing withdrawal of the state from sensitive social and economic sectors itself promotes greater moral hazard. Needless to say, this has not happened through direct state action—neoliberalism at least nominally abhors this. Rather, this has occurred through the vacuum created by state retraction and the filling of this vacuum with market rationality that appears on its face to promote open information and competition but may in fact encourage substantial risk shifting from private to public and from wealthy to poor.

The state, in shaping economic life through its apparent absence, reflects deep assumptions about right and wrong and plays directly on social structures and differences. Offering political economists direct qualitative and empirical evidence on how state deregulation has itself helped institutionalize ideas about right and wrong at the reputational expense of one of our most trusted professions, the ethnography of New Delta is a case study in the production and distribution of moral hazard.

The school's parent company is the first level at which to answer this. As a holding of the private equity firm Venture Partners Group, Law Corp has as its true financial mission the creation of value for off-site private equity investors who are either institutional investors or high net worth individuals or families. The average shelf life of a private equity holding (either the company itself or the firm's relationship with it) ranges from five to six years only.[55] In the meantime, standard private equity practice is to maximize value by cutting costs and, if possible, reducing workforce. To do this, private equity firms play an unusually larger role in their subsidiaries' governance than do officers of other corporate organizations.[56]

As reported by my informants, VPG and Law Corp's direct presence in the life of New Delta was a matter of some controversy. As one former professor said, the photos of all VPG firm managers initially featured prominently on campus:

I know in the old building we had . . . . our local board pictures up, and then they actually had pictures of the VPG board; there's probably seven or eight partners, and I don't remember which ones. . . . There's always different ones. But you know they were making sure their investments were going well, apparently, and because it was so new.

In one instance, a group of consultants helping with the initial ABA site visit took issue with the prominence of off-site executive governance. Kate explained that,

From the beginning, Law Corp was super-hyper involved. I remember even the t-shirts we were first given back before the first "mock" site visit, the shirt had the school logo and name and on the sleeve, Law Corp was proudly affixed. The mock site team told the administrators that the Law Corp logo needed to come off; the administrators thought they were joking, but one of the mock site team members told them that they were serious. So, I think, from that point, Law Corp tried to act like a "support," and in fact they behaved that way for a while, at least until we got accreditation in 2010.

In other cases, students and faculty were themselves acutely aware of their precarious position as holdings of a private equity venture. For some this began as an expectation of greater customer satisfaction or higher quality:

RT: You said the initial impression was that it might be a good thing. What gave you that?

Walt: I say that because they obviously have to make their money, so they obviously want . . . You would think their best interests would be the student and try to make it the best learning possibility because, obviously, that's how they make their money is by having people go there and want to go there and want to stay there. Obviously, they have shareholders to answer to. What made me realize the opposite is that they didn't care about the student. All they cared about was enrollment. They didn't really care about the quality. That's what changed my perspective. There are definitely some quality people that go there, but there are definitely some people that should not be there. I think that, overall, hurts the reputation of the school.

And so moral hazard at New Delta began with its very governance structure where school decisions over admissions, academic standards, curriculum, and student opportunities were influenced by—and at times subservient to—fulfilling promises to capital investors. The risk incurred by these foundational investors—placing millions of dollars in funds attached to law school economics—was softened by shifting this risk to other stakeholders—notably students and faculty.[57] Not only that, but implementation of this financial hierarchy at the local level necessitated that incentives be applied to local administrative decision making.

Budgetary decisions made by local New Delta administration were, at least in the minds of several of my informants, the result of incentive structures and vertical pressures. The vertical pressure applied from Law Corp and VPG above the law school level itself is different from horizontal pressures experienced locally by the school in its academic or professional communities. In describing the curriculum changes, Myra clearly conveyed feeling this vertical pressure:

My understanding is we were told . . . "You're running out of time, so forget about getting it right; we just have to get it done. If you don't vote yes to get it done, corporate is going to make it happen anyway, and you will be told how it's going to happen."

I actually think that that threat is probably the reason that the third vote passed, because, like, "Well, at least we have some control over it because our colleagues have created this, rather than being told how it's going to run." *I think because we were coerced, more than anything, the integrated curriculum on a third vote passed.*[58]

The experience of this pressure translated into local policies to satisfy the home office. If the policy cascade describes a domino effect in rule making among stratified institutions, the application of corporate pressure on local administrators can be said to hasten moral hazard along the same path.

This observation rests on the transmissibility of moral hazard. If the latter is a condition of separation between risk and consequence, law and policy have important roles in this.[59] They provide the normative structure that enables such separation. But, as policy cascades through regulatory levels and bureaucratic institutions, it also encounters forces that disperse moral hazard along the way. In this sense, moral hazard is more than simply a condition of separation from one's resulting harm. It is also the experience of that separation by those affected by it. Through the experience of this, affected individuals such as students or home owners may be, and I would argue in this case *are*, encouraged to produce their own moral hazard.

Preliminary support for this claim is readily apparent. As the earlier discussion would suggest, the school charged its students premium tuition rates.[60] During the years of this study, NDSL tuition averaged approximately $40,000 per year compared to $39,000 at University of Illinois, $43,000 at University of San Diego, and $50,000 at Harvard. Furthermore, student outcomes at New Delta, although promising in the school's early low-growth days, had fallen considerably. The school's first-time bar passage rate fell from 97 to 31 percent between 2009 and 2015. And its reported full-time employment rate appeared to drop from 97 to 40 percent between 2010 and 2014. Many students would have great difficulty paying down the $250,000 to $280,000 debt (at repayment) incurred during attendance. In pure, economic rational choice terms—balancing the probability and cost of failure against the probability and benefit of success— the cost of the degree should not, in most cases, have been worth it.[61] If return on investment—minimally the likelihood of paying back one's debt plus recouping opportunity costs from attending school—were the only measure of "success," students probably never should have enrolled at New Delta.[62]

But the results of this calculation applied only to students. Until recently, the school itself and others like it suffered few if any consequences for student failure. They are paid up front via Title IV. Those moneys, immanently public in origin, are converted on student enrollment into private funds and disappear only to be repaid in smaller fractions as income tax at the end of the year. Although oversight regarding this arrangement has been delegated to the Council, its primary approach during this fieldwork was to accredit broadly and let the market decide.[63] And yet, thanks to Title IV, access to which accreditation is in the first place meant to police, law schools have been largely shielded from market pricing and competition constraints.

Remaining at the local level, moral hazard may be further transmitted via faculty. By embracing the school's imprecated mission statement, this group of as many as forty-four legal academics came to view their work as "serving the underserved"—largely racial minority and low-income students and their future clients—and thus expanding access to legal profession and services. Even among the critics who viewed this skeptically as "drinking the Kool-Aid," simply remaining on as faculty helped to perpetuate the arrangement.

Paradoxically critical to this picture is the trope of the individual "caring" professor. Though not per se sinister, the trope of caring can be, and in this context was, dually predatory. By touting its faculty as caring student-minded teachers, the company gained advantage from the individual professor's time and energy relative to the wider legal and legal academic professions.[64] Caring in this way was an externality to be selected for in recruitment and used in marketing value. And at the same time, it allowed this external resource to occlude the prospect of failure increased by dropping admissions standards. In several conversations, caring emerged as a trope. For Sonia, it helped explain why she continued in a role she might otherwise have withdrawn from earlier:

What makes me sleep well at night is every time I touch these students' minds and open them up to seeing the plight and how we can make a difference in people's lives and so forth. That's really what drives me, not so much having, commanding a large salary but again to help these students.

A second explained how successful the faculty had been in choosing colleagues who cared about students. Amid a larger conversation reflecting critically on her participation in the business model, Hilary stopped herself:

I feel like I've been bashing the school, but there were a lot of good things about it as well. . . . I don't know if I've ever told you this story before, but I was at a . . . conference one time, and I was waiting . . . I was the last one to leave or something, so I was waiting. I was sitting in the hotel bar waiting for my flight instead of sitting at the airport. I overheard these professors, and they taught legal writing . . . but they were talking about how ridiculous being student centered is. One woman laughed and said, "Yeah! Students pay my mortgage. That's about it." It was just horrible! She was not from a for-profit school, but I thought that was just horrible.

I don't think that any of our faculty ever has even that thought cross their mind. I think that the faculty was truly there because of the mission of the school. Let's teach these students who can't get into other law schools. Get them practice ready so they can go out there, pass the bar, and just hit the ground running. I think the faculty had a great desire to do that, and I think that if we had been given the proper tools, and maybe if the curriculum hadn't changed, then maybe we would have continued with that success. The school did have a lot of success early on.

Further sustaining the production of moral hazard, faculty and staff alike were participants in what appeared to many as increasingly inferior offerings following ABA accreditation. Such lower-budget developments included a unilateral adoption of trimesters to enroll students in all three terms of the year, move them through the school more quickly, and make more efficient use of faculty teaching time. So detrimental to teaching and learning were the trimesters that New Delta administration made an abrupt about-face in the spring of 2015 to announce a return to the traditional semester system. As Albert told me,

The trimester is gone away, and I think the problem with that is just everybody was just exhausted. There was no, there was no winter breaks. There's no breaks between semesters. You felt like you're on a treadmill all the time, and for what? For people to get through law school because "they save some money"?[65] . . . I just think we needed to slow things down; I think it's much better for the students. Ultimately, it just didn't work. It's to their credit; they're going back to it.

Another was less sanguine about the lessons to be learned from this back and forth. "I think a lot of people feel that it's just the way the business operates," she said. "These impactful decisions are made quickly and without a whole lot of input from the rest of us, or input that is considered and matters in any real way." Such changes in programming also had an impact on student organizations and opportunities, with funds for the main student body organization reduced and temporarily withheld during a low cash flow period, also in 2015. "They will never admit how bad things are," said one student leader, "which frustrates me because we could probably help them."

Educational experience seemed to further suffer from the loss of key faculty amid the changes. If the initial wave of departures was involuntary—through firings—the second was perhaps fallout from the first. After Jesús, Oscar, and

Rose—all highly respected among their colleagues—were already fired, four junior faculty left voluntarily to other teaching or study opportunities. At that time, students seemed to be of the mind that the losses were all high-quality educators. This understanding, according to my informant Roberta, became a push factor—not only for transfer but also for a speedier graduation.

As if this were not hard enough on the psyche of the students, the school then offered contract buyouts—voluntary paid layoffs—to another round of faculty the following year. And while the initial offer sought ten volunteers, it ultimately found more. By late spring of that year students received the message that several faculty had "chosen" to leave the school for family and other personal reasons and that this had no implications for the health and well-being of the institution itself. Students like Walt saw it differently:

This semester has been very frustrating. We got an email a few weeks ago, maybe a month ago, from the dean, essentially telling us that they were giving professors the "opportunity" to be bought out of their contracts. . . . From what I heard, thirteen professors signed up. You look at that, "Why are these professors so quick to jump ship?" Obviously, we're going down that road.

Obviously, the ones that they're hoping that they'll step forward are the ones that make the most money, and it means the ones that have been there the longest, the ones that have the most teaching experience; those seemed to be the ones that we're losing.

New Delta's choice to casualize faculty by increased use of adjuncts, visitors, and former students added to these feelings of dilution. For at least some, such as an upper-division working student named Valerie, the result in educational quality became palpable:

Valerie: Several of my core bar-tested courses have been taught by faculty who openly admitted in class that they have absolutely no background in it and that they have been told they are teaching three days prior. Heavy reliance on "flipping the classroom" and YouTube videos substituted lecture . . . Most concerning was the number of mistakes made by the professor; if you get levels of scrutiny mixed up, maybe I don't want you grading my Con Law II final. This has been the case in several classes where depending on "who you get" makes all the difference.

RT: Very sorry to hear this. Was there a point in time where this shifted or started? Was this from beginning to end?

Valerie: Over the course of my time at the school?

RT: Right.

Valerie: I think it has become more frequent since the school has started hiring more adjunct faculty, especially those whose practice takes precedence over class. This trimester one of my professors has been absent from five classes, three for a trial booked months in advance and two for a European vacation. The subject is bar tested.

This reported decline in quality, although experienced locally as the result of potentially unsuited faculty instruction in important law subject areas, was the result of decisions first made at the very top of the organizational pyramid. Traveling from VPG to Law Corp to NDSL and finally to faculty, policy choices favoring local austerity were intended to promote global revenue maintenance in times of substantial crisis in the legal education economy. In this regard, moral hazard, the separation of risk creation and its consequences, was transmitted in traceable fashion from global to local levels of the institution.

Conclusion

The deregulatory framework allowing law schools like New Delta to operate under the banner of open access has permitted the creation of substantial moral hazard. This should be particularly concerning insofar as this moral hazard may be tentatively observed as transmissible to new graduating classes of first-time attorneys. Making it further problematic is the very mission New Delta and other Law Corp schools set for themselves. Assuming that mission, to "serve the underserved" and increase "access to justice," is genuine, the observations of this chapter suggest these institutions may do worse than fall short. They may, by placing disproportionately minority, economically marginal, and nontraditional students at higher risk of experiencing the predicament of moral hazard in their ultimate postgraduate careers, exacerbate the problem of access.

The mechanism by which this occurs, the policy cascade, is a process whereby policy objects promulgated at institutional centers like the Department of Education or ABA Council set off the development of new policy objects further down the chain of institutional assemblages. Because of the structure of federal regulatory power in the United States, this progression could also be described as movement down a power gradient—an incline from higher to lower levels of institutionally secure power positions. Such imagery takes seriously the enduring role of sovereign institutions even in the face of Foucauldian concepts such as *disciplinary power* or *governmentality*. Whereas the latter capture local street-level exercises of outsourced state power, they do not wholly replace the power of institutions in a highly bureaucratic policy environment. Moreover, when looking closely—via ethnography or otherwise—at the regulatory field of U.S. higher education, it becomes even more apparent that sovereign power maintains hegemony precisely through the efficient mechanism of the policy cascade. Disciplinary power requires ongoing energy and resource expenditure at the lower levels. Like their metaphorical namesakes, policy cascades do not. Set in motion at the higher levels of the regulatory state, they seem to "flow" un-inhibited down a path of least resistance until, ultimately, they shape everyday life for actors—in this case vulnerable students—on the ground.

These observations speak to the larger relation between neoliberalism and access. Proponents of a reduced or outsourced state have long argued that a strong social welfare network leads to an increase in moral hazard. As in the private insurance debates of the nineteenth century, these writers have blamed the loss-distributing function—and thus risk-distributing function—of such safety nets for creating incentives for risky behavior. On this basis they have argued somewhat successfully for deregulation and market rationality in many areas of social life.[66] But, as the preceding pages have suggested by contrast a more *marketized* approach to education in for-profit law schools like New Delta has sustained and exacerbated the moral hazard they now partake in.

Conclusion

The Trouble with Differentiation

L AW has the capacity to remake the world in its own image. Recognizing this, legal profession and education have for decades sought ethnoracial and socioeconomic diversity through active recruitment. But diversity generated by policy that creates lower-quality and higher-cost opportunities must be examined from up close. The anthropology of policy has offered a toolbox by which to conduct that examination in this book. Here, participant observation, informant accounts, and close readings of policy doctrine combined to show the complexities of "access." Chief among those has been a tendency for law schools to inflect access through existing political economy—one that places faith in the market as normative substitute for social protection. In the context of law school admissions, *it is as if the groups long excluded from the legal profession are expected to suddenly and spontaneously be well equipped to make discerning judgments over and bargains with institutions of expert professional training*. The result is not immediate access to the profession for marginal groups but rather immediate access to marginal groups on the part of increasingly commercial education institutions. Once law schools have embraced neoliberal access in this way, they imply to their graduates aiming for careers in lawmaking, advocacy, and dispute resolution that this is "how the world works."

Legal education is capable of more than reproducing extant political economy. Law schools could, for example, impart the tools to "engineer" a more *just* one. To do that, they might place the moral stability of their financial and knowledge practices at front and center of their self-governance. As the case of New Delta begins to illustrate, the market-based differentiation many embrace can easily fail in this respect. Rather than encouraging instructors to experiment with humanistic, moral, and civic–minded teaching, this kind of differentiation—even when it espouses social justice—appears to call for austerity and responsibilization, embedding in turn the logic of neoliberalism at the center of professional training and socialization.

Difference and Differentiation

Key to that logic is an approach to "difference" that seems to run counter to substantive access to justice in broader perspective. Under this approach, ethno-racial and socioeconomic differences have a role in the legal profession, but they appear adjunct or apart from the more mainstream professional channels of training and advancement. Differences espoused as "market leading" by law schools like New Delta—differences like "practice orientation" and "student outcome centeredness"—are ones that still carry certain stigma in legal academia and profession. Even now, high-ranking public policy school graduates continue to be preferred in most professional recruitment channels. Meanwhile, by embracing ethnoracially diverse communities for recruitment, New Delta has raised minority enrollments well above those of other programs—especially those in the top tier. Here, in short, law school "differentiation" and sociocultural "difference" have not coincidentally become twined.

More broadly, differentiation without proper regulation may be exacerbating a "hemispheric" or "apartheid" landscape for legal education. There, ethnoracial and economic diversity becomes the responsibility of a bottom tier whereas professional elitism and high income remain the province of the top. For students in the bottom hemisphere, career service counseling offices can do only so much. Employers advertising in these offices are fewer and smaller than their counterparts posting jobs at higher-ranked law schools. Career advisors then hail the virtues of individual networking and branding, a move that embraces all too well the rise of "human capital"—of "labor" as individualized, self-invested capital.[1] Moreover, failure to obtain jobs among these students becomes a matter of *personal* responsibility rather than *structural* disadvantage in a "competitive" employment marketplace.

Differentiation through advanced faith in the normativity of markets has helped produce these conditions. Partially abrogating its regulatory role—where better quality and recruitment standards could at least assure "diverse" law school students that they will be taught at a high level—the ABA Council of the Section of Legal Education during this research drifted toward deference to a self-regulating law school market. The most direct remedy, therefore, might be more robust regulatory policy. In early 2016, the U.S. Department of Education was considering removal of the ABA's accreditation power over law schools in general.[2] Later, it cut off funding to one for-profit law school for allegedly misrepresenting outcome data.[3] Meanwhile the ABA has proposed tightening Standards 316 on bar passage and 501 on admissions.[4] Whether or not these actions produce lasting change, any new policy to remedy current realities carries a heavy burden. Several features make such solutions especially challenging.

Race and Remedies

The first challenge is broader, systemic racial inequality. In the United States, following the desegregation and civil rights era, higher education put in place affirmative action programs seeking to ensure the racial diversity of colleges, universities, and professional schools. This came after realization that "separate is inherently unequal" in education and other public services, but it also reflected an epiphany that racial integration necessitated economic upward mobility through equal opportunity in bachelor's and graduate degree programs.

Initial approaches to equal opportunity in higher education focused on numbers. As lawsuits against the University of California and University of Washington, among others, revealed, universities were setting aside percentages of incoming class seats so that minority candidates could be assured at least a few spots in their programs.[5] This policy resulted in rapid diversification of law schools such as the University of Texas and University of Michigan. But, ultimately, some white students denied admission to these programs felt they were now being excluded on the basis of race. Citing this as a double standard, they argued that such exclusions resulted in a denial of equal protection guaranteed under the U.S. Constitution's Fourteenth Amendment.[6] By and large, they were successful, and institutions of higher education were barred from using bare quotas.

In the next phase, college and university programs shifted to more holistic approaches that factored racial diversity in as but one factor for admission. These approaches were also challenged but repeatedly upheld at the high court.[7] Critics have come to believe this rollback on affirmative action created unintended consequences, such as the privileging of upper- and middle-class African American and African immigrant students over disadvantaged ones most in need, as well as the steering of lower-class students generally toward for-profit vocational and technical schools.

Thinking back to legal education, would bottom-tier law schools—let alone for-profit ones—succeed among minority students if affirmative action or other diversity policies had remained more robust over the past few decades? A suggestion running throughout this book has been that greater diversity of students in the for-profit legal education sector is a direct outcome of neoliberal access and not an indication of increased social justice. The markers of poorer stability, lower quality, higher risk, and greater professional stigma seem here to attach disproportionately to ethnoracial and socioeconomically diverse students. One possible effect might be a racialization of for-profit law schools and their alumni networks themselves. Viewed by the professional community as the "bottom" in quality and accepted by the wider public as tolerable because diverse, the for-profit embrace of diversity not only pairs differentiation with difference; it ensures that difference in this case can be read as "racial difference" in particular.

Alternatives to Access

In higher education generally, diversity policy over the last several decades migrated from "equality of opportunity" to "equality of access."[8] Equal opportunity meant that minority students would be guaranteed positions at even the highest levels of education, but their outcomes would be a matter of individual ambition and diligence. With the retreat of robust affirmative action, an equal access approach has become the norm; it guarantees access to the general area of study but makes no promises about standardized quality of education, reputation, or transmitted cultural capital. Neoliberal access, further, marketizes this emphasis on access so that the most active new venues of inclusion for minority students are those that position themselves as "market challengers" or "innovators." In the undergraduate sector, for-profit and online colleges and trade schools have long assumed this role. In professional legal education, they have done so only recently. Guaranteeing educational access through new, untested, and potentially "predatory formations" of advancement can have an effect opposite to what was intended by guaranteeing opportunity.[9] But tightened regulatory oversight of these institutions would likely come at an immediate cost to access and could eliminate or restrict some of the immediate agents of nominal diversity among ABA programs. Would a better-regulated legal education sector, therefore, look again like the homogenized exclusive legal education of yesterday?

Present-day diversity is itself not a predicament we should idealize. Having 250 percent more ethnoracial minority students in law school in 2013 than there were in 1987 is facially a good thing.[10] But having so much of this diversity concentrated in the bottom quintile of institutions, and a sizeable percentage of that concentrated among for-profits, merits deep reflection.[11] Schools least likely to produce high-level outcomes (including the policy makers to effect change) have embraced minority students, but those most likely to produce such results still, relatively speaking, have not.

There was, however, a time when diversity marginally increased among elite ABA law schools. In the 1960s, law school cohorts at UC Berkeley and Harvard went from having nearly no ethnoracial minority students to quickly having measurable numbers.[12] This resulted from new civil rights era affirmative action practices implemented when federal government administration of and spending on social programs was at its highest. As recent analyses show, this was also an era when socioeconomic inequality in the United States was near an all-time low.[13]

Such practices cannot be replicated under current constitutional law. The courts that made this determination have said they considered history, sociology, and psychology and found overt "positive discrimination" more harmful than beneficial in the long run.[14] The resulting policies emphasizing access over opportunity are preferred because, it is said, even a bifurcated educational and professional landscape enables "access" to upward mobility and specific, ultimately white-collar, employment niches.

But at what *cost*? Many minority students, we now know, pay a high premium for the privilege of access enjoyed at greater quality and less cost by others across legal education.[15] The ethnographic case of New Delta School of Law, I hope, reflects some of the ways in which students experience this through encounters with curriculum, faculty, and the outlying professional community.

Law and Neoliberalism

Law school teaching in the United States has long separated justice and morality. There is doctrine and its application through legal hard skills, and there is finesse manifested through legal soft skills. Still minimal in the formal training of lawyers among ABA schools is a systematic reflection on the moral ordering lawyers participate in. Though work prosecuting and defending criminal suspects, or litigating against negligent corporations, undeniably implicates questions of right and wrong or good and bad, the pedagogy producing these vocations submerges those binaries beneath rules and processes. And there may be valid, historically rooted reasons to keep it this way in the classroom.

But what happens when whole institutions conduct their business under this separation? When, as some have done, law schools tell disgruntled alumni to take responsibility for their own decisions—reproducing the logic of responsibilization—they relieve themselves of a moral burden. When they cater to prospective matriculants as would-be customers, they reduce the student–teacher relationship to one of commercial transaction.

Students may learn that this is the proper way to relate to society as lawyers. Then, advising parties in a divorce, or advising corporations in mergers and acquisitions, they bring a morally unburdened approach backed by the credibility and hegemony of a professional law degree and professional community. With this in mind, we might consider with Annelise Riles that lawyers are, in fact, one of the most important vectors for neoliberal norm structuring and implementation in the global economy.[16] Although the case of New Delta is an extreme one in the way profits from the professional degree trade are distributed, I have suggested here that this is simply the far end of a spectrum that includes most proximately other "high-cost" fourth-tier law programs, as well as many upper-level law schools.

Legal reasoning and advocacy, as they are currently structured in American common-law legal education, have been well suited to this role. They break apart apparent patterns in the way social life gives rise to conflict and look instead for individual "facts" in each separate situation for application of relevant rules. Under the common law, if such rules are not already explicitly articulated, they are said to be "discovered" in the logic of lines of previous case resolutions.[17] Human interactions that give rise to conflict become transactions where intention is demonstrated by palpable so-called objective evidence. In the study of negligence, for example "reasonable care" has largely been reduced to a calculus borrowed from utilitarian political economy.

It is therefore worth emphasizing that New Delta School of Law reflects a confluence of legal and economistic thinking characteristic of our age. Contrary to how elite law school critics might frame them—as a circumscribed ghetto of legal academia—the for-profit law schools simply take more seriously and manifest more literally the decades-old marriage of law and economics in

Western thought. Less institutions of "higher learning," they act more as sites for knowledge capitalism.[18]

Morals and Models

Still, for-profit law schools are comprised of people who, for better or worse, come in to work most days thinking they are "serving the underserved" of the world around them. This belief is not without the manufacturing traces left by corporate directors, public relations firms, and marketing specialists. Belief in the goodness of their daily effort is itself a moralizing act on the part of the many employees making up the institution captured in this study. In other words, the question of morality arises not only from above but also from the ground up, and it must be interrogated carefully in a serious look at the social status of these institutions.

Even as the law school industry appears to be shifting weekly as of this writing, one stable trend has been a tendency among the 200 nonprofit ABA law schools to distance themselves from the few for-profit programs existing in their midst. The majority criticize and shun for-profits as morally defective because their after-cost revenues—not distinguishable in size or source from others—are sent off to corporate private equity shareholders. This extraction of value, most educators would say, is unbecoming of an academic institution. Nonprofit law schools, private and public, keep their surplus value within the walls of the institution and therefore allow their growth to benefit the students themselves.

Yet this distinction may not be conclusive. For years—particularly during the 2000s when law jobs were abundant and student applications at their peak—law schools served as so-called cash cows of their respective university homes. By 2011, the outgoing dean of the University of Baltimore School of Law claimed that his parent institution retained as much as 45 percent of his law school's tuition revenues.[19] Even if that accounting can be disputed, the general practice of subsidizing nonlucrative academic units with law school tuition has been widely acknowledged at universities.[20]

The claim that nonprofits retain surplus value to the benefit of current students misses a key point. The wider law school industry creates moral hazard not just because of where it *sends* student tuition moneys but also because it *assesses* tuition using certain extrinsic factors and unverifiable claims. Brian Tamanaha laid out the evidence for this, including deceptive reporting practices for graduate employment rates, arguments that the $150,000 law degree has re-deeming edification value for even those without legal employment, and the use of student tuition moneys to fund lavish faculty "research" bonuses.[21] This critical emphasis on employment outcomes has been criticized by other senior academics such as Erwin Chemerinsky as overly economistic,[22] but economic reductionism in this regard has been prompted in the first instance by messaging that touts the long-term financial value of the law degree.[23]

Meanwhile, as assertions about long-term net value and edification for non-law careers emanate, students continue to take on nondischargeable loan debt for decades to come. In a world where as many as half of all law graduates cannot find legal employment[24] and where the average annual income of a lawyer hovers around $62,000,[25] the claims referenced in the preceding paragraphs—apart from the economic model they justify—are themselves a great source of law school moral hazard. To the extent that, amid wider questions about law's political economy, nonprofit schools and their faculty wish to distinguish for-profit law schools as the true culprits of the "law school scam," they may be conducting a significant sleight of hand. Emphasizing the unusual (and, to many, mysterious) business model of for-profit schools, critics point to poor employment statistics and falling bar passage rates to suggest these are the worst moral players in their arena. This rhetorical move binds the question of morality to the question of business model and encourages those not intimately familiar with this sector to forestall questions about substantive distinction at the for-profit law programs while focusing on the formal difference in "model." With this rhetorical piece in place, observers of the current law school industry may be asked to overlook, excuse, or reinterpret similar substantive policies and practices in place among nonprofit programs.

The word *industry* has been deliberate here. For important reasons dealt with in this book, this probably cannot really be considered a true market. As even staunch law and economics writers might agree, a true market functions (and thrives) on the relative open flow of information. Richard Posner himself has said, in a different context,

We would think it wrong (and inefficient) if the law permitted a seller in hawking his wares to make false or incomplete representations of their quality. . . . Shouldn't a person be allowed to protect himself from disadvantageous transactions by ferreting out concealed facts about individuals which are material to the implicit or explicit representations that to those individuals make concerning their moral qualities. . . . they want to manipulate the world around them by selective disclosure of facts about themselves. It is not clear why society should assign the property right in such information to the individual to whom it pertains.[26]

In the case of ABA law schools offering questionable employment numbers and claims about nonlaw career benefits to justify exorbitant student debt, any so-called market is not a well-functioning one. This implicates all ABA schools and not simply those that are "for profit." For this reason, the distinctive dilemma of for-profit law schools must arise from something besides just their business model.[27]

Although for-profit JD programs share most of the same substantive practices leading to moral hazard at the nonprofits, what the former appear to do very differently is *organizational culture*. As I suggested in Chapter 2, this differentiation in culture comes through corporate policy mandated from above—that is, from a corporate nerve center separate from any of the consortium JD programs. That center, in turn, is governed by private equity fund managers who borrow and cross-apply lessons derived from a variety of other commercial sectors and contexts.

Application of corporate policies borrowed from noneducation sectors such as industrial manufacturing to an academic institution requires a significant amount of work. Paramount among that is the transformation of policy into culture. Whereas culture in its "natural state" may be made up of symbols and practices common to a community or group, culture in this ideological modality really belongs to those at the center—executives, high administrators, and so forth. Those in charge set corporate policy; strategize the proper means of delivery to faculty, staff, and students; and narrate the importance of such policies in terms of culture using the pronouns "we," "us," and "ours" to engender feelings of solidarity and mutual aspiration. The imperative to generate a new integrated first-year curriculum described in Chapter 4 is the starkest example of this, though others can well be seen in the use of "Talent Plus" for faculty recruitment in Chapter 1, the elimination of faculty titles in Chapter 4, or the elimination of tenured faculty in Chapter 6.

The efficacy of policy as culture goes further than simple maintenance of organizational distinction and integrity. At its most potent level, the ideological power of corporate policy encourages highly educated, often highly critical, law faculty to view their role in the organization and the industry as a benevolent one. Although other fourth-tier law schools with low median LSAT and GPA indicators attrited a percentage of their first-year class well before the bar exam, faculty in this study took pride in the provision of academic success counseling and the offering of student second chances. This, in turn, was justified by a diverse student body, with self-reported numbers ranging from 35 to 42 percent "diversity" students over the years. African American, Native American, and Latino/Latina students all were better represented here than at other schools, and for this reason flexibility on academic attrition was considered to serve a diversity submission. Faculty took special comfort in the benevolence of this approach.

Yet few openly acknowledged or discussed the ways in which such features preserved revenues while maintaining enrollment of some who, many felt, would not pass a state bar exam. For such students, timely repayment of federal or private loans would become a challenge. Embracing their role as a benevolent one, then, New Delta faculty were themselves contributors to this. Emphasizing student centeredness and service to the underserved, corporate ideology worked to ensure that feelings of moral hazard remained at bay. It accomplished this in part by capitalizing on the discourse of crisis in legal education where "crisis" meant not simply the decline in applications and enrollments beginning around 2011 but also a pedagogical crisis looming well before this downturn. There, underscored by respected research such as the Carnegie Foundation's "Educating Lawyers" report from 2007, legal academics began to note, observe, and comment on the growing gap between a narrow set of skills offered in U.S. law schools and the wide array of skills required among U.S. legal service providers.[28] Skills such as drafting and client counseling, as well as law firm and case management, were all essential to the concrete practice of law and yet nowhere to be found in most curricula until perhaps a student's third year of study. In addition to embracing no-frills programming and low-performing students, faculty at New Delta also took pride in their efforts to produce "practice-ready" students through the infusion of even first-year doctrinal courses with practical exercises such as contract negotiations and drafting.

And yet, professional ethics was ever attenuated by the problem of moral hazard. In medical school, new students are initiated in the famous white coat ceremony that kicks off the first year of every career. In that ritual, students are asked to recite the Hippocratic Oath, which states in part a commitment to "do no harm." This commitment appears to transcend discrete professional establishments such as hospitals, clinics, and trauma centers and rather governs the behavior of U.S. medical doctors in *every* situation in which their skills are relied on by everyday people in need of medical care.[29]

The legal profession in the United States is a different matter. There, an adversarial system of justice inherited from British common law demands "zealous" advocacy on both sides of any dispute. In some cases there appears to be clear culpability or guilt, but attorneys for both sides are expected to prosecute or defend their case rigorously. In other cases there can be no clear assignment or no asymmetrical assignment of blame, and the requirement of zealous advocacy is part of what helps bring the truth of the matter to light.

Advocates, in other words, must dwell in moral liminality. The choice to do so with more or less reflection does little to diminish its philosophical significance.

All of this being said, the faculty of New Delta School of Law operated under a related but different moral liminality. Relatedly, the righteousness of their role as educators of the marginalized—racial, ethnic, and class minorities in the legal profession—could not be confirmed until those students had lived out a portion of their professional careers in the outlying community. The school and its business and admissions models were a "work in progress"—hence sudden adjustments to that model were relatively common and undisturbing. But differently, the risk generated by their work as educators was immediately palpable. Without proper financial counseling, students took out maximal student loan funds, and some drove Land Rovers or BMWs on the assumption they were only borrowing against future earnings.

Faculty remained silent on the problem of financial risk for a variety of possible reasons. First, they may have been ignorant. Although most knew the cost of annual tuition fell in the upper $40,000 bracket, most had attended law school twenty years earlier and had neither incurred nor lived under similar financial burdens. Second, if aware, they were discouraged from drawing critical attention to the economic model. Doing so would only frighten students, and this in turn would harm revenue and job security. Third, many felt that they were already doing their best to help. Beyond teaching, most advised dozens of students as part of a mentoring program. Beyond mentoring, faculty advised a large number of student organizations ranging from the International Law Society to the Asian Pacific American Law Student Association. This feeling—of often going "beyond" one's anticipated professional role—is key to understanding the moral economy of New Delta School of Law.

The *beyondness* of responsibility fulfillment, common among educators from the grade school and high school, to the undergraduate and graduate levels, has become a fixture of the Western teaching establishment. Attesting to this is an annual income tax deduction offered by the U.S. Internal Revenue Service for an amount of personal expenditures made by teachers on K–12 classroom expenses.[30] This deduction is a potent symbol of the neoliberal approach to education: rather than publicly funding teachers to the fullest extent necessary when students are most vulnerable—at the primary and secondary levels—we expect the lowest-paid teachers to privately forward the costs of classroom supplies and seek not full reimbursement but a deduction that simply reduces taxable income by a small amount. Recent cases of corruption and cheating among schoolteachers at these levels is further suggestive.[31] In an environment when educators are asked to *give* so much of their personal time, effort, and resources, even the most rational individuals may seek recompense in the moral uncertainties generated by this system.

Faculty at a law school like New Delta might be different than, say, faculty at USC Gould School of Law or Georgetown Law Center. Although the former's financial and status incentives to teach are lower, their demands, increased by corporate efficiency concerns and academically precarious students, are higher. Whereas this study does not directly test this observation, it finds evidence to suggest these psychic and emotional trade-offs form an important part of the moral economy studied here.

Impacting Students

In understanding how all this has an impact on students, we must ask whether a law faculty can fulfill its responsibility of properly socializing[32] students into professional conduct when it is itself implicated in producing significant moral hazard? The answer depends on two possible separations.

The first falls between the professor's own moral position and the lessons he or she imparts on students. This potential gap is not unique to academic law, though it may arguably be more poignant here. Could an instructor at West Point teach the Geneva Conventions if he or she participated in war crimes on the ground during Vietnam? Must a professor of business ethics be free and clear of involvement in the Savings and Loan, Enron, or Lehman Brothers scandals? Or does involvement in those moments offer an instructor some kind of valuable added perspective? Does it make a difference whether the ethical dilemma is still ongoing? For professors at NDSL, whom I isolate here due to their close ongoing contact with students, the question would be whether instruction they offer—formal or informal—in law and ethics is sound given the ethically dubious predicament of legal education generally and for-profit legal education in particular.

The second separation falls between morality—practical or metaphysical questions about "right" and "wrong"—and professional ethics—the rules and best practices that govern a far narrower conception of "right" as "right for" this particular enterprise. Here, it may matter whether we view legal ethics as on one hand the theories of right versus wrong that govern everyone with a legal education or on the other hand those governing only the practice of law itself.

One of the aims of this book is to support the first view. Legal professional ethics are more than just what is practically required to maintain bar membership or what is clearly stated in the Model Rules of Professional Conduct. JDs sit on corporate boards, state legislatures, venture capital funds, television production teams, armed conflict compliance reviews, and myriad other bodies. Because lawyers hold such significant places in our world, professional ethics and wider considerations of morality belong on a single continuum. Many might respond normatively that law is founded on the separation of the moral world from the legal. Many more might say the same descriptively. But few would deny the substantial *work* that goes into imparting this separation on students of law. As Beth Mertz has handily shown, that work can be the most vexing part of first-year teaching and learning.[33] To the extent the legal profession casts itself as being "in the service of" community, society, or the nation, it cannot logically then erect a wall between its governing ethics and wider considerations of justice.

If professional ethics cannot sit apart from justice, legal educators cannot separate their own moral hazard from what they teach students. Their students—particularly the ones who paid full sticker price[34] to attend the school—are the human embodiment of their risk creation. Now sitting on the shoulders of a new generation of lawyers, moral hazard may color their negotiations of right and wrong. In this study alone, for example, law students cited loan discharge—shifting the financial burden back onto the public—as their best hope for emerging from this transaction with a future.[35]

Conclusion

I have suggested that ABA-accredited for-profit law programs are one early outcome of market-based differentiation and that the results have been as described here. I have secondarily emphasized the role of market deference on the part of regulators and the challenges this poses for rectification. Deference has special appeal in the current climate of neoliberal governance. There, state involvement in commerce should simply be to guarantee basic rights and liberties while staying out of social entitlements and, most importantly, moral values. Morality, the logic goes, can be sorted out through a well-functioning market.[36] Under this reasoning, the moral "goodness" or "badness" of for-profit law schools is irrelevant. Of greatest consequence is the *value* those schools are capable of offering students. In quantitative terms, this value would be assessed on the basis of employment and income outcomes. Several have made strong cases in recent years for students to adopt this kind of risk–utility balancing.[37] They have provided valuable instruction into how such balancing should be set up taking into account quantitative information such as tuition "discount pricing," law school employment reporting practices, structural features in the legal services market, and the narrowness of discounted loan repayment programs.

Assuming better access to information on the quantitative and qualitative value of the degree offered, some believe low-performing law schools will simply fail and close.[38] As applications drop, as schools compete for competent students, and as the competence of students is widely indexed in numbers such as bar passage, programs forced to accept the lowest-performing students will run afoul of current ABA Standards,[39] risk deaccreditation, and risk losing access to Title IV federal loans moneys. At the same time, even without these threats, under current conditions schools near the bottom of median LSAT and GPA numbers will become harder pressed to fill first-year seats at sustainable levels. But as Chapter 1 explained, market discipline has been slow to correct behavior as these institutions emphasize open access.

For lower-performing students—those with lower LSAT and GPA scores— marginal cost differences are unimportant because the alternatives to law school are nowhere near as putatively profitable. That this lower-performing group tends to include lower-income and nontraditional students only heightens this "all in" consumer approach. Students in this book like Keshia, who chose law school over living in her car, are a case in point for this thinking.

A wider implication of this has already been seen in profiles of more recent law school applicant pools. Although applications came down overall, this drop has resulted more from a loss of students near the middle and top of LSAT scores.[40] In short, lower-performing students continued to apply while higher performing students became more cautious—some say under more nuanced risk–utility thinking inspired by the critical accounts cited earlier. Structurally, of course, the absence of higher-performing students only shifted the hierarchy of acceptance indicators downward.

Faith in the deregulatory approach must also confront for-profit law school conditions specifically. Here, the unique business model does matter. Founded to enrich private equity investors, they are incentivized to extract maximum value but cannot pass on savings to students. Doing so runs counter to the underlying logic of private equity.[41] Meanwhile, absent substantive new policy, schools operating in this fashion will continue to allow private investors access to public moneys in the form of student loan proceeds.

This story was a dark one made darker by the absence of a supreme "bad" actor. Serving as participants, staff, educators, administrators, managers, executives, and regulators played integral roles. Yet, individually, no single person, nor one class of actors, alone could be deemed "responsible." A few on the ground seemed convinced otherwise. "A for-profit law school could be great," some said, "it was just executed poorly by so-and-so." Like many elsewhere, I came to view the problem more diffusely as an attenuation of the "social"—a subordination of collective reflection and its moral concomitants to the individualized economics of capital. Long seen by other writers across different areas of contemporary life, this absence was particularly striking here, among expert wielders of law and policy raising the flag of social justice.

But for social researchers darkness brings possibility. This ethnographic glimpse at law school political economy reveals a need for closer study of professional education and its oversight policy. As we acknowledge this need, space opens up for the disciplines to lend insight. For those interested in "studying through," in better understandings of the moral and political nuances of policy in action, the time is here to join the conversation.

Appendix
List of Abbreviations

- AALS Faculty Appointments Registry (FAR)
- Academic Success Program (ASP)
- Alternative Admissions Model Program for Legal Education (AAMPLE)
- American Bar Association (ABA)
- American Bar Association Council of the Section of Legal Education and Admissions to the Bar (Council)
- American Bar Association, Section of Legal Education and Admission to the Bar, *Standards and Rules of Procedure for Approval of Law* Schools (ABA Standards)
- Association for Private Sector Colleges and Universities (APSCU)
- Association of American Law Schools (AALS)
- Continuing Legal Education (CLE)
- Chief executive officer (CEO)
- Curriculum vitae (CV)
- Department of Education (ED)
- Department of Justice (DOJ)
- First-Year Student (1L)
- Free Application for Federal Student Aid (FAFSA)
- General Electric (GE)
- Higher Education Act (HEA)
- Human Resources (HR)
- Law Corp Futures (LCF)

- Law School Admissions Council (LSAC)

- Law School Admissions Test (LSAT)

- Lawyering Process (LP)

- Legal Research and Writing (LRW)

- Massachusetts School of Law at Andover (MSL)

- Multi-Year Bar Accelerated Review (myBAR)

- New England Association of Schools and Colleges (NEASC)

- New Delta School of Law (NDSL)

- Nothing But Objectivity (NOBI)

- Public Relations (PR)

- Reduction in force (RIF)

- Standard operating procedure (SOP)

- Undergraduate grade point average (UGPA)

- University of Phoenix (UOP)

- Unlock Potential (UP)

- Venture Partners Group (VPG)

- Veterans Affairs (VA)

Notes

Introduction

1. Emphasis added. All faculty, staff, and student informant interviews were conducted by the author in confidence, and informant names have been changed by mutual agreement. Interviews with public figures in legal education have retained original informant names. Changes to direct quotations are denoted by brackets except where the true identities of New Delta School of Law, Law Corp, or Venture Partners Group were originally referenced.

2. Emphasis added.

3. For more on "diversity" in neoliberal education policy and practice, see Bonnie Urciuoli, "Neoliberal Education: Preparing the Student for the New Workplace," in *Ethnographies of Neoliberalism*, ed. Carol Greenhouse (Philadelphia: University of Pennsylvania Press, 2010): 170–175.

4. All mentions of the American Bar Association in relation to accreditation here refer to the American Bar Association Council of the Section on Legal Education and Admissions to the Bar—an entity related to, but separate from the main ABA professional organization. Although scholarly and popular texts refer consistently to "ABA accreditation," it is the Council and not the ABA itself that administers the accreditation process. This process includes a school site visit, a report from the site visit team to the accreditation committee, a recommendation from the accreditation committee to the Council, a hearing including school representatives before the Council, and finally an accreditation decision from the Council.

5. Karen Ho, "Finance," in *A Companion to Moral Anthropology*, ed. Didier Fassin (Oxford, UK: Wiley Blackwell, 2012): 414.

6. *Elite* here and throughout is intended ethnographically to denote the way in which participants saw themselves relative to the outlying legal community. Among law schools, there would be another hegemonic sense of *elite* to describe the "top ten" JD programs in relation to all other law schools.

7. All references to school rankings throughout this book should be understood ethnographically and critically. *U.S. News*, the predominant authority referenced on law school rankings, has changed to using the term *ranking not published* (or RNP) for the lower-ranking tiers in recent years. Ry Rivard, "Lowering the Bar," *Inside Higher Ed*, January

16, 2015; retrieved on October 27, 2015, from www.insidehighered.com/news/2015/01/16/law-schools-compete-students-many-may-not-have-admitted-past.

8. Although technically formed as contract buy-outs and framed locally as cases of voluntary retirements, these were generally understood in light of the company's own stated policies on "reductions in force." See, for example, Chapter 6.

9. Henry J. Reske, "One Antitrust Battle Over: Judge Approves Consent Decree between ABA, DOJ," *ABA Journal*, August 1996: 44.

10. Though not specifically aimed at for-profits, the ABA did begin to propose new requirements in 2016 that would discipline consistent low bar passage performance.

11. As of this writing, however, the U.S. Department of Education has elected to freeze Title IV student loans for attendance at at least one for-profit law school leading in turn to accusations of institutional misfeasance and a student class action suit.

12. For a history of this term emerging out of the insurance industry of the nineteenth century, see Tom Baker, "On the Genealogy of Moral Hazard," *Texas Law Review* 75 (1996): 237–292.

13. This belief can be traced back to at least the writings of Aristotle. See Richard Posner, *The Economics of Justice* (Cambridge, MA: Harvard University Press, 1983). See also Ken Cooper-Stephenson and Elaine Gibson, *Tort Theory* (York, Ontario: Captus Press, 1993): 30–31.

14. See, for example, Brian Tamanaha, *Failing Law Schools* (Chicago: University of Chicago Press, 2012); and William D. Henderson, "A Blueprint for Change," *Pepperdine Law Review* 40 (2013): 494–495.

15. Several of these standards, student–faculty ratio expectations for instance, have already been altered in response to these critiques.

16. Admittedly, not all differentiation is created equal. For Tamanaha, the Massachusetts School of Law (MSL), with its more austere faculty model and course offerings resulting in lower tuition for students, is closer to the ideal type. If more new law schools were to adopt this model, he writes, students might be able to receive the practical training a lawyer needs without the unnecessary bells and whistles of faculty research or policy discussions. MSL has never attained ABA accreditation and is rather endorsed only by the regional New England Association of Schools and Colleges (NEASC). Thorough discussions about the impact of the MSL model on legal education should therefore consider how the status change from regional- to ABA-accredited (and thus Title IV–eligible) law program and new availability of public finance income streams might alter the seemingly populist value structure of currently unaccredited programs. For-profit law schools like New Delta are already ABA accredited, and they already result from a move toward differentiation following the landmark antitrust investigation, lawsuit, and settlement previously referenced. Although not the kind of differentiation Tamanaha envisions, NDSL and its ilk instantiate the limits of a deregulatory differentiation when left up to the disciplinary forces of the free market.

17. See, generally, Henry Giroux, *Neoliberalism's War on Higher Education* (Chicago: Haymarket Books, 2014); Eric Gould, *The University in a Corporate Culture* (New Haven, CT,

and London: Yale University Press, 2011); and Stanley Aronowitz, *The Knowledge Factory: Dismantling the Corporate University and Creating True Higher Learning* (Boston: Beacon Press, 2000).

18. I am mindful of its roots in the political economic thinking of Hayek and Friedman, of its popularization in the policy wars of Reagan and Thatcher, and of theoretical critiques of it by David Harvey, Aiwa Ong, Pierre Bourdieu, and Henry Giroux, among many others. David Harvey, *A Brief History of Neoliberalism* (Oxford, UK: Oxford University Press, 2005); Aihwa Ong, *Neoliberalism as Exception: Mutations in Citizenship and Sovereignty* (Durham, NC: Duke University Press, 2006); Pierre Bourdieu, "The Essence of Neoliberalism," *Le Monde Diplomatique*, December 1998; and Giroux, *Neoliberalism's War on Higher Education.*

19. I thank Richard Gilman-Opalsky for reminding me that "market fundamentalism" as such is not particularly unique to *neo*liberalism, and I specify that I am interested in the marriage between market fundamentalism and contemporary regulatory theory and action.

20. Wendy Brown, *Undoing the Demos: Neoliberalism's Stealth Revolution* (Cambridge, MA, and London: MIT/Zone Books, 2015): 9. I thank Jothie Rajah for prompting me to assimilate this line of thought.

21. Although many decry the "corporatization of the university" in recent decades, some have said we are now well past that phase into an era of university financialization.

22. Adoption of neoliberal thinking belies an historical sleight of hand. The economic liberalism of Euro-American centuries past—embodied most notably in the policy approaches of Franklin Roosevelt—saw economic exchange as "embedded" in social relations. Corporate governance and securities exchanges were then kept subservient to the needs of social cohesion such as public health, democratic legitimacy, and civil rights. The neoliberal philosophy of today—so widespread as to be almost invisible to young people coming of age under its purview—does the opposite: It finds the legitimacy of social relations in their compatibility with the "free exchange" of economic life. For a more critical view on the "embeddedness" approach to economics in social science see Ho, "Finance": 425.

23. Jennifer M. Gidley, Gary P. Hampson, Leone Wheeler, and Elleni Bereded-Samuel, "From Access to Success: An Integrated Approach to Quality Higher Education Informed by Social Inclusion Theory and Practice," *Higher Education Policy* 23 (2010): 123–147.

24. Sue Kilpatrick and Susan Johns, "Institutional Responses to Social Inclusion in Australian Higher Education: Responsible Citizenship or Political Pragmatism?" *Widening Participation and Lifelong Learning* 16 (2014): 27–46.

25. Karl Polanyi, *The Great Transformation* (Boston: Beacon Press, 2001): 76.

26. Ibid.

27. Nancy Fraser, "A Triple Movement?" *New Left Review*, June 2013: 128–129.

28. Jarrett Zigon, "Narratives," in *A Companion to Moral Anthropology*, ed. Didier Fassin (West Sussex, UK: Wiley-Blackwell, 2012): 205.

29. Joel Best and Eric Best, *The Student Loan Mess: How Good Intentions Created a Trillion-Dollar Problem* (Berkeley: University of California Press, 2014): 63.

30. Before 1976, student loans *could* be discharged or canceled through bankruptcy filings. Beginning in 1978, a series of statutory changes made discharge increasingly unavailable. In its place, a program of "income-based repayment" or IBR has emerged to assess longer repayment schedules for lower-income earners based on prescribed debt-to-income ratios.

31. Although the Department of Education is abbreviated in some ABA documents as "DOE," I have chosen to retain the official administrative abbreviation of "ED" throughout this book.

32. See, for example, Harper Lee, *To Kill a Mockingbird* (New York: HarperCollins Press, 1960); and John Grisham, *Runaway Jury* (New York: Doubleday, 1996).

33. Eugene Gaetke, "Lawyers as Officers of the Court," *Vanderbilt Law Review* 42 (1989): 41.

34. In California, where I am a member of the state bar, Business and Professions Code section 6068 imposes duties to exercise *moral* judgment in the execution of professional duties. For instance, an attorney is

(g) Not to encourage either the commencement or the continuance of an action or proceeding from any corrupt motive of passion or interest.

and

(h) Never to reject, for any consideration personal to himself or herself, the cause of the defenseless or the oppressed.

California Business and Professions Code § 6068(g–h).

35. See Annelise Riles, *Collateral Knowledge: Legal Reasoning in the Global Financial Markets* (Chicago: University of Chicago Press, 2011): 13.

36. Cris Shore and Susan Wright, "Policy: A New Field of Anthropology," in *Anthropology of Policy: Critical Perspectives on Governance and Power*, eds. Cris Shore and Susan Wright (London and New York: Routledge, 1997): 11.

37. Geoffrey Wood and Mike Wright, "Private Equity: A Review and Synthesis," *International Journal of Management Reviews* 11 (2009): 361.

38. It has since grown in popularity.

39. See, for example, Alexander Osterwalder et al., *Value Proposition Design: How to Create Products and Services Customers Want* (Hoboken, NJ: John Wiley & Sons, 2014); and Cindy Barnes, Helen Blake, and David Pinder, *Creating and Delivering Your Value Proposition: Managing Customer Experience for Profit* (London: Kogan Page, 2009).

40. This is not to suggest that such students were incapable or undeserving of law school admission but that many had been deliberately excluded by most other American law programs for a variety of reasons whose merits can be debated.

41. Joao Biehl, *Vita: Life in a Zone of Social Abandonment* (Berkeley: University of California Press, 2005).

42. "Grab the Bleach: St. John's University School of Law," *Third Tier Reality*, August 22, 2010; retrieved on August 28, 2015, from http://thirdtierreality.blogspot.com/2010/08/grab-bleach-st-johns-university-school.html.

43. "The Four Tiers: T13, Trap, No-Name, and Joke," *Outside the Law School Scam*, June 14, 2013; retrieved on August 28, 2015, from http://outsidethelawschoolscam.blogspot.com/2013/06 /the-four-tiers-t13-trap-no-name-and-joke.html.

44. Pierre Bourdieu, *Outline of a Theory of Practice*, trans. Richard Nice (New York: Cambridge University Press, 1977); Emile Durkheim, *The Division of Labor in Society* (New York: The Free Press, 1997); Emile Durkheim, *The Rules of Sociological Method*, trans. Steven Lukes (New York: The Free Press, 2013); Franz Fanon, *The Wretched of the Earth* (New York: Grove Press, 1963); Michel Foucault, *Discipline and Punish: The Birth of the Prison*, trans. Alan Sheridan (New York: Vintage Books, 1979); and Immanuel Wallerstein, *The Modern World-System: Capitalist Agriculture and the Origins of the European World-Economy in the Sixteenth Century* (New York: Academic Press, 1976).

45. Tamanaha, *Failing Law Schools*: 135–137; and Paul Campos, *Don't Go to Law School (Unless)* (Self-published, 2012): 34–36.

46. Arjun Appadurai, "Disjuncture and Difference in the Global Cultural Economy," *Theory, Culture & Society* 7 (1990): 295–310.

47. Mihaela Papa and David Wilkins, "Globalization, Lawyers, and India: Toward a Theoretical Synthesis of Globalization Studies and the Sociology of the Legal Profession," *International Journal of the Legal Profession* 18 (2011): 175–209.

48. See Luz Herrera, "Educating Main Street Lawyers," *Journal of Legal Education* 63 (2013): 197. See also George Leef, "Why The Legal Profession Says LegalZoom Is Illegal," *Forbes,* October 14, 2014; retrieved on August 20, 2015, from www.forbes.com/sites/georgeleef/2014/10/14 /why-the-legal-profession-says-legalzoom -is-illegal.

49. "Clients will continue to demand efficiency and responsiveness from their lawyers. They expect lawyers to create efficient internal processes, completing work quickly and for less cost. They expect lawyers to use technology to perform tasks previously done by junior associates, and some corporate clients refuse to pay for the work of first-year associates." Board of Governors, Challenges to the Profession Committee, "The New Normal: The Challenges Facing the Legal Profession" (Madison: State Bar of Wisconsin, 2011): 7.

50. Campos and Tamanaha, in their own ways, have promoted greater informational availability on the belief that this is foundational to a well-functioning law admissions market. Henderson has focused on the pedagogical and curricular reforms that would promote greater job outcomes for legal study. If lower-tiered schools were forced to charge according to reputation, this would incentivize educational differentiation to the point that schools like New Delta might specialize in teaching specific skills or practice areas. All three believe in the antiseptic effect a well-informed marketplace might have over legal education in what they agree to be its current state of crisis. Tamanaha, *Failing Law Schools*: xii–xiii; and Campos, *Don't Go to Law School (Unless)*: xii. See also Henderson, "A Blueprint for Change": 504:

[W]e are underserving our students by permitting them to incur so much educational debt when the education we offer does not adequately map onto the workplace they are entering. The model of three years of generalist training to become an artisan lawyer is no longer a realistic or sufficient career preparation for most law graduates. The problem here is not the cost of legal education per se; rather, it is the value of legal education as it is currently constructed.

51. Bryant Garth, "Crises, Crisis Rhetoric, and Competition In Legal Education: A Sociological Perspective on the (Latest) Crisis of the Legal Profession and Legal Education," *Stanford Law & Policy Review* 24 (2013): 504.

52. Ibid.

53. Ibid.

54. Erwin Chemerinsky and Carrie Menkel-Meadow, "Don't Skimp on Legal Training," *New York Times*, April 14, 2014; retrieved on October 27, 2015, from www.nytimes .com/2014/04/15/opinion/dont-skimp-on-legal-training.html. Dean Chemerinsky's critics, including some of those already mentioned, reflect disappointment that such a revered public interest– and social justice–minded academic and advocate would aspire to elitism while refusing to acknowledge the realities of the many middle- and lower-tiered schools and their students. Tamanaha, *Failing Law Schools*: 183; and Karen Sloan, "UC Irvine Debuts at No. 30 on US News List—Missing Goal," *The National Law Journal*, March 9, 2015, retrieved on August 20, 2015, from www.nationallawjournal.com/id=1202720102826/ UC-Irvine-Debuts-at-No-30-on-US-News-ListmdashMissing-Goal#ixzz3jOGMlRZH.

55. Hegemony for the Italian writer Antonio Gramsci was

the "spontaneous" consent given by the great masses of the population to the general direction imposed on social life by the dominant fundamental group; this consent is "historically" caused by the prestige (and consequent confidence) which the dominant group enjoys because of its position and function within the world of production.

Antonio Gramsci, *Selections from the Prison Notebooks*, eds. and trans. Quentin Hoare and Geoffrey Nowell Smith (New York: International Publishers, 1971): 12.

56. Brown, *Undoing the Demos*: 31.

57. Scott DeVito, "Letter to the Editor," *The New York Times*, November 2, 2015.

58. C. Wright Mills, *White Collar* (London and New York: Oxford University Press, 1951); and Talcott Parsons, "Law as an Intellectual Stepchild," *Sociological Inquiry* 47 (1977).

59. Caroll Seron, *The Business of Practicing Law* (Philadelphia: Temple University Press, 1996); and Yves Dezelay and Bryant Garth, *Dealing in Virtue: International Commercial Arbitration and the Construction of a Transnational Legal Order* (Chicago: University of Chicago Press, 1998).

60. Deborah Rhode, *The Trouble with Lawyers* (Oxford, UK, and New York: Oxford University Press, 2015).

61. John Susskind, *The End of Lawyers? Rethinking the Nature of Legal Services* (Oxford, UK, and New York: Oxford University Press, 2010).

62. Riles, *Collateral Knowledge*.

63. Ibid.: 13.

64. Bill Maurer, *Mutual Life, Limited: Islamic Banking, Alternative Currencies, Lateral Reason* (Princeton, NJ: Princeton University Press, 2005).

65. Karen Ho, *Liquidated: An Ethnography of Wall Street* (Durham, NC: Duke University Press, 2009).

66. Carol Greenhouse, *The Paradox of Relevance* (Philadelphia: University of Pennsylvania Press, 2011).

67. Elizabeth Mertz, *The Language of Law School: Learning to "Think Like a Lawyer"* (Oxford, UK: Oxford University Press, 2007): 16.

68. Ibid.: 27.

69. Didier Fassin, "Introduction: Toward a Critical Moral Anthropology," in *A Companion to Moral Anthropology*, ed. Didier Fassin (West Sussex, UK: Wiley-Blackwell, 2012): 4–5.

70. Some in this debate may prefer a kind of distanced approach to morality where "good" and "bad" are judged best by individual "success" or "failure" (for example: Did they really *not* get jobs? Don't they feel more prestigious afterwards *anyway*?) rather than a more *social* sense of virtue or progress. But there are ethics to legal education and profession beyond simply learning the rules of engagement and mastering their application for advancement in an academic or professional "field." Drawing from a rich tradition in both interpretive anthropology and the anthropology of law and policy, it is now widely acceptable and indeed welcome to represent interpretations of an institutional dispute—particularly one with such lopsided power dynamics—from the perspective of those with "weaker" institutional voices and power, especially as those constitute a majority of this law school population. The space for what some would call "activist anthropology" has been building since the days of Franz Boas and his academic progeny and has grown in recent discussions about indigenous rights, race and antiracism, and the boycott movement.

71. Shore and Wright, "Policy": 11.

72. As Shore and Wright have further noted, the ethnographic study of policy takes the anthropology of expertise in a new direction. Whereas traditional anthropology featured the field-worker as expert studying "primitive" or lay individuals, the anthropology of law inverted this by having an uninformed ethnographer studying the insider community of lawyers or judges—"studying up" as Laura Nader famously called it. Laura Nader, "Up the Anthropologist: Perspectives Gained from Studying Up," in *Reinventing Anthropology*, ed. Dell H. Hymes (New York, Pantheon Books, 1972): 284–311. In the discipline of public policy studies, scholars have identified a relatively neat bifurcation between "top-down" and "bottom-up" approaches in the literature. Marcia K. Meyers, Norma M. Riccucci, and Irene Lurie, "Achieving Goal Congruence in Complex Environments: The Case of Welfare Reform," *Journal of Public Administration Research and Theory: J-PART*, 11 (2001): 167.

73. All informants interviewed were affiliates of NDSL, Law Corp, or their parent fund Venture Partners Group (VPG) for some time during the fieldwork for this project. But my interview sample includes both former and current affiliates as of the time of interview. Similarly, informant affiliations will have certainly changed by the time this book appears in print. To better preserve the confidentiality of my informants, I have chosen to omit distinctions between former and current faculty and staff as of the interview stage. Data

fidelity lost in dropping this distinction is, in my view, outweighed by the significant access strict confidentiality afforded me in conducting this project.

74. The phrase *managed precarity* appears in a 2015 article by Caitlin Hewitt-White, describing a policy to weaken schoolteacher labor unionism in Ontario, Canada. In that context, the author describes the selective termination of teachers and their replacement with casual education contract workers. Caitlin Hewitt-White, "The OSSTF Anti-Bill 115 Campaign: An Assessment from a Social Movement Unionism Perspective," *Alternate Routes: A Journal of Critical Social Research* 26 (2015): 176. My definition of the term *managed precarity*, meanwhile, emphasizes its *management* potential: It is in this study a condition that permits management within a private for-profit enterprise to better manage a workforce considered to be otherwise hostile—due to tenure, left-leaning political sensibilities, and faith in faculty governance—to its directives.

Chapter 1

1. William Sullivan, Anne Colby, Judith Welch Wegner, Lloyd Bond, and Lee Shulman, *Educating Lawyers: Preparation for the Profession of Law—Summary* (Stanford, CA: The Carnegie Foundation for the Advancement of Teaching, 2007).

2. For Saskia Sassen, *predatory formations* are "a mix of elites and systemic capacities with finance a key enabler, that push toward acute concentration." Saskia Sassen, *Expulsions: Brutality and Complexity in the Global Economy* (Cambridge, MA, and London: Harvard University Press, 2014): 13.

3. See, for example, Judith Butler and Athena Athanasiou, *Dispossession: The Performative in the Political* (Cambridge, UK: Polity Press, 2013): 43; and Guy Standing, *The Precariat Charter: From Denizens to Citizens* (London and New York: Bloomsbury, 2014).

4. Richard Gilman-Opalsky, *Precarious Communism: Manifest Mutations, Manifesto Detourned* (New York: Minor Compositions, 2014): 5n5.

5. For more on "shareholder value" and job insecurity see Ho, *Liquidated*: 126.

6. Durkheim, *The Division of Labor*: 60–62.

7. Ibid.: 242–243.

8. Wood and Wright, "Private Equity": 364.

9. See American Bar Association, Section of Legal Education and Admissions to the Bar, *Standards and Rules of Procedure for Approval of Law* Schools 2014–2015, Standard 501(b) (Chicago: ABA).

10. American Bar Association, "ABA National Lawyer Population Survey Historical Trend in Total National Lawyer Population 1878–2015," 2015. Retrieved on September 1, 2015, from www.americanbar.org/content/dam/aba/administrative/market_research/total-national-lawyer-population-1878-2015.authcheckdam.pdf.

11. Steven Seidenberg, "Unequal Justice: U.S. Trails High-Income Nations in Serving Civil Legal Needs," *ABA Journal*, June 1, 2012; retrieved on September 1, 2012, from www.abajournal.com/magazine/article/unequal_justice_u.s._trails_high-income_nations_in_serving_civil_legal_need.

12. Ibid.

13. Tamanaha, *Failing Law Schools*: 119–120; and Campos, *Don't Go to Law School (Unless)*: 47–48.

14. Peter James Kolovos, "Antitrust Law and Nonprofit Organizations: The Law School Accreditation Case," *N.Y.U. Law Review* 71 (1996): 690.

15. Ibid.: 689.

16. Ibid.: 690.

17. Complaint at 5-7, *United States v. American Bar Association*, No. 1:95CV01211 (D.D.C. June 27, 1995).

18. Kolovos, "Antitrust Law": 692.

19. This is a pseudonym.

20. These origins are significant in part because Catholic law schools were historically also mission-based lower-tiered programs available to ethnic minorities in the United States at a time when established secular law schools excluded those groups. See William W. Fisher, Morton J. Horowitz, and Thomas A. Reed, *American Legal Realism* (New York: Oxford University Press, 1993): 271.

21. Local publication; source information omitted.

22. Most U.S. law schools accept foreign LLB degree holders, as these are equivalent in rank, despite being considered an undergraduate rather than a graduate credential.

23. Association of American Law Schools, "Faculty Appointments Register (FAR)." Retrieved on September 3, 2015, from www.aals.org/services/faculty-recruitment-services/far/.

24. The LLM degree is a "masters of legal letters", and serves as a legal "graduate" degree. It is often obtained by foreign jurists seeking an advanced U.S. credential and permits those individuals to sit for a state bar exam. But, it is also a popular finishing degree for aspiring legal academics. Unlike other disciplines requiring a "doctorate" for tenure-line university teaching, most law faculty, including all those with JD and LLM degrees, are not permitted to be called "doctor." Holders of the SJD or JDS, the most advanced legal graduate degree, are given this title.

25. Talent Plus, "About Us." Retrieved on September 4, 2015, from www.talentplus.com/about-us-footer.

26. Jim Collins, *Good to Great* (New York: HarperBusiness, 2001): 13.

27. These were usually individualized employee goals tied to monetary incentives. The term applied more to administrative roles within the organization.

28. The Norwegian Africanist scholars Marianne Millstein and David Jordhus-Lier have written about casualization "from below" in the context of nongovernmental organizations serving as labor brokers in urban developing communities of Cape Town, South Africa. Marianne Millstein and David Jordhus-Lier, "Making Communities Work? Casual Labour Practices and Local Civil Society Dynamics in Delft, Cape Town," *Journal of Southern African Studies* 38 (2012): 183–201. That practice differs from the kind described here as "upward casualization." Whereas the former involves third-party nongovernmental actors serving as brokers, the latter takes place internally within the workforce of a single enterprise at the behest of management. Brokerage, in a sense, may be irrelevant to upward

casualization insofar as the lower-level casual labor supply is already present, available, and self-motivated to enter this system. Although I do not foreclose the likelihood that this concept can apply to industry-wide labor dynamics, this study supports its description only at the level of a single enterprise.

29. Edna Bonacich, "A Theory of Ethnic Antagonism: The Split Labor Market," *American Sociological Review* 37:5 (1972): 547–559.

30. John W. Curtis, "Trends in Faculty Employment Status, 1975–2011," Association of American University Professors, March 20, 2013. Retrieved on January 18, 2017, from www .aaup.org/sites/default/files/Faculty_Trends_0.pdf.

31. Aronowitz, *The Knowledge Factory*:74–76; Giroux, *Neoliberalism's War on Higher Education*: 16–17; and Gould, *The University in a Corporate Culture*: 126–130.

32. American Bar Association, Section of Legal Education and Admissions to the Bar, *Standards and Rules of Procedure for Approval of Law Schools* 2012–2013, Interpretation 402-2, 30–31; retrieved on September 6, 2015, from www.americanbar.org/content/dam/ aba/publications/misc/legal_education/Standards/2012_2013_aba_standards_and_rules .authcheckdam.pdf.

33. Jeffrey E. Lewis, "Memorandum Regarding Proposed Revisions to Standards: Chapters 1, 3, and 4, and Standards 203(b) and 603(d) to the Council of the Section of Legal Education and Admissions to the Bar," July 24, 2013: 56–57. Retrieved on September 4, 2015, from www.americanbar.org/content/dam/aba /administrative/legal_education_ and_admissions_to_the_bar/council_reports_and_resolutions/august_2013_open_ session/2013_src_memo%20to_council_re_ch%201_%203_%204_and%20s203_b_and_ s603_d.authcheckdam.pdf.

34. Ibid.: 59–60.

35. "Resolution of Faculty of Brooklyn Law School Regarding Proposed Changes to Existing ABA Standards Regarding Security of Position, Academic Freedom, and Attraction and Retention of Faculty." Retrieved on October 30, 2015, from www.americanbar .org/content/dam/aba/migrated/2011_build/legal_education/committees/standards_ review_documents/20110620_comment_security_of_position_brooklyn_law_school_ faculty.authcheckdam.pdf.

36. In the United States, unlike many other countries, judges must also be members of the bar.

37. See, for example, Susan C. Wawrose, "What Do Legal Employers Want to See in New Graduates? Using Focus Groups to Find Out," *Ohio Northern University Law Review* 39 (2013): 532, 538.

38. The LSAT is scored on a scale of 120 to 180 points. The lowest score possible, one assigned for simply sitting for the exam, is 120. UGPA, meanwhile, is scored on a scale of 0 to 4.0, although students, particularly from high grade inflation schools, frequently graduate with a GPA of more than 4.0.

39. Text on file with author.

40. The move to make law school into a two-year program had already been debated in the wider legal education community, but it gained new traction and has been imple-

mented in a number of schools amid the latest "crisis." See, for example, Vivia Chen, "The Careerist: Third-Rate Law Schools Try Harder," *The American Lawyer*, March 17, 2014.

41. See, for example, Chris Durrance, John DiMaggio, and Martin Smith, "College, Inc." *Frontline*, Aired May 4, 2010 (Boston: WGBH Educational Foundation, 2010).

42. See Durrance, DiMaggio, and Smith, "College, Inc."

43. Tamanaha, *Failing Law Schools*, 143–144.

44. For more on strategic and remedial uses of scholarship offerings, see ibid., 85, 164–165.

45. "IRAC" is an acronym standing for *issue, rule, analysis,* and *conclusion.* It is described as the standard template for all "legal" writing.

46. Top-Law-Schools.com, "Law School Admissions Forum, AAMPLE programs-Anyone ever taken? Good/bad?" Retrieved on May 26, 2015, from www.top-law-schools .com/forums /viewtopic.php?t=36681.

47. Ibid.

48. Ibid.

49. Karen Sloan, "Lawsuit: Infilaw Paying Law Grads to Put off Bar Exam," *National Law Journal*, June 4, 2015. Retrieved on September 8, 2015, from www.nationallawjournal .com/id=1202728422268/Lawsuit-Infilaw-Paying-Law-Grads-To-Put-Off-Bar-Exam?slreturn= 20150808153226.

50. Technological infrastructure could also potentially have tax benefits as its inevitable rapid depreciation in value might be written off in filings.

51. I use *fetishized* here to mean admired as an embodiment of the ideology to which New Delta participants subscribed.

52. For more on the concept, see William Pietz, "The Problem of the Fetish," *Res* 9 (Spring 1985): 12–13.

53. "Flipping" consists of changing the predominant course delivery method so that students watch instructional video lectures on-line ahead of time and then use classroom time to solve problems or ask questions.

54. For more on the normative role of "best practices" under neoliberalism, see Brown, *Undoing the Demos*, 2015: 136–150: "Formally, they are nonnormative, pure means, 'exemplary behaviors modeled into processes.' But this is only the surface of the matter" (136).

55. Although nonprofit educational institutions are exempted from public performance infringement claims, for-profit entities are not. See Copyright Act 1976, 17 U.S.C. §110(1) (1976).

56. In at least one instance, a visiting assistant professor was named associate dean of academic affairs, a position widely understood as "second in command" to the law school dean and one regularly in charge of course scheduling and faculty support.

Chapter 2

1. See E. B. Tylor, *Primitive Culture: Researches into the Development of Mythology, Philosophy, Religion, Art, and Custom Vol. 1* (Cambridge, UK: Cambridge University Press, 1870): 1, suggesting, "Culture . . . is that complex whole which includes knowledge, belief, art,

morals, law, custom, and any other capabilities and habits acquired by man as a member of society." See also A. L. Kroeber and Clyde Klukohn, *Culture: A Critical Review of Concepts and Definitions* (New York: Vintage Books, 1952): 181, proposing that "culture consists of patterns, explicit and implicit, of and for behaviour acquired and transmitted by symbols, constituting the distinctive achievements of human groups, including their embodiment in artifacts"; Ruth Benedict, *Patterns of Culture* (New York: Mentor Books, 1952): 46, arguing that culture is the sum "pattern of thought and action" in a society; and Clifford Geertz, *The Interpretation of Cultures* (New York: Basic Books, 1973): 4. Geertz offers an interpretive definition of culture as the "webs of significance" spun by individuals that make up a community.

2. See, for example, Ruth Benedict, *The Chrysanthemum and the Sword: Patterns of Japanese Culture* (Cleveland, OH: Meridian Books, 1967). For more examples of anthropological knowledge put to use in military defense, see Duncan Bell, "Writing the World: Disciplinary History and Beyond," *International Affairs* 85 (2009): 3–22.

3. See, for example, Kevin T. Jackson, "The Scandal beneath the Financial Crisis: Getting a View from a Cultural–Moral Mental Model." *Harvard Journal of Law and Public Policy* 33 (2010): 736–778.

4. Leonidas Donskis and Zygmunt Bauman, *Moral Blindness: The Loss of Sensitivity in Liquid Modernity* (Cambridge, MA: Polity Press, 2013): 164.

5. Carol Leonnig, "How HUD Mortgage Policy Fed the Crisis," *The Washington Post*, June 10, 2008. See also Raymond Brescia, "Wells Fargo Settlement: An Important Victory For Minority Homeowners, Communities," PBS.org; retrieved on September 22, 2014, from www.pbs.org/wnet/need-to-know/opinion/wells-fargo-settlement-an-important-victory-for-minority-homeowners-communities/14150/; and Michael Powell, "Bank Accused of Pushing Mortgage Deals on Blacks," *New York Times*, June 6, 2009.

6. Best and Best, *The Student Loan Mess*.

7. Application of the term *subprime* to education finance grew as aggregate student loan debt surpassed $1 trillion in 2012. On "subprime education," see Matthew A. McGuirre, "Subprime Education: For-Profit Colleges and the Problem with Title IV Federal Student Aid," *Duke Law Journal* 62 (2012): 119–160. For more on aggregate student debt, see Best and Best, *The Student Loan Mess*: 106.

8. Karl Marx and Friedrich Engels, *The German Ideology* (New York: Prometheus Books, [1932] 1998).

9. Max Weber, *The Protestant Ethic and the Spirit of Capitalism*, trans. Talcott Parsons (New York: Routledge, 2001).

10. Georg Lukacs, *History and Class Consciousness: Studies in Marxist Dialectics* (Cambridge, MA: MIT Press, 1972).

11. Emphasis added.

12. Susan Donaldson James, "Evil Charisma: Osama Bin Laden, Hitler and Manson Had It," *ABC News.com*, May 5, 2011; retrieved on September 22, 2014, from http://abcnews.go.com/Health /osama-bin-ladens-evil-charisma-recalls-adolf-hitler/story?id=13520863.

13. Riaz Tejani, "Are We All for Profit?" *New Legal Realism Conversations*; retrieved on September 22, 2014, from http://newlegalrealism.wordpress.com/2014/08/.

14. Retrieved on August 6, 2014.

15. Leonard H. Goodman and Richard W. Rabinowitz, "Lawyer Opinion on Legal Education: A Sociological Analysis," *Yale Law Journal* 64 (1955). Goodman and Rabinowitz showed that legal practitioners in a variety of professional contexts harbored disdain for the low level of practical training they received in law school. That same year, the *American Bar Association Journal* published several pieces criticizing existing clinical education and proposing a novel student law firm as solution; see William C. Mathes, "The Practice Court: Practical Training in Law School," *ABA* Journal 42:4, April 1956; and C. Clinton Clad, "The Gap in Legal Education: A Proposed Bridge," *ABA Journal* 41:1 (January 1955).

16. Sullivan et al., *Educating Lawyers*.

17. See, generally, Randolph N. Jonakait, "The Two Hemispheres of Legal Education and the Rise and Fall of Local Law Schools," *New York Law School Law Review* 51 (2007): 863–905.

18. Nicole Black, "The Myth of the Upper-Middle-Class Lawyer," *GP Solo* 29:5, American Bar Association, 2012.

19. This informal "tier" system characterizes American legal education discourse and results from law school rankings. These rankings assess all 200-some American Bar Association accredited law schools and traditionally applied numerical ranks to the first 100. The remaining schools were once classified collectively as "third tier" and "fourth tier." *U.S. News and World Report* has become the dominant rankings source, but newer sources, including *Above the Law* and *Brian Leiter's Law School Reports*, have been offering alternative rankings in recent years.

20. See Gerald Hess, "Heads and Hearts: The Teaching and Learning Environment in Law School," *Journal of Legal Education* 52 (2002): 75–111.

21. Borrowing from quantitative natural and social sciences, education scholars have come to describe this more succinctly as "bimodal distribution."

22. Bryant Garth has argued that faculty scholarship should remain a requirement for even lower-tiered law schools to promote market participation of faculty scholars and, in turn, higher-quality research through competition. Bryant Garth, "Legal Education Reform: New Regulations, Markets, and Competing Models of Supposed Deregulation," *The Bar Examiner*, December (2014): 23.

23. See, generally, Chapter 1 of this book.

24. Regardless of the precise theory (fairness, equality, and so on) or form (procedure, substance), justice in general deals with the "righting of wrongs" and may not be the sole province of law. Legal expertise is the product of education, training, and experience in law. In the last half-century, formal education has become the sole pathway to legal expertise, and legal expertise has been widely viewed as a sure pathway to social mobility and wealth. More recently, observers have noted that expertise alone is insufficient and that it must be coupled with social or cultural "capital," with law schools trying to offer this. See, for example, Mertz, *The Language of Law School*, or Dezelay and Garth, *Dealing in Virtue*.

To attract students, fourth-tier law school such as the one described here, less endowed with cultural capital than their top-tier counterparts, espoused social justice and high-lighted student opportunities to "give back."

25. Jack Welch, quoted in Chris Durrance, John DiMaggio, and Martin Smith. "College, Inc." *Frontline*. Aired May 4, 2010. Boston: WGBH Educational Foundation, 2010.

26. Best and Best, *The Student Loan Mess*: 158.

27. Ibid.: 115.

28. See Rosa Luxemburg, *The Accumulation of Capital*, trans. Agnes Schwarzschild (London and New York: Routledge, [1951] 2003): 12. "Capitalist methods of production do more than awaken in the capitalist this thirst for surplus value whereby he is impelled to ceaseless expansion of reproduction. Expansion becomes in truth a coercive law, an economic condition of existence for the individual capitalist."

29. See Figure I.1.

30. The question to the group was, "What on the charter is resonating for you today?" Volunteers were then selected to share and speak in depth.

31. To preserve the anonymity of informants in this study, both statements here are hypothetical composites of actual meetings statements.

32. See, among others, Emile Durkheim, *The Elementary Forms of Religious Life* (New York: Free Press. 1995); Gregory Bateson, *Naven* (Palo Alto, CA: Stanford University Press, 1936); and Mary Douglas, *Purity and Danger: An Analysis of Concepts of Pollution and Taboo* (New York: Praeger, 1966).

33. Ibid.

34. Ibid.

35. Daniel Goleman, *Emotional Intelligence: Why It Can Matter More Than I.Q.* (New York: Bantam Books, 1995).

36. Daniel Goleman, "What Makes a Leader?" *Harvard Business Review* 76 (1998): 93–102.

37. Ibid.

38. Ibid.

39. See Chapter 5 of this book.

40. Synonyms have been used here to avoid reproduction of potential intellectual property.

41. General Electric website. Retrieved on August 15, 2014, from www.ge.com/en/company/companyinfo/quality/whatis.htm .

42. It is also significant that both are among the top 100 U.S. defense contractors. See General Services Administration, "Top 100 Contractors Report 2013'; retrieved on September 23, 2014, from www.fpds.gov/downloads/top_requests. /Top_100_Contractors_Report_Fiscal_Year_2013.xls.

43. This number reached nearly 40 percent during peak enrollments in 2011–2012.

44. Mertz, *The Language of Law School*.

45. Shaila Dewan, "Moral Hazard: A Tempest-Tossed Idea," *The New York Times*, February 25, 2012.

Chapter 3

1. Martha Neil, "Bloody Thursday: 6 Major Law Firms Ax Attorneys," *ABA Journal*, February 12, 2009; retrieved on May 28, 2015, from www.abajournal.com/news/article/bloody_thursday_4_major_law_firms_ax_attorneys_more_layoffs_at_others.

2. Ryan Davis, "'Bloody Thursday' Claims 748 at U.S. Law Firms," *Law360.com*, February 12, 2009; retrieved on May 28, 2015, from www.law360.com/articles/87260/bloody-thursday-claims-748-at-us-law-firms.

3. Martha Neil, "February Free Fall: Major Law Firms Lay off Another 2,000-Plus Attorneys and Staff," *ABA Journal*, February 26, 2009; retrieved on May 28, 2015, from www.abajournal.com/news/article /february_freefall_firms_ax_attorneys_freeze_pay.

4. Debra Cassens Weiss, "2009's Toll: More Than 10,000 Law Firm Layoffs and Lower Pay Trend," *ABA Journal*, May 28, 2009; retrieved on May 28, 2015, from www.abajournal.com/news/article /2009s_toll_more_than_10000_law_firm_layoffs/.

5. "Crash Course: The Origins of the Financial Crisis," *The Economist*, September 7, 2013; retrieved on September 17, 2015, from www.economist.com/news/schoolsbrief/21584534-effects-financial-crisis-are-still-being-felt-five-years-article.

6. Drew Combs, "RocknRolla," *The American Lawyer*, August 7, 2009; retrieved on May 28, 2015, from www.americanlawyer.com/id=1202484507958/RocknRolla#ixzz3movnX488.

7. David Segal, "What They Don't Teach Lawyers, Lawyering," *The New York Times*, November 9, 2011; retrieved on September 17, 2015, from www.nytimes.com/2011/11/20/business /after-law-school-associates-learn-to-be-lawyers.html.

8. Tamanaha, *Failing Law Schools*, 113.

9. Jürgen Habermas, *The Theory of Communicative Action. Vol. 2: Lifeworld and System: A Critique of Functionalist Reason*, trans. Thomas McCarthy (Boston: Beacon Press, 1987): 117:

> No matter whether one starts with Mead from basic concepts of social interaction or with Durkheim from basic concepts of collective representation, in either case society is conceived from the perspective of acting subjects as the *lifeworld of a social group*. In contrast, from the observer's perspective of someone not involved, society can be conceived only as a *system of actions* such that each action has a functional significance according to its contribution to the maintenance of the system.

10. Tamanaha, *Failing Law Schools*: 160–162.

11. Patricia Cohen, "The Long Haul Degree," *The New York Times*, April 16, 2010; retrieved on September 17, 2015, from www.nytimes.com/2010/04/18/education/edlife/18phd-t.html?_r=0.

12. As described in Chapter 1, ABA Standard 402 mandates "sufficient" faculty for accreditation. This term was defined with a range of 1:30 to 1:20 up until 2014, when these numerical ratios were removed.

13. David Segal, "Is Law School a Losing Game?" *The New York Times*, January 8, 2011; retrieved on May 28, 2015, from www.nytimes.com/2011/01/09/business/09law.html?_r=0.

14. See, generally, Best and Best, *The Student Loan Mess*.

15. These sources began to dry up during the credit crisis of the late 2000s, so to remain viable Law Corp itself was forced to offer debt financing for existing students. Law Corp did this in part knowing that once it achieved ABA accreditation, as it did in 2010, federal loan applications would be fair game.

16. Best and Best, *The Student Loan Mess*, 13–14.

17. Michael Simkovic and Frank McIntyre, "The Economic Value of a Law Degree" (April 13, 2013). HLS Program on the Legal Profession Research Paper No. 2013-6; retrieved on September 18, 2015, from http://ssrn.com/abstract=2250585.

18. Blake Ellis, "My College Degree Is Worthless," *CNN.com*; retrieved on September 18, 2015, from http://money.cnn.com/2014/11/02/pf/college/for-profit-college-degree/; Catherine Rampell, "The Investment in For-Profit Colleges Isn't Paying Off," *The Washington Post*, September 25, 2014; retrieved on September 18, 2015, from www.washingtonpost.com/opinions/catherine-rampell-the-investment-in-for-profit-colleges-isnt-paying-off/2014/09/25/0c4aaf24-44ec-11e4-b47c-f5889e061e5f_story.html; and Barry Yeoman, "The High Price of For-Profit Colleges," *Academe*, May–June 2011; retrieved on September 18, 2015, from www.aaup.org/article /high-price-profit-colleges#.Vfw7lmDscRk.

19. In September 2016 the parent company of ITT Tech announced a full shutdown of all operations after federal regulators sanctioned the organization for financial irregularities and prevented it from receiving additional federal loan dollars. Danielle Douglas-Gabrielle, "ITT Tech Parent Company to Cease All Operations," *The Washington Post*, September 14, 2016; retrieved on September 22, 2016, from www.washingtonpost.com/news/grade-point/wp/2016/09/14/itt-tech-parent-company-to-cease-all-operations/.

20. Tamanaha, *Failing Law Schools*; and Campos, *Don't Go to Law School* (*Unless*). To the extent that I embrace these writers more than others such as Chemerinsky or Garth, it is because Tamanaha and Campos had most significance in the minds of local actors on this topic.

21. The book, published by the University of Chicago Press, was Tamanaha's ninth monograph, though it differed considerably from his previous works. Although the author had already gained respect for well-received writings on jurisprudence and legal theory, *Failing* was an empirically grounded exposé about law school admissions, billing, and teaching practices themselves.

22. Tamanaha, *Failing Law Schools*: xii.

23. Ibid.

24. Paul Caron, "Brian Tamanaha's Revenge," *TaxProf Blog*. August 20, 2012; retrieved on June 4, 2015, from http://taxprof.typepad.com/taxprof_blog/2012/08/tamanahas-.html.

25. Borrowing from the *altermondialiste* movement of the 2000s decade, I use this term to describe a position not against regulation per se but against the extant form of regulation long prevalent at the ABA Council on the Section of Legal Education. This form has been described by many as "captured" by legal educators, the very profession meant to fall under is normative purview.

26. Tamanaha, *Failing Law Schools*: 173.

27. "Law School Accreditation 11-10-11," YouTube video, 1:25:27, from the 2011 National Lawyers Convention, Professional Responsibility & Legal Education Practice Group Panel, Washington, DC, November 10, 2011. Posted by the Federalist Society and retrieved on October 21, 2015, from https://youtu.be/7iXQzulAqdI.

28. Bryant Garth, "Legal Education Reform": 22.

29. Ibid.

30. John P. Heinz and Edward O. Laumann, *Chicago Lawyers: The Social Structure of the Bar* (New York and Chicago: Russell Sage and American Bar Foundation, 1982): 331–332.

31. Former president of the American Bar Foundation, former dean of Indiana University, dean emeritus at Southwestern Law School, and current professor at the UC Irvine School of Law, Garth has engaged legal education from a variety of intellectual and administrative subject positions.

32. Tamanaha, *Failing Law Schools*: 88–89.

33. Jerry Organ, "Further Understanding the Transfer Market—A Look at the 2014 Transfer Data," *The Legal Whiteboard Blog*; retrieved on September 18, 2015, from http://lawprofessors.typepad.com/legalwhiteboard/2014/12/further-understanding-the-transfer-market-a-look-at-the-2014-transfer-data.html. According to Organ, the total number of transfers in 2013 was 2,501 students, compared with 2,438 in 2012 and 2,187 in 2014.

34. I considered my involvement to help the students in this way a form of activist or engaged anthropology of the kind written on with some frequency in recent years. See, for example, Charles R. Hale, "Activist Research v. Cultural Critique: Indigenous Land Rights and the Contradictions of Politically Engaged Anthropology," *Cultural Anthropology* 21 (2006): 96–120.

35. Enrollments would have been judged "shortfall" in terms of the high volume expectation of NDSL and Law Corp executives at the height of the law school enrollment bubble—the same that resulted in a move to a larger, more expensive facility in 2011–2012.

36. Joe Palazollo, "Number of LSAT Takers Continues to Slide," *Wall Street Journal Blog*, October 24, 2014; retrieved on September 30, 2015, from http://blogs.wsj.com/law/2014/10/24 /number-of-lsat-takers-continues-to-slide/.

37. Daniel O. Bernstine, "The State of Law School Admissions: Where Are We in 2014?" *The Bar Examiner*, June 2014: 13.

38. Ibid.

39. Tamanaha, *Failing Law Schools*: 50.

Chapter 4

1. Julie Froud and Karel Wiliams, "Private Equity and the Culture of Value Extraction," *New Political Economy* 12 (2007): 1469–1523.

2. Ibid.

3. Charles Arthur, "Do We Really Need All Those Endless Updates to iTunes?" *The Guardian*, December 17, 2014; retrieved on September 30, 2015, from www.theguardian.com/technology/2014/dec/07/do-we-need-all-those-itunes-updates.

4. E. Allan Farnsworth, *An Introduction to the Legal System of the United States*, 4th ed. (New York: Oxford University Press, 2010): 11.

5. Ibid.

6. Ibid,: 19.

7. Some schools, like the University of Chicago, had begun awarding the JD decades earlier. Many of the other elite programs (for example, Stanford and Berkeley) actually phased out their JD before reintroducing it much later. See David Perry, "How Did Lawyers Become Doctors? From the LL.B to the J.D." *Precedent* (Winter 2013): 26–30.

8. Ibid.

9. Tamanaha, *Failing Law Schools*: 24–26. See also Robert Stevens, *Law School: Legal Education in America from the 1850s to the 1980s* (Chapel Hill: University of North Carolina Press, 1983): 92–94.

10. The hiring of management consultants in the higher education context is a fascinating development amid the wider changes sweeping U.S. universities and colleges and could rightly occupy an entire separate volume.

11. Nobi website; retrieved on June 12, 2015, from www.nobigroup.com/whoweare .html.

12. Fernanda Zamudio-Suaréz, "Lawmakers in 2 States Propose Bills to Cut Tenure," *The Chronicle of Higher Education*, January 13, 2017. Retrieved on January 19, 2017, from www.chronicle.com/article/Lawmakers-in-2-States-Propose/238890.

13. Tamanaha, *Failing Law Schools*: 50.

14. Catherine Ho, "An End to Tenure at Law Schools," *The Washington Post*, August 18, 2013; and James Huffman, "Law Schools: Reform or Go Bust," *Newsweek*, February 20, 2015.

15. Tamanaha, *Failing Law Schools*: 29.

16. Sullivan et. al., *Educating Lawyers*.

17. Robert W. Gordon, "The Geologic Strata of the Law School Curriculum," *Vanderbilt Law Review* 60 (2007): 340.

18. William Blackstone, *Commentaries on the Laws of England* (Oxford, UK: Clarendon Press, 1765–1769); and James Kent, *Commentaries on American Law* I, 1st ed. (New York: O. Halsted, 1826).

19. Sullivan et al, *Educating Lawyers*.

20. Ibid.

21. Emphasis added.

Chapter 5

1. A focus group is a small body of informants gathered by social researchers for the purpose of collective questioning and information gathering. These have been used in scholarly research, but more commonly they are used for commercial market research. See, generally, H. Russell Bernard, *Social Research Methods: Qualitative and Quantitative Approaches*, 2nd edition. (Thousand Oaks, CA, and London: Sage, 2013): 197–199.

2. The very discussion of a deadline indicated a need to report back to outside entities by a designated date, whether or not faculty, staff, and students were comfortable with the timeline.

3. See Chapter 4 of this book.

4. To its great credit, however, the school often had one of its own graduates among the top three—in several instances the single best—bar scorer in the state.

5. See Chapter 3 of this book. This number is taken as a proportion of the total 1L cohort who successfully finished the first year and would have advanced to the second.

6. This implied that any challenges to leadership that day might result in reduction in discretionary approval of faculty resource expenditures.

7. One might wonder at this stage why any vote was taken at all, or why a second and third were necessary if leadership was already decided. Law Corp used a system of "individual strategic objectives" (ISOs) whereby executives tied managerial performance to individual goals. Some faculty believed that the New Delta dean had a corporate-mandated ISO requiring her to achieve faculty legitimacy for the new program and certainly had one for delivering a new program as such.

8. As described in Chapter 6, this point was further underscored with the firing of two more critical senior faculty at the conclusion of the 2.0 debacle.

Chapter 6

1. For more on this rule, see Chapter 7.

2. In the year after I concluded this fieldwork, portions of the school's building were rented out as temporary space to major TV networks for broadcasting during a major sporting event, and the building itself was "wrapped" in consumer advertising. Both were, ostensibly, for a sum of money to count toward the 10 percent of privately sourced revenue.

3. A termination clause is a contractual term that spells out the party's conditions for termination. A forum selection clause is a contractual term that prescribes the jurisdiction in which a dispute must be adjudicated.

4. For more on the phrase "lawyer up" see Riaz Tejani, "Efficiency Unbound: Processual Deterrence for a New Legal Realism," *UC Irvine Law Review* (forthcoming).

5. The NDSL Faculty Handbook, as amended on October 12, 2012, provides for a formal posttenure review process.

6. Documents on file with author.

7. See Chapter 5.

8. Under the law of defamation, for example, statements made in pursuit of litigation are subject to an absolute privilege, meaning that they are not actionable even if they create reputational harm.

9. Randy J. Kozel and David Rosenberg, "Solving the Nuisance-Value Settlement Problem: Mandatory Summary Judgment," *Virginia Law Review* 90 (2004): 1850.

10. Although this gloss on the dean's use of the "better mousetrap" seemed to prevail ethnographically, some among those present at its utterance believed well into the controversy that it had been used simply as part of the common colloquialism "to build a better

mousetrap" intended to mean improvement on a simple, ubiquitous, familiar product. In other words, they felt, she just meant improving an item already difficult to improve. I do not intend to evaluate the "true" meaning of the usage here and reproduce primarily its ethnographic meaning for those on the ground.

11. This move toward casualization parallels wider trends in higher education growing not only in their own frequency but in the frequency with which they have been reported and criticized in the popular and trade press. See, for example, Marc Bousuet, "'Scientific American': Academic Labor Market 'Gone Seriously Awry,'" *Chronicle of Higher Education*, February 23, 2010; retrieved on October 28, 2015, from http://chronicle.com/blogs/ brainstorm /scientific-american-academic-labor-market-gone-seriously-awry/21425; and Maria Maisto, "Unionization of Instructors Is Crucial for Colleges," *New York Times*, May 14, 2015, retrieved on October 28, 2015, from www.nytimes.com/roomfordebate/2015/ 05/14/should-graduate-students-and-adjuncts-unionize-for-better-pay/unionization-of-instructors-is-crucial-for-colleges.

Chapter 7

1. See, generally, Heinz and Laumann, *Chicago Lawyers*.

2. This observation has been a common feature in anti–affirmative action arguments. See, for example, *Grutter v. Bollinger,* 539 U.S. 306 (2003). Clarence Thomas dissent:

When blacks take positions in the highest places of government, industry, or academia, it is an open question today whether their skin color played a part in their advancement. The question itself is the stigma—because either racial discrimination did play a role, in which case the person may be deemed "otherwise unqualified," or it did not, in which case asking the question itself unfairly marks those blacks who would succeed without discrimination.

Here, my argument is not against affirmative diversification in general but rather the version of it combined with educational austerity to offer a differential quality of learning for ethnoracially and socioeconomically diverse students.

3. Altering a two-decade trend of leniency, the ED finally cut off loans to one for-profit law school in early 2017. U.S. Department of Education, "Charlotte School of Law Denied Continued Access to Federal Student Aid Dollars" (press release), December 19, 2016, retrieved on January 15, 2017, from www.ed.gov/news/press-releases/ charlotte-school-law-denied-continued-access-federal-student-aid-dollars.

4. 34 C.F.R. §602.

5. American Bar Association Section of Legal Education and Admissions to the Bar, *Standards and Rules of Procedure for Approval of Law Schools* 2014–2015: 1-46, 89-108.

6. Revisions to ABA Standard 509 now require accurate disclosure of gainful employment and other applicant-relevant data.

7. This expectation required that all law schools have primarily tenure-track faculty who are assessed largely on the basis of their scholarly output. Both tenure and scholarship, critics say, are expensive and do not necessarily benefit students. See Tamanaha, *Failing Law Schools*: 28–29, 54–61; and Gordon Russell, "The ABA Section on Legal Education

Revisions of the Law Library Standards: What Does It All Mean?" *Law Library Journal* 106 (2014).

8. In the case of tenure, an association of American law deans circulated a letter calling the accreditation requirement an "abuse of power" by the Section on Legal Education. Doug Lederman, "Law Deans Criticize Their Accreditor," *Inside Higher Ed*, April 21, 2006; retrieved on October 21, 2015, from www.insidehighered.com/news/2006/04/21/aba.

9. Tamanaha, *Failing Law Schools*: 26–27.

10. Ibid.: 155–159.

11. Ibid.: 133–134.

12. "Law School Accreditation 11-10-11.".

13. Experts in law and economics have long said informational transparency may be requisite to a healthy market. See Posner, *The Economics of Justice*: 240–242.

14. Tamanaha, *Failing Law Schools*: 130–132.

15. M7 Financial, *Graduate Program Credit Ratings for Law Schools (2014–2015)*; retrieved on May 26, 2015, from www.m7financial.com/resources/.

16. Stephanie Francis Ward, "Department of Education Flags 5 Law Schools' Debt-to-Income Ratios, Including 3 in Infilaw System," *ABA Journal*, January 11, 2016; retrieved on January 15, 2017, from www.abajournal.com/news/article/department_of_education_flags_5_law_schools_debt-to-income_ratios_including.

17. See Tamanaha, *Failing Law Schools*: 186–187; see also Paul Campos, *Don't Go to Law School (Unless)*: 57.

18. See generally Mertz, *The Language of Law School*; and Elizabeth Mertz, "Teaching Lawyers the Language of Law: Legal and Anthropological Translations," *John Marshall Law Review* 34 (2000): 99.

19. Ho, *Liquidated*: 147.

20. Ibid.: 130. For public corporations, shareholder value is determined by significant budgetary reporting and auditing by third-party financial firms. See Elisse B. Walter and Matthew A. Daigler, "Gatekeepers Are the Key to Good Governance," *Forbes*, June 21, 2010; retrieved on October 28, 2015, from www.forbes.com/2010/06/21/shareholders-risk-gatekeepers-elisse-walter-leadership-governance-ethisphere.html. Although the rise of shareholder value was unequivocally bad for workers in many long-standing industries, at least the justifications for this today have to be articulated and well-documented for public companies under policies since established by the Sarbanes-Oxley Act of 2002. See Sarbanes-Oxley Act of 2002; Pub.L. 107–204, 116 Stat. 745. In private equity, however, ownership remains "private," and the same decisions about waste and efficiency are not subject to the same reporting. See See David P. Stowell, *An Introduction to Investment Banks, Hedge Funds, and Private Equity* (New York: Academic Press/Elsevier, 2010): 291. Under this system, reduction of a company's workforce or infrastructure *for the sole purpose* of boosting revenues for investors would not be unheard of, nor raise any alarm bells. Indeed, within the short timelines on which private equity companies are typically held, such practices have become commonplace. See Walter Hamilton, "Private-Equity Industry: A Bad Rep,

but Is It Deserved?" *Los Angeles Times*, January 12, 2012; retrieved on October 28, 2015, from http://articles.latimes.com/2012/jan/12 /business /la-fi-private-equity-20120112.

21. Ibid.: 130–131.

22. American Bar Association, Section of Legal Education and Admissions to the Bar, *Standards and Rules of Procedure for Approval of Law* Schools 2014–2015, Standard 405 (b–d).

23. Importantly, however, the coincidence of these developments is not direct evidence of causation.

24. Susan K. Boyd, *The ABA's First Section: Assuring a Qualified Bar* (Chicago: American Bar Association, 1993): 15–16.

25. Standard 501 (b) (2014-2015).

26. Standard 501 (a) merely requires, "sound admission policies and practices," and does not preclude the kind of formal, extra vetting that AAMPLE in theory represents.

27. Recent discussions suggest Standard 316 may become a problem as well. Proposed language requires as a condition for accreditation that 75 percent of graduates from each school pass a state bar within two years of graduation. This tightens and simplifies existing rules that have allowed many low-performing law schools, not only for-profits, to evade discipline. See Stephanie Francis Ward, "Committee OKs Proposal to Tighten ABA Bar Pass Standards; Some Members Hope More Will Be Done," *ABA Journal*, September 12, 2016; retrieved on January 15, 2017, from www.abajournal.com/news/article/committee_oks_proposal_to_tighten_aba_bar_pass_standards_some_members_hope.

28. Developed in 2013, Standard 509 states, "A law school shall publicly disclose on its website, in the form and manner and for the time frame designated by the Council, the following information:

1. admissions data;
2. tuition and fees, living costs, and financial aid;
3. conditional scholarships;
4. enrollment data, including academic, transfer, and other attrition;
5. numbers of full-time and part-time faculty, professional librarians, and administrators;
6. class sizes for first-year and upper-class courses; number of seminar, clinical and co-curricular offerings;
7. employment outcomes; and
8. bar passage data."

29. See Julia Glum, "For-Profit Colleges: Gainful Employment Rule Takes Effect, Sparking Change for Schools and Students," *International Business Times*, July 1 2015; retrieved on October 31, 2015, from www.ibtimes.com/profit-colleges-gainful-employment-rule-takes-effect-sparking-change-schools-students-1992233.

30. Ward, "Department of Education Flags 5 Law Schools' Debt-to-Income Ratios, Including 3 in Infilaw System."

31. See Department of Education, "Obama Administration Announces Final Rules to Protect Students from Poor-Performing Career College Programs," *Ed.gov*, October

30, 2015; retrieved on October 28, 2015, from www.ed.gov/news/press-releases/obama-administration-announces-final-rules-protect-students-poor-performing-career-college-programs.

32. Above the Law, "Stats of the Week: New 'Gainful Employment' Rule the Death Knell for For-Profit Law Schools?" July 10, 2015; retrieved on October 28, 2015, from http://abovethelaw.com /2015/07/stats-of-the-week-new-gainful-employment-rule-the-death-knell-for-for-profit-law-schools/.

33. "For-Profit Groups Sue to Block Gainful Employment Rules," *Inside Higher Ed*, November 7, 2014.

34. Meyers, Riccucci, and Lurie, "Achieving Goal Congruence in Complex Environments": 167.

35. Michael Stratford, "New Fodder for 90/10 Debate," *Inside Higher Ed*, October 13, 2014; retrieved on October 23, 2015, from www.insidehighered.com/news/2014/10/13/more-profit-colleges-would-fail-9010-rule-if-veterans-benefits-are-included-analysis.

36. Kate O'Gorman, "The 90-10 Rule: Why Predatory Schools Target Veterans," *New-GIBill.org*, May 7, 2012; retrieved on October 23, 2015, from www.newgibill.org/blog/the-90-10-rule-why-predatory-schools-target-veterans.

37. Some states have now begun to close this loophole by limiting state tuition benefits from going to for-profits. See National Conference of State Legislatures, "For-Profit Colleges and Universities," July 3, 2013; retrieved on October 23, 2014, from www.ncsl.org/research/education /for-profit-colleges-and-universities.aspx.

38. See Chapter 6. The school's partnership with the Law Society (Bar) of Botswana faded once it was determined this would not lead to a consistent income stream.

39. See Barbara Glesner Fines, *Law School Materials for Success* (Chicago: CALI e-Langdell Press, 2013): 9.

40. Campos, *Don't Go to Law School (Unless)*: 57.

41. Ibid.: 63; and Tamanaha, *Failing Law Schools*: 146–147.

42. Campos, *Don't Go to Law School (Unless)*: 63–64; and Tamanaha, *Failing Law Schools*: 146.

43. Jacob Gershman, "Law Schools Face New Rules on Reporting Graduates' Success," *The Wall Street Journal*, March 17, 2015; retrieved on October 23, 2015, from www.wsj.com/articles /law-schools-face-new-rules-on-reporting-graduates-success-1426629126.

44. Ibid.

45. Ibid.

46. Reinhold, Susan. "Local Conflict and Ideological Struggle: Positive Images and Section 28." Unpublished PhD thesis, University of Sussex, 1994. Cited in Shore and Wright, "Policy": 14.

47. Matthew Sherman, "A Short History of Financial Deregulation in the United States," Center for Economic Policy and Research, July 2009; retrieved on October 23, 2015, from www.cepr.net/documents /publications/dereg-timeline-2009-07.pdf.

48. *City of Los Angeles v. Wells Fargo Bank*, Complaint and Demand for Jury Trial (C. D. Cal. December 5, 2013), 27.

49. Ibid.

50. Tracy Alloway, "Why Would Anyone Want to Restart the Credit Default Swaps Market? Saving Single-Name Credit Default Swaps?" *Bloomberg Business*, May 11, 2015; retrieved on October 23, 2015, from www.bloomberg.com/news/articles/2015-05-11/why-would-anyone-want-to-restart-the-credit-default-swaps-market-.

51. Baker, "On the Genealogy of Moral Hazard": 238–239.

52. Ibid.

53. Ibid.

54. Ibid.: 254–255.

55. Amy Or, "Average Private Equity Hold Times Drop to 5.5 Years," *The Wall Street Journal*, June 10, 2015; retrieved on October 23, 2015, from http://blogs.wsj.com/privateequity/2015/06/10/average-private-equity-hold-times-drop-to-5-5-years/.

56. Wood and Wright, "Private Equity": 361.

57. This is not illegal and is rather common in corporate finance. But it rarely has such a direct impact on students and professional trainees.

58. Emphasis added.

59. Baker, "On the Genealogy of Moral Hazard": 238–239.

60. By *premium*, I mean rates at or above those paid by students at "top" law schools.

61. This simplified risk–utility balancing excludes "optimism bias," or the idea that students tend to overestimate their chances for success despite the high risk of loss counterbalancing that. See Tamanaha, *Failing Law Schools*: 143–144.

62. For a sharp critical note about "return on investment" as a trope of neoliberal knowledge capitalism, see Brown, *Undoing the Demos*: 23.

63. New regulatory discipline from both the ABA and ED against one for-profit law school in late 2016 suggested this approach was, at least momentarily, reversing. See Department of Education, "Charlotte School of Law Denied Continued Access to Federal Student Aid Dollars."

64. These additional services were not additionally compensated despite distinguishing the school in the market from its competitors.

65. The "savings" referenced here was a complicated one. Among most ABA law schools developing two-year JD programs at the time, students graduating quickly did not save on law school tuition. Schools still required the same number of units to be completed in the same number of semesters, but more classes were available during breaks so that the academic calendar omitted conventional vacation breaks. These programs were still marketed as "saving" money in the sense that students incurred fewer "opportunity costs" abstaining from employment and required fewer ad hoc overhead expenses such as apartment rental while in residence.

66. Coeval passage of the Affordable Care Act may serve as a counterexample.

Conclusion

1. Brown, *Undoing the Demos*: 109.

2. Stephanie Francis Ward, "ABA Threatened with 1-Year Suspension of Law School Accreditation Powers," *ABA Journal*, June 24, 2016; retrieved on January 15, 2017, from

www.abajournal.com/news/article/aba_threatened_with_1-year_suspension_of_law_school_accreditation_powers/.

3. Daniel Douglas-Gabriel, "Education Department Denies Federal Student Aid to For-Profit N.C. Law School," *The Washington Post*, December 19, 2016; retrieved on January 15, 2017, from www.washingtonpost.com/news/grade-point/wp/2016/12/19/feds-deny-financial-aid-funding-to-for-profit-n-c-law-school/?utm_term=.c158c366fc5a.

4. Kyle McEntee and David Frakt, "Comments on Proposed Revisions to Standards 316 and 501," (Memo to ABA Section on Legal Education and Admissions to the Bar); retrieved on January 15, 2017, from www.americanbar.org/content/dam/aba/administrative/legal_education_and_admissions_to_the_bar/council_reports_and_resolutions/comments/201607_comment_s316_s501_law_school_transparency.authcheckdam.pdf.

5. *Regents of the University of California v. Bakke*. 438 U.S. 265 (1978); and *Defunis v. Odegaard*, 416 U.S. 312 (1974).

6. *Regents of the University of California v. Bakke.*

7. *Hopwood v. Texas*, 78 F.3d 932 (5th Cir. 1996); and *Grutter v. Bollinger*, 539 U.S. 306 (2003).

8. Milton Friedman and Rose Friedman, "Free to Choose," in *Justice: a Reader*, ed. Michael Sandel. (New York: Oxford University Press): 51–53.

9. On "predatory formations," see Saskia Sassen, *Expulsions: Brutality and Complexity in the Global Economy* (Cambridge, MA, and London: Harvard University Press, 2014): 13.

10. American Bar Association, Section on Legal Education and Admissions to the Bar, "Total Minority JD Employment"; retrieved on July 6, 2016, from www.americanbar.org/groups/legal_education/resources/statistics.html.

11. Deborah Cassens Weiss, "Law School Diversity Improves, but Not at Most Prestigious Schools," *ABA Journal*, February 12, 2015; retrieved on July 5, 2016, from www.abajournal.com/news/article/law_school_diversity_improves_but_not_at_most_prestigious_schools.

12. William Kidder, "The Struggle for Access from Sweatt to Grutter: A History of African American, Latino, and American Indian Law School Admissions, 1950–2000," *Harvard BlackLetter Law Journal* 19 (2003): 10.

13. Drew Desilver, "U.S. Income Inequality, on Rise for Decades, Is Now Highest since 1928," Pew Research Center, December 5, 2013; retrieved on July 6, 2016, from www.pewresearch.org/fact-tank/2013/12/05/u-s-income-inequality-on-rise-for-decades-is-now-highest-since-1928/.

14. Clarence Thomas, dissent, *Grutter v. Bollinger*.

15. This has been the effect of what Aaron Taylor describes as the use of "diversity" more generally as a survival tool for law schools during the economic crisis. Aaron Taylor, "Diversity as Law School Survival Strategy," February 2015. Saint Louis University Legal Studies Research Paper No. 2015-1; retrieved on July 6, 2016, from http://ssrn.com/abstract=2569847.

16. Riles, *Collateral Knowledge*: 11.

17. This has been the approach of "legal positivism," a diverse school of Western legal philosophy believing that there are discoverable rules constituting the law as a whole.

18. Michael A. Peters, "Classical Political Economy and the Role of Universities in the New Knowledge Economy," *Globalisation, Societies and Education*, 1:2 (2003): 153–168.

19. Debra Cassens Weiss, "Is Baltimore Law School a Cash Cow? University President Disputes Ousted Dean's Figures" *ABA Journal*, August 2, 2011.

20. Segal, "Is Law School a Losing Game?"

21. The vast majority of legal academics are not engaged in, nor trained to engage in, advanced empirical research methodologies that might otherwise justify calling these expenditures "research grants" rather than simply publication "bonuses."

22. Chemerinsky and Menkel-Meadow, "Don't Skimp on Legal Training."

23. Simkovic and McIntyre, "The Economic Value of a Law Degree."

24. Elizabeth Olson, "Burdened with Debt, Law School Graduates Struggle in Job Market," *The New York Times*, April 26, 2015; retrieved on October 27, 2015, from www.nytimes .com/2015/04/27 /business/dealbook/burdened-with-debt-law-school-graduates-struggle-in-job-market.html.

25. CNNMoney.com, "Go to Law School. Rack up Debt. Make $62,000," July 15, 2014; available at http://money.cnn.com /2014/07/15/pf/jobs/lawyer-salaries/.

26. Posner, *The Economics of Justice*: 233.

27. One could assert, however, that simply concealing the practice of tuition gaming under cover of "nonprofit" status shows bad faith and therefore belongs to a higher class of culpability. I take no position on that here.

28. See, for example, Kenneth D. Chestek, "MacCrate (in)Action: The Case for Enhancing the Upper-Level Writing Requirement in Law Schools" (March 20, 2006); retrieved on July 6, 2016, from http://ssrn.com/abstract=892447; and Susan Sturm and Lani Guinier, "The Law School Matrix: Reforming Legal Education in a Culture of Competition and Conformity," 516 *Vanderbilt Law Review* 60 (2007).

29. See Erich H. Loewy, "Oaths for Physicians—Necessary Protection or Elaborate Hoax?" *MedGenMed* 9 (2007), 7; retrieved on October 28, 2015, from www.ncbi.nlm.nih.gov/ pmc/articles/PMC1925028/.

30. Internal Revenue Code §§ 62(a)(2)(D) and 62(d)(1).

31. Emma Brown, "Nine Atlanta Educators in Test-Cheating Case Are Sentenced to Prison," *The Washington Post*, April 14, 2015; retrieved on October 27, 2015, from www .washingtonpost.com/local/education/eight-atlanta-educators-in-test-cheating-case-sentenced-to-prison/2015/04/14/08a9d26e-e2bc-11e4-b510-962fcfabc310_story.html.

32. Sullivan et al., *Educating Lawyers*.

33. Mertz, *The Language of Law School*.

34. Tamanaha, *Failing Law Schools*.

35. See Chapter 7.

36. This has been aptly criticized by, among others, Michael Sandel, *What Money Can't Buy: The Moral Limits of Markets* (New York: Farrar, Straus and Giroux, 2012).

37. Tamanaha, *Failing Law Schools*, 2012; and Campos, *Don't Go to Law School (Unless)*.

38. Bryant Garth, "Legal Education Reform"; and Chemerinsky and Menkel-Meadow, "Don't Skimp on Legal Training."

39. ABA Standard 501 (2014–2015).

40. Rivard, "Lowering the Bar."

41. Froud and Wiliams, "Private Equity and the Culture of Value Extraction."

References

Above the Law. "Stats of the Week: New 'Gainful Employment' Rule the Death Knell for For-Profit Law Schools?" July 10, 2015. Retrieved on October 28, 2015, from http://abovethelaw.com/2015/07/stats-of-the-week-new-gainful-employment-rule-the-death-knell-for-for-profit-law-schools/.

Alloway, Tracy. "Why Would Anyone Want to Restart the Credit Default Swaps Market? Saving Single-Name Credit Default Swaps?" *Bloomberg Business*. May 11, 2015. Retrieved on October 23, 2015, from www.bloomberg.com/news/articles/2015-05-11/why-would-anyone-want-to-restart-the-credit-default-swaps-market-.

American Bar Association Section of Legal Education and Admissions to the Bar. *Standards and Rules of Procedure for Approval of Law Schools* 2012–2013. Chicago, IL: ABA.

———. *Standards and Rules of Procedure for Approval of Law Schools* 2014–2015. Chicago, IL: ABA.

———. "Total Minority JD Employment." Retrieved on July 6, 2016, from www.americanbar.org/groups/legal_education/resources/statistics.html.

———. "ABA National Lawyer Population Survey: Historical Trend in Total National Lawyer Population 1878–2015." 2015. Retrieved on September 1, 2015, from www.americanbar.org/content/dam/aba/administrative/market_research/total-national-lawyer-population-1878-2015.authcheckdam.pdf.

Appadurai, Arjun. "Disjuncture and Difference in the Global Cultural Economy." *Theory, Culture & Society* 7 (1990): 295–310.

Aronowitz, Stanley. *The Knowledge Factory: Dismantling the Corporate University and Creating True Higher Learning*. Boston: Beacon Press, 2000.

Arthur, Charles. "Do We Really Need All Those Endless Updates to iTunes?" *The Guardian*. December 17, 2014. Retrieved on September 30, 2015, from www.theguardian.com/technology/2014/dec/07/do-we-need-all-those-itunes-updates.

Association of American Law Schools. "Faculty Appointments Register (FAR)." Retrieved on September 3, 2015, from www.aals.org/services/faculty-recruitment-services/far/.

Baker, Tom. "On the Genealogy of Moral Hazard." *Texas Law Review* 75 (1996).

Barnes, Cindy, Helen Blake, and David Pinder. *Creating and Delivering Your Value Proposition: Managing Customer Experience for Profit*. London: Kogan Page, 2009.

Bateson, Gregory. *Naven*. Palo Alto, CA: Stanford University Press, 1936.

Bell, Duncan. "Writing the World: Disciplinary History and Beyond." *International Affairs* 85 (2009).

Benedict, Ruth. *Patterns of Culture*. New York: Mentor Books, 1952.

———. *The Chrysanthemum and the Sword: Patterns of Japanese Culture*. Cleveland, OH: Meridian Books, 1967.

Bernard, H. Russell. *Social Research Methods: Qualitative and Quantitative Approaches*, 2nd edition. Thousand Oaks, CA, and London: Sage, 2013.

Bernstine, Daniel O. "The State of Law School Admissions: Where Are We in 2014?" *The Bar Examiner*. June 2014.

Best, Joel, and Eric Best. *The Student Loan Mess: How Good Intentions Created a Trillion-Dollar Problem*. Berkeley: University of California Press, 2014.

Biehl, Joao. *Vita: Life in a Zone of Social Abandonment*. Berkeley: University of California Press, 2005.

Black, Nicole. "The Myth of the Upper-Middle-Class Lawyer." *GP Solo* 29:5. American Bar Association, 2012.

Blackstone, William. *Commentaries on the Laws of England*. Oxford, UK: Clarendon Press, 1765–1769.

Board of Governors, Challenges to the Profession Committee. "The New Normal: The Challenges Facing the Legal Profession." Madison: State Bar of Wisconsin, 2011.

Bonacich, Edna. "A Theory of Ethnic Antagonism: The Split Labor Market," *American Sociological Review* 37:5 (1972).

Bourdieu, Pierre. *Outline of a Theory of Practice*. Translated by Richard Nice. New York: Cambridge University Press, 1977.

———. "The Essence of Neoliberalism." *Le Monde Diplomatique*. December 1998.

Bousuet, Marc. "'Scientific American': Academic Labor Market 'Gone Seriously Awry,'" *Chronicle of Higher Education*. February 23, 2010. Retrieved on October 28, 2015, from http://chronicle.com/blogs/brainstorm/scientific-american-academic-labor-market-gone-seriously-awry/21425

Boyd, Susan K. *The ABA's First Section: Assuring a Qualified Bar*. Chicago: American Bar Association, 1993.

Brescia, Raymond. "Wells Fargo Settlement: An Important Victory for Minority Homeowners, Communities." PBS.org. Retrieved on September 22, 2014, from www.pbs.org/wnet/need-to-know/opinion/wells-fargo-settlement-an-important-victory-for-minority-homeowners-communities/14150/.

Brown, Emma. "Nine Atlanta Educators in Test-Cheating Case Are Sentenced to Prison." *The Washington Post*. April 14, 2015. Retrieved on October 27, 2015, from www.washingtonpost.com/local/education/eight-atlanta-educators-in-test-cheating-case-sentenced-to-prison/2015/04/14/08a9d26e-e2bc-11e4-b510-962fcfabc310_story.html.

Brown, Wendy. *Undoing the Demos: Neoliberalism's Stealth Revolution*. Cambridge, MA, and London: MIT/Zone Books, 2015.

Butler, Judith and Athena Athanasiou. *Dispossession: The Performative in the Political*. Cambridge, UK: Polity Press, 2013.

California Business and Professions Code § 6068(*g–h*).

Campos, Paul. *Don't Go to Law School (Unless): A Law Professor's Guide to Maximizing Opportunity and Minimizing Risk*. Self-published, 2012.

Caron, Paul. "Brian Tamanaha's Revenge." *TaxProf Blog*. August 20, 2012. Retrieved on June 4, 2015, from http://taxprof.typepad.com/taxprof_blog/2012/08/tamanahas-.html.

Chemerinsky, Erwin and Carrie Menkel-Meadow. "Don't Skimp on Legal Training." *New York Times*. April 14, 2015. Accessed October 27, 2015. http://www.nytimes.com/2014/04/15/opinion/dont-skimp-on-legal-training.html.

Chen, Vivia. "The Careerist: Third-Rate Law Schools Try Harder." *The American Lawyer*. March 17, 2014.

Chestek, Kenneth D. "MacCrate (in)Action: The Case for Enhancing the Upper-Level Writing Requirement in Law Schools." March 20, 2006. Available at http://dx.doi.org/10.2139/ssrn.892447.

City of Los Angeles v. Wells Fargo Bank. Complaint and Demand for Jury Trial (C.D. Cal. December 5, 2013).

Clad, C. Clinton. "The Gap in Legal Education: A Proposed Bridge." *ABA Journal* 41:1 (January 1955).

CNNMoney.com. "Go to Law School. Rack up Debt. Make $62,000." July 15, 2014. Available at http://money.cnn.com/2014/07/15/pf/jobs/lawyer-salaries/.

Cohen, Patricia. "The Long Haul Degree." *The New York Times*. April 16, 2010. Retrievedd on September 17, 2015, from www.nytimes.com/2010/04/18/education/edlife/18phd-t.html?_r=0.

Collins, Jim. *Good to Great*. New York: HarperBusiness, 2001.

Combs, Drew. "RocknRolla." *The American Lawyer*. August 7, 2009. Retrieved on May 28, 2015, from www.americanlawyer.com/id=1202484507958/RocknRolla#ixzz3movnX488.

Cooper-Stephenson, Ken, and Elaine Gibson. *Tort Theory*. York, Ontario: Captus Press, 1993.

Copyright Act 1976. 17 U.S.C. §110(1) (1976).

"Crash Course: The Origins of the Financial Crisis." *The Economist*. September 7, 2013. Retrieved on September 17, 2015, from www.economist.com/news/schoolsbrief/21584534-effects-financial-crisis-are-still-being-felt-five-years-article.

Curtis, John W. "Trends in Faculty Employment Status, 1975–2011." Association of American University Professors. March 20, 2013. Retrieved on January 18, 2017, from www.aaup.org/sites/default/files/Faculty_Trends_0.pdf.

Davis, Ryan. "'Bloody Thursday' Claims 748 at U.S. Law Firms." *Law360.com*, February 12, 2009. Retrieved on May 28, 2015, from www.law360.com/articles/87260/bloody-thursday-claims-748-at-us-law-firms.

Defunis v. Odegaard, 416 U.S. 312 (1974).

Department of Education. "Obama Administration Announces Final Rules to Protect Students from Poor-Performing Career College Programs." *Ed.gov*. October 30, 2015. Retrieved on October 28, 2015, from www.ed.gov/news/press-releases/obama-administration-announces-final-rules-protect-students-poor-performing-career-college-programs.

———. "Charlotte School of Law Denied Continued Access to Federal Student Aid Dollars" (press release). December 19, 2016. Retrieved on January 15, 2017, from www.ed.gov/news/press-releases/charlotte-school-law-denied-continued-access-federal-student-aid-dollars.

Desilver, Drew. "U.S. Income Inequality, on Rise for Decades, Is Now Highest since 1928." Pew Research Center. December 5, 2013. Retrieved on July 6, 2016, from www.pew research.org/fact-tank/2013/12/05/u-s-income-inequality-on-rise-for-decades-is-now-highest-since-1928/.

DeVito, Scott. "Letter to the Editor" *New York Times*. November 2, 2015.

Dewan, Shaila. "Moral Hazard: A Tempest-Tossed Idea." *New York Times*. February 26, 2012.

Dezelay, Yves, and Bryant Garth. *Dealing in Virtue: International Commercial Arbitration and the Construction of a Transnational Legal Order*. Chicago: University of Chicago Press, 1998.

Donskis, Leonidas, and Zygmunt Bauman. *Moral Blindness: The Loss of Sensitivity in Liquid Modernity*. Cambridge, MA: Polity Press, 2013.

Douglas, Mary. *Purity and Danger: An Analysis of Concepts of Pollution and Taboo*. New York: Praeger, 1966.

Douglas-Gabrielle, Danielle. "ITT Tech Parent Company to Cease All Operations," *The Washington Post*, September 14, 2016. Retrieved on September 22, 2016, from www .washingtonpost.com/news/grade-point/wp/2016/09/14/itt-tech-parent-company-to-cease-all-operations/.

———. "Education Department Denies Federal Student Aid to For-Profit N.C. Law School," *The Washington Post*, December 19, 2016; retrieved on January 15, 2017, from www.washingtonpost.com/news/grade-point/wp/2016/12/19/feds-deny-financial-aid-funding-to-for-profit-n-c-law-school/?utm_term=.c158c366fc5a.

Durkheim, Emile. *The Elementary Forms pf Religious Life*. New York: Free Press, 1995.

———. *The Division of Labor in Society*, trans. W. D. Halls. New York: The Free Press, 1997.

———. *The Rules of Sociological Method*. Translated by Steven Lukes. New York: The Free Press, 2013.

Durrance, Chris, John DiMaggio, and Martin Smith. "College, Inc." *Frontline*. Aired May 4, 2010. Boston: WGBH Educational Foundation, 2010.

Ellis, Blake. "My College Degree is Worthless." *CNN.com*. Retrieved on September 18, 2015, from http://money.cnn.com/2014/11/02/pf/college/for-profit-college-degree/.

Fanon, Franz. *The Wretched of the Earth*. New York: Grove Press, 1963.

Farnsworth, E. Allan. *An Introduction to the Legal System of the United States*, 4th edition. New York: Oxford University Press, 2010.

Fassin, Didier. "Introduction: Toward a Critical Moral Anthropology." In *A Companion to Moral Anthropology*. Edited by Didier Fassin. West Sussex, UK: Wiley-Blackwell, 2012.

Fines, Barbara Glesner. *Law School Materials for Success*. Chicago: CALI e-Langdell Press, 2013.

Fisher, William W., Morton J. Horowitz, and Thomas A. Reed. *American Legal Realism*. New York: Oxford University Press, 1993.

"For-Profit Groups Sue to Block Gainful Employment Rules." *Inside Higher Ed.* November 7, 2014.

Foucault, Michel. *Discipline and Punish: The Birth of the Prison.* Translated by Alan Sheridan. New York: Vintage Books, 1979.

"The Four Tiers: T13, Trap, No-Name, and Joke." *Outside the Law School Scam.* June 14, 2013. Retrieved on August 28, 2015, from http://outsidethelawschoolscam.blogspot .com/2013/06/the-four-tiers-t13-trap-no-name-and-joke.html.

Fraser, Nancy. "A Triple Movement?" *New Left Review.* June 2013.

Friedman, Milton, and Rose Friedman. "Free to Choose." In *Justice: A Reader,* ed. Michael Sandel. New York: Oxford University Press, 2007: 51–53.

Froud, Julie, and Karel Wiliams. "Private Equity and the Culture of Value Extraction." *New Political Economy* 12 (2007): 1469–1523.

Gaetke, Eugene. "Lawyers as Officers of the Court." *Vanderbilt Law Review* 42 (1989).

Garth, Bryant. "Crises, Crisis Rhetoric, and Competition in Legal Education: A Sociological Perspective on the (Latest) Crisis of the Legal Profession and Legal Education." *Stanford Law & Policy Review* 24 (2013): 504.

———. "Legal Education Reform: New Regulations, Markets, and Competing Models of Supposed Deregulation." *The Bar Examiner.* December 2014: 22.

Geertz, Clifford. *The Interpretation of Cultures.* New York: Basic Books, 1973.

Geertz, Clifford. "Thick Description: Toward an Interpretive Theory of Culture." in *The Interpretation of Cultures.* New York: Basic Books, 1973.

General Electric website. Retrieved on August 15, 2014, from www.ge.com/en/company/ companyinfo/quality/whatis.htm.

General Services Administration. "Top 100 Contractors Report 2013." Retrieved on September 23, 2014, from www.fpds.gov/downloads/top_requests/Top_100_Contractors_ Report_Fiscal_Year_2013.xls.

Gershman, Jacob. "Law Schools Face New Rules on Reporting Graduates' Success." *The Wall Street Journal.* March 17, 2015. Retrieved on October 23, 2015, from www.wsj.com/ articles /law-schools-face-new-rules-on-reporting-graduates-success-1426629126.

Gidley, Jennifer M., Gary P. Hampson, Leone Wheeler, and Elleni Bereded-Samuel. "From Access to Success: An Integrated Approach to Quality Higher Education Informed by Social Inclusion Theory and Practice." *Higher Education Policy* 23 (2010).

Gilman-Opalsky, Richard. *Precarious Communism: Manifest Mutations, Manifesto Detourned.* New York: Minor Compositions, 2014.

Giroux, Henry. *Neoliberalism's War on Higher Education.* Chicago: Haymarket Books, 2014.

Glum, Julia. "For-Profit Colleges: Gainful Employment Rule Takes Effect, Sparking Change for Schools And Students." *International Business Times.* July 1 2015. Retrieved on October 31, 2015, from www.ibtimes.com/profit-colleges-gainful-employment-rule-takes-effect-sparking-change-schools-students-1992233.

Goleman, Daniel. *Emotional Intelligence: Why It Can Matter More Than I.Q.* New York: Bantam Books, 1995.

Goleman, Daniel. "What Makes a Leader?" *Harvard Business Review* 76 (1998): 93–102.

Goodman, Leonard H. and Richard W. Rabinowitz. "Lawyer Opinion on Legal Education: A Sociological Analysis." *Yale Law Journal* 64 (1955).

Gordon, Robert W. "The Geologic Strata of the Law School Curriculum." *Vanderbilt Law Review* 60 (2007).

Gould, Eric. *The University in a Corporate Culture*. New Haven. CT, and London: Yale University Press, 2011.

"Grab the Bleach: St. John's University School of Law." *Third Tier Reality*. August 22, 2010. Retrieved on August 28, 2015, from http://thirdtierreality.blogspot.com/2010/08/grab-bleach-st-johns-university-school.html.

Gramsci, Antonio. *Selections from the Prison Notebooks*. Edited and translated by Quentin Hoare and Geoffrey Nowell Smith. New York: International Publishers, 1971.

Greenhouse, Carol. *The Paradox of Relevance*. Philadelphia: University of Pennsylvania Press, 2011.

Grisham, John. *Runaway Jury*. New York: Doubleday, 1996.

Grutter v. Bollinger. 539 U.S. 306 (2003).

Habermas, Jürgen. *The Theory of Communicative Action. Vol. 2: Lifeworld and System: A Critique of Functionalist Reason*. Translated by Thomas McCarthy. Boston: Beacon Press, 1987.

Hale, Charles R. "Activist Research v. Cultural Critique: Indigenous Land Rights and the Contradictions of Politically Engaged Anthropology." *Cultural Anthropology* 21 (2006): 96–120.

Hamilton, Walter. "Private-Equity Industry: A Bad Rep, But Is It Deserved?" *Los Angeles Times*. January 12, 2012. Retrieved on October 28, 2015, from http://articles.latimes.com/2012/jan/12/business/la-fi-private-equity-20120112.

Harvey, David. *A Brief History of Neoliberalism*. Oxford, UK: Oxford University Press, 2005.

Heinz, John P., and Edward O. Laumann, *Chicago Lawyers: The Social Structure of the Bar*. Chicago: Russell Sage Foundation and American Bar Foundation, 1982.

Henderson, William D. "A Blueprint for Change." *Pepperdine Law Review* 40 (2013).

Herrera, Luz. "Educating Main Street Lawyers." *Journal of Legal Education* 63 (2013).

Hess, Gerald. "Heads and Hearts: The Teaching and Learning Environment in Law School." *Journal of Legal Education* 52 (2002).

Hewitt-White, Caitlin. "The OSSTF Anti-Bill 115 Campaign: An Assessment from a Social Movement Unionism Perspective." *Alternate Routes: A Journal of Critical Social Research* 26 (2015).

Higher Education Act §1150. Title IV. § 481(b)(6).

Ho, Catherine. "An End to Tenure at Law Schools." *The Washington Post*, August 18, 2013.

Ho, Karen. *Liquidated: An Ethnography of Wall Street*. Durham, NC: Duke University Press, 2009.

———. "Finance." In *A Companion to Moral Anthropology*. Edited by Didier Fassin. Oxford, UK: Wiley Blackwell, 2012.

Hopwood v. Texas. 78 F.3d 932 (5th Cir. 1996).

Huffman, James. "Law Schools: Reform or Go Bust." *Newsweek*, February 20, 2015.

Internal Revenue Code §§ 62(a)(2)(D) and 62(d)(1).

Jackson, Kevin T. "The Scandal beneath the Financial Crisis: Getting a View from a Moral-Cultural Mental Model." *Harvard Journal of Law and Public Policy* 33 (2010): 736–778.

James, Susan Donaldson. "Evil Charisma: Osama Bin Laden, Hitler and Manson Had It." *ABC News.com*, May 5, 2011. Retrieved on September 22, 2014, from http://abcnews.go.com/Health/osama-bin-ladens-evil-charisma-recalls-adolf-hitler/story?id=13520863.

Jonakait, Randolph N. "The Two Hemispheres of Legal Education and the Rise and Fall of Local Law Schools." *New York Law School Law Review* 51 (2007): 863–905.

Kent, James. *Commentaries on American Law* I, 1st edition. New York: O. Halsted, 1826.

Kidder, William. "The Struggle for Access from Sweatt to Grutter: A History of African American, Latino, and American Indian Law School Admissions, 1950–2000." *Harvard BlackLetter Law Journal* 19 (2003): 10.

Kilpatrick, Sue and Susan Johns. "Institutional Responses to Social Inclusion in Australian Higher Education: Responsible Citizenship or Political Pragmatism?" *Widening Participation and Lifelong Learning* 16 (2014).

Kolovos, Peter James. "Antitrust Law and Nonprofit Organizations: The Law School Accreditation Case." *N.Y.U. Law Review* 71 (1996).

Kozel, Randy J., and David Rosenberg. "Solving The Nuisance-Value Settlement Problem: Mandatory Summary Judgment." *Virginia Law Review* 90 (2004).

Kroeber, A. L., and Clyde Klukohn. *Culture: A Critical Review of Concepts and Definitions*. New York: Vintage Books, 1952: 181.

"Law School Accreditation 11-10-11." YouTube video, 1:25:27, from the 2011 National Lawyers Convention, Professional Responsibility & Legal Education Practice Group Panel, Washington, DC, November 10, 2011. Posted by the Federalist Society and retrieved on October 21, 2015, from https://youtu.be/7iXQzulAqdI.

Lederman, Doug. "Law Deans Criticize Their Accreditor." *Inside Higher Ed.* April 21, 2006. Retrieved on October 21, 2015, from www.insidehighered.com/news/2006/04/21/aba.

Lee, Harper. *To Kill a Mockingbird*. New York: HarperCollins Press, 1960.

Leef, George. "Why the Legal Profession Says LegalZoom Is Illegal." *Forbes*. October 14, 2014. Retrieved on August 20, 2015, from www.forbes.com/sites/georgeleef/2014/10/14/why-the-legal-profession-says-legalzoom -is-illegal.

Leonnig, Carol. "How HUD Mortgage Policy Fed the Crisis." *The Washington Post*, June 10, 2008.

Levmore, Saul. "Probabilistic Recoveries, Restitution, and Recurring Wrongs." *Journal of Legal Studies* 19 (1990).

Lewis, Jeffrey E. "Memorandum Regarding Proposed Revisions to Standards: Chapters 1, 3, and 4, and Standards 203(b) and 603(d) to the Council of the Section of Legal Education and Admissions to the Bar." July 24, 2013. Retrieved on September 4, 2015, from www.americanbar.org/content/dam/aba/administrative/legal_education_and_admissions_to_the_bar/council_reports_and_resolutions/august_2013_open_session/2013_src_memo%20to_council_re_ch%201_%203_%204_and%20s203_b_and_s603_d.authcheckdam.pdf.

Loewy, Erich H. "Oaths for Physicians—Necessary Protection or Elaborate Hoax?" *Med-GenMed* 9 (2007). Retrieved on October 28, 2015. from www.ncbi.nlm.nih.gov/pmc/articles/PMC1925028/.

Lukacs, Georg. *History and Class Consciousness: Studies in Marxist Dialectics.* Cambridge, MA: MIT Press, 1972.

Luxemburg, Rosa. *The Accumulation of Capital.* Translated by Agnes Schwarzschild. London and New York: Routledge, [1951] 2003.

Maisto, Maria. "Unionization of Instructors Is Crucial for Colleges." *New York Times.* May 14, 2015. Retrieved on October 28, 2015, from www.nytimes.com/roomfordebate/2015/05/14/should-graduate-students-and-adjuncts-unionize-for-better-pay/unionization-of-instructors-is-crucial-for-colleges.

Marx, Karl, and Friedrich Engels. *The German Ideology.* New York: Prometheus Books, [1932] 1998.

Mathes, William C. "The Practice Court: Practical Training in Law School." *ABA Journal* 42 (1956): 333–336, 397–398.

Maurer, Bill. *Mutual Life, Limited: Islamic Banking, Alternative Currencies, Lateral Reason.* Princeton, NJ: Princeton University Press, 2005.

McEntee, Kyle and David Frakt, "Comments on Proposed Revisions to Standards 316 and 501," (Memo to ABA Section on Legal Education and Admissions to the Bar); retrieved on January 15, 2017, from www.americanbar.org/content/dam/aba/administrative/legal_education_and_admissions_to_the_bar/council_reports_and_resolutions/comments/201607_comment_s316_s501_law_school_transparency.authcheckdam.pdf.

McGuirre, Matthew A. "Subprime Education: For-Profit Colleges and the Problem with Title IV Federal Student Aid." *Duke Law Journal* 62 (2012): 119–160.

Mertz, Elizabeth. "Teaching Lawyers the Language of Law: Legal and Anthropological Translations." *John Marshall Law Review* 34 (2000).

————. *The Language of Law School: Learning to "Think Like a Lawyer."* London and New York: Oxford University Press, 2007.

Meyers, Marcia K., Norma M. Riccucci, and Irene Lurie. "Achieving Goal Congruence in Complex Environments: The Case of Welfare Reform." *Journal of Public Administration Research and Theory: J-PART* 11 (2001).

Mills, C. Wright. *White Collar.* London and New York: Oxford University Press, 1951.

Millstein, Marianne, and David Jordhus-Lier. "Making Communities Work? Casual Labour Practices and Local Civil Society Dynamics in Delft, Cape Town." *Journal of Southern African Studies* 38 (2012).

M7 Financial. *Graduate Program Credit Ratings for Law Schools (2014–2015).* Retrieved on May 26, 2015, from www.m7financial.com/resources/.

Nader, Laura. "Up the Anthropologist: Perspectives Gained from Studying Up." In *Reinventing Anthropology.* Edited by Dell H. Hymes. New York: Pantheon Books, 1972.

National Conference of State Legislatures. "For-Profit Colleges and Universities." July 3, 2013. Retrieved on October 23, 2014, from www.ncsl.org/research/education/for-profit-colleges-and-universities.aspx.

Neil, Martha. "Bloody Thursday: 6 Major Law Firms Ax Attorneys." *ABA Journal* February 12, 2009. Retrieved on May 28, 2015, from www.abajournal.com/news/article/bloody_thursday_4_major_law_firms_ax_attorneys_more_layoffs_at_others.

———. "February Free Fall: Major Law Firms Lay off Another 2,000-Plus Attorneys and Staff." *ABA Journal.* February 26, 2009. Retrieved on May 28, 2015, from www.abajournal.com/news/article/february_freefall_firms_ax_attorneys_freeze_pay.

NOBI website. Retrieved on June 12, 2015, from www.nobigroup.com/whoweare.html.

O'Gorman, Kate. "The 90-10 Rule: Why Predatory Schools Target Veterans." *NewGIBill.org.* May 7, 2012. Retrieved on October 23, 2015, from www.newgibill.org/blog/the-90-10-rule-why-predatory-schools-target-veterans.

Olson, Elizabeth. "Burdened with Debt, Law School Graduates Struggle in Job Market." *New York Times.* April 26, 2015. Retrieved on October 27, 2015, from www.nytimes.com/2015/04/27/business/dealbook/burdened-with-debt-law-school-graduates-struggle-in-job-market.html.

Ong, Aihwa. *Neoliberalism as Exception: Mutations in Citizenship and Sovereignty.* Durham, NC: Duke University Press, 2006.

Or, Amy. "Average Private Equity Hold Times Drop to 5.5 Years." *The Wall Street Journal.* June 10, 2015. Retrieved on October 23, 2015, from http://blogs.wsj.com/privateequity/2015/06/10/average-private-equity-hold-times-drop-to-5-5-years/.

Organ, Jerry. "Further Understanding the Transfer Market—A Look at the 2014 Transfer Data." *The Legal Whiteboard Blog.* Retrieved on September 18, 2015, from http://lawprofessors.typepad.com/legalwhiteboard/2014/12/further-understanding-the-transfer-market-a-look-at-the-2014-transfer-data.html.

Osterwalder, Alexander, Yves Pigneur, Gregory Bernarda, Alan Smith, and Trish Papadakos. *Value Proposition Design: How to Create Products and Services Customers Want.* Hoboken, NJ: John Wiley & Sons, 2014.

Palazollo, Joe. "Number of LSAT Takers Continues to Slide." *Wall Street Journal Blog.* October 24, 2014. Retrieved on September 30, 2015, from http://blogs.wsj.com/law/2014/10/24/number-of-lsat-takers-continues-to-slide/.

Papa, Mihaela, and David Wilkins. "Globalization, Lawyers, and India: Toward a Theoretical Synthesis of Globalization Studies and the Sociology of the Legal Profession." *International Journal of the Legal Profession* 18 (2011): 175–209.

The Paper Chase. directed by James Bridges (1973; Beverly Hills, CA :Twentieth Century Fox, 2003), DVD.

Parsons, Talcott. "Law as an Intellectual Stepchild." *Sociological Inquiry* 47 (1977).

Perry, David. "How Did Lawyers Become Doctors? From the LL.B to the J.D." *Precedent* (Winter 2013).

Peters, Michael A. "Classical Political Economy and the Role pf Universities in the New Knowledge Economy." *Globalisation, Societies and Education.* 1:2 (2003): 153–168.

Pietz, William. "The Problem of the Fetish." *Res* 9 (Spring 1985): 12–13.

Polanyi, Karl. *The Great Transformation.* Boston: Beacon Press, 2001.

Posner, Richard. *The Economics of Justice.* Cambridge, MA: Harvard University Press, 1983.

Powell, Michael. "Bank Accused of Pushing Mortgage Deals on Blacks." *New York Times*. June 6, 2009.

Rampell, Catherine. "The Investment in For-Profit Colleges Isn't Paying Off." *The Washington Post*. September 25, 2014. Retrieved on September 18, 2015, from www.washingtonpost .com/opinions/catherine-rampell-the-investment-in-for-profit-colleges-isnt-paying-off/2014/09/25/0c4aaf24-44ec-11e4-b47c-f5889e061e5f_story.html.

Reske, Henry J. "One Antitrust Battle Over: Judge Approves Consent Decree between ABA, DOJ." *ABA Journal*. August 1996.

Regents of the University of California v. Bakke. 438 U.S. 265 (1978).

Reinhold, Susan. "Local Conflict and Ideological Struggle: Positive Images and Section 28." Unpublished PhD thesis, University of Sussex, 1994. Cited in Shore and Wright, "Policy." 14.

"Resolution of Faculty of Brooklyn Law School Regarding Proposed Changes to Existing ABA Standards Regarding Security of Position, Academic Freedom, and Attraction and Retention of Faculty." Retrieved on October 30, 2015, from www.americanbar .org/content/dam/aba/migrated/2011_build/legal_education/committees/standards_ review_documents/20110620_comment_security_of_position_brooklyn_law_school_ faculty.authcheckdam.pdf.

Rhode, Deborah, *The Trouble with Lawyers*. Oxford, UK, and New York: Oxford University Press, 2015.

Riles, Annelise. *Collateral Knowledge: Legal Reasoning in the Global Financial Markets*. Chicago: University of Chicago Press, 2011.

Rivard, Ry. "Lowering the Bar." *Inside Higher Ed*. January 16, 2015. Retrieved on October 27, 2015, from www.insidehighered.com/news/2015/01/16/law-schools-compete-students-many-may-not-have-admitted-past.

Russell, Gordon. "The ABA Section on Legal Education Revisions of the Law Library Standards: What Does It All Mean?" *Law Library Journal* 106 (2014).

Sandel, Michael. *What Money Can't Buy: The Moral Limits of Markets*. New York: Farrar, Straus and Giroux, 2012.

Sarbanes-Oxley Act of 2002. Pub.L. 107–204. 116 Stat. 745.

Sassen, Saskia. *Expulsions: Brutality and Complexity in the Global Economy*. Cambridge, MA, and London: Harvard University Press, 2014.

Segal, David. "Is Law School a Losing Game?" *The New York Times*. January 8, 2011. Retrieved on May 28, 2015, from www.nytimes.com/2011/01/09/business/09law.html?_r=0.

———. "What They Don't Teach Lawyers, Lawyering." *The New York Times*. November 9, 2011. Retrieved on September 17, 2015, from www.nytimes.com/2011/11/20/business/ after-law-school-associates-learn-to-be-lawyers.html.

Seidenberg, Steven. "Unequal Justice: U.S. Trails High-Income Nations in Serving Civil Legal Needs." *ABA Journal*. June 1, 2012. Retrieved on September 1, 2012, from www .abajournal.com/magazine/article/unequal_justice_u.s._trails_high-income_nations_ in_serving_civil_legal_need.

Seron, Caroll. *The Business of Practicing Law*. Philadelphia: Temple University Press, 1996.

Sherman, Matthew. "A Short History of Financial Deregulation in the United States." Center for Economic Policy and Research. July 2009. Retrieved on October 23, 2015, from www.cepr.net/documents/publications/dereg-timeline-2009-07.pdf.

Shore, Cris, and Susan Wright. "Policy: A New Field of Anthropology." In *Anthropology of Policy: Critical Perspectives on Governance and Power*. Edited by Cris Shore and Susan Wright. London and New York: Routledge, 1997.

Simkovic, Michael and Frank McIntyre. "The Economic Value of a Law Degree" (April 13, 2013). HLS Program on the Legal Profession Research Paper No. 2013-6. Retrieved on September 18, 2015, from http://ssrn.com/abstract=2250585.

Sloan, Karen. "UC Irvine Debuts at No. 30 on US News List—Missing Goal." *The National Law Journal*. March 9, 2015. Retrieved on August 20, 2015, from www.nationallawjournal.com/id=1202720102826/UC-Irvine-Debuts-at-No-30-on-US-News-ListmdashMissing-Goal#ixzz3jOGMlRZH.

———. "Lawsuit: Infilaw Paying Law Grads to Put off Bar Exam." *National Law Journal*. June 4, 2015. Retrieved on September 8, 2015, from www.nationallawjournal.com/id=1202728422268/Lawsuit-Infilaw-Paying-Law-Grads-To-Put-Off-Bar-Exam?slreturn=20150808153226. Standing, Guy. *The Precariat Charter: From Denizens to Citizens*. London and New York: Bloomsbury, 2014.

Stevens, Robert. *Law School: Legal Education in America from the 1850s to the 1980s*. Chapel Hill: University of North Carolina Press, 1983.

Stowell, David P. *An Introduction to Investment Banks, Hedge Funds, and Private Equity*. New York: Academic Press/Elsevier, 2010.

Stratford, Michael. "New Fodder for 90/10 Debate." *Inside Higher Ed*. October 13, 2014. Retrieved on October 23, 2015, from www.insidehighered.com/news/2014/10/13/more-profit-colleges-would-fail-9010-rule-if-veterans-benefits-are-included-analysis.

Sturm, Susan, and Lani Guinier. "The Law School Matrix: Reforming Legal Education in a Culture of Competition and Conformity." 516 *Vanderbilt Law Review* 60 (2007).

Sullivan, William M., Anne Colby, Judith Welch Wegner, Lloyd Bond, and Lee Shulman. *Educating Lawyers: Preparation for the Profession of Law—Summary*. Stanford, CA: The Carnegie Foundation for the Advancement of Teaching, 2007.

John Susskind, *The End of Lawyers? Rethinking the Nature of Legal Services*. Oxford, UK, and New York: Oxford University Press, 2010.

Talent Plus. "About Us." Retrieved on September 4, 2015, from www.talentplus.com/about-us-footer.

Tamanaha, Brian. *Failing Law Schools*. Chicago: University of Chicago Press, 2012.

Taylor, Aaron. "Diversity as Law School Survival Strategy." February 2015. Saint Louis University Legal Studies Research Paper No. 2015-1. Retrieved on July 6, 2016, from http://ssrn.com/abstract=2569847.

Tejani, Riaz. "Are We All for Profit?" *New Legal Realism Conversations*, August 27, 2014. Retrieved on September 22, 2014, from http://newlegalrealism.wordpress.com/2014/08/.

———. "Efficiency Unbound: Processual Deterrence for a New Legal Realism." *U.C. Irvine Law Review* 6 (2016).

Top-Law-Schools.com. "Law School Admissions Forum, AAMPLE programs-Anyone ever taken? Good/bad?" Retrieved on May 26, 2015, from www.top-law-schools.com/forums/viewtopic.php?t=36681.

Tylor, E. B. *Primitive Culture: Researches into the Development of Mythology, Philosophy, Religion, Art, and Custom Vol. 1.* Cambridge, UK: Cambridge University Press, 1870.

United States v. American Bar Association. Complaint. No. 1:95CV01211. (D.D.C. June 27, 1995).

Urciuoli, Bonnie. "Neoliberal Education: Preparing the Student for the New Workplace." In *Ethnographies of Neoliberalism.* Edited by Carol Greenhouse. Philadelphia: University of Pennsylvania Press, 2010.

Wallerstein, Immanuel. The *Modern World-System: Capitalist Agriculture and the Origins of the European World-Economy in the Sixteenth Century.* New York: Academic Press, 1976.

Walter, Elisse B., and Matthew A. Daigler. "Gatekeepers Are the Key to Good Governance." *Forbes.* June 21, 2010. Retrieved on October 28, 2015, from www.forbes.com/2010/06/21/shareholders-risk-gatekeepers-elisse-walter-leadership-governance-ethisphere.html.

Ward, Stephanie Francis. "ABA Threatened with 1-Year Suspension of Law School Accreditation Powers," *ABA Journal,* June 24, 2016; retrieved on January 15, 2017, from www.abajournal.com/news/article/aba_threatened_with_1-year_suspension_of_law_school_accreditation_powers/.

———. "Department of Education Flags 5 Law Schools' Debt-to-Income Ratios, Including 3 in Infilaw System," *ABA Journal,* January 11, 2016. Retrieved on January 15, 2017, from www.abajournal.com/news/article/department_of_education_flags_5_law_schools_debt-to-income_ratios_including.

Wawrose, Susan C. "What Do Legal Employers Want to See in New Graduates? Using Focus Groups to Find Out." *Ohio Northern University Law Review* 39 (2013).

Weber, Max. *The Protestant Ethic and the Spirit of Capitalism.* Translated by Talcott Parsons. New York: Routledge, 2001.

Weiss, Debra Cassens. "2009's Toll: More Than 10,000 Law Firm Layoffs and Lower Pay Trend." *ABA Journal.* May 28, 2009. Retrieved on May 28, 2015, from www.abajournal.com/news/article/2009s_toll_more_than_10000_law_firm_layoffs/.

———. "Is Baltimore Law School a Cash Cow? University President Disputes Ousted Dean's Figures." *ABA Journal.* August 2, 2011.

———. "Law School Diversity Improves, but Not at Most Prestigious Schools." *ABA Journal.* February 12, 2015. Retrieved on July 5, 2016, from www.abajournal.com/news/article/law_school_diversity_improves_but_not_at_most_prestigious_schools.

Wood, Geoffrey, and Mark Wright. "Private Equity: A Review and Synthesis." *International Journal of Management Reviews* 11 (2009).

Yeoman, Barry. "The High Price of For-Profit Colleges." *Academe.* May–June 2011. Retrieved on September 18, 2015, from www.aaup.org/article/high-price-profit-colleges#.Vfw7lmDscRk.

Zamudio-Suaréz, Fernanda. "Lawmakers in 2 States Propose Bills to Cut Tenure," *The Chronicle of Higher Education*. January 13, 2017. Retrieved on January 19, 2017, from www.chronicle.com/article/Lawmakers-in-2-States-Propose/238890.

Zigon, Jarrett. "Narratives." In *A Companion to Moral Anthropology*. Edited by Didier Fassin. West Sussex, UK: Wiley-Blackwell, 2012.

Index

AALS. *See* Association of American Law
Schools
AAMPLE. *See* Alternative Admissions Model
Program for Legal Education
ABA. *See* American Bar Association Council of
the Section of Legal Education and Admissions to the Bar
ABA Journal, 169
ABA Standards and Rules of Procedure for Approval of Law Schools, 179
Above the Law, 170, 235n19
academic freedom, 24, 41, 75, 136, 175, 177
access: economic costs of, 8–9; to federal loan
moneys, 8, 15, 31, 55–56, 91–92, 107, 178, 179,
180, 184, 185, 199–200, 218, 219, 238n15, 242n3;
to housing, 58, 195–96; to justice, 1–2, 8, 9, 15,
31, 69, 203, 205, 206, 208; to legal education,
24, 25, 31, 91–92, 95–96, 109, 178, 183–84, 200,
201, 205, 208–9, 231n20, 235n24; to legal services, 1–2, 19, 30, 31, 68, 200; moral costs of, 9;
as neoliberal, 7, 8, 9, 11, 204, 205–6, 208
accreditation site visits, 6, 120, 177, 185–87, 197,
223n4
activist anthropology, 229n70, 239n34
adjunct faculty, 31, 39–41, 42, 43, 44–45, 122, 175,
202–3
affirmative action, 207–8, 209, 242n2
agency vs. structure, 87–88
Alternative Admissions Model Program for Legal
Education (AAMPLE), 50–52, 55, 98, 107, 110,
183–84, 244n26
American Bar Association Council of the Section
of Legal Education and Admissions to the
Bar, 102, 106, 109, 169, 178, 195, 203, 223n4; accreditation of for-profit law schools, 2, 4–5,
8, 25, 29, 31, 32–33, 41–42, 66, 80, 89, 111–12,
178, 179, 199–200, 218, 246n63; accreditation of MSL, 31–32, 224n16; accreditation of
NDSL, 2, 32–33, 66, 80, 89, 91, 107, 110, 111–12,
120, 149, 154, 156, 159, 167–68, 177, 185–87, 194,
197, 199–200, 201, 224n16, 238n15; accreditation site visits, 6, 120, 177, 185–87, 197, 223n4;
admissions standards, 183–84, 207, 244n26;
bar passage standards, 207, 224n10, 244n27;
criticisms of, 94–96, 97, 179–80, 181, 206–7,
238n25; disclosure standards, 184–85, 242n6,
244n28; distance education rules, 53, 56;
establishment of, 114; faculty governance
standards, 70, 137, 167–68, 186; gainful
employment (GE) rules, 179, 180, 184, 192–93,
242n6; law library resources standards, 179;
and marketization, 4–5, 199–200, 206–7, 218;
relations with ED, 6, 20; scholarship standards, 5, 95, 179, 242n7; Standard 205(b), 167;
Standard 306, 53; Standard 316, 207, 244n27;
Standard 402, 41, 42, 237n12; Standard 405,
41–42, 123–24, 182–83; Standard 501, 183–84,
207, 244n26; Standard 509, 184–85, 242n6,
244n28; student-faculty ratio standards, 5,
31, 41, 89, 224n15, 237n12; tenure standards,
29, 41–42, 95, 122, 123–24, 179, 182–83, 242n7,
243n8
American Bar Association Journal, 235n15
American Gilded Age, 7
American Revolution, 113
anthropology of law, 229nn70,72
anthropology of policy, 20–21, 194, 205, 229n70
Appadurai, Arjun: "Disjuncture and Difference in
the Global Cultural Economy," 14
Aristotle, 224n13
Asian Pacific American Law Student Association, 215

Association of American Law Schools (AALS),
21, 39, 55, 114; Faculty Appointment Registry
(FAR), 36; Faculty Placement Bulletin, 36;
Faculty Recruitment Conference, 33, 36,
44, 45
Association of Private Sector Colleges and Universities (APSCU), 179
Australia: higher education and marginal groups
in, 7; neoliberal access in, 7

BarBri, 188–89
bar passage, 5, 29, 181, 212, 214, 218; ABA standards
regarding, 207, 224n10, 244n27; NDSL pas-
sage rate, 12, 67, 82, 90, 101, 103, 108, 109, 118,
135, 137–38, 142, 149, 176, 177, 183–84, 190–92,
193, 199, 241n4
becoming vs. being a lawyer, 25, 178, 180–81
Benedict, Ruth: on culture, 234n1
Best, Joel and Eric, 8
beyondness of responsibility, 215–16
Biehl, Joao: on social abandonment, 11
bimodal distribution, 87, 99, 235n21
Blackstone, William, 128
Bloody Thursday layoffs, 85
Boas, Franz, 229n70
Bonacich, Edna: on split labor market theory, 40
Botswana, 24–25, 160–63, 245n38
Brian Leiter's Law School Reports, 235n19
Brooklyn Law School, 41
Brown, Wendy: on neoliberalism, 6, 16

Campos, Paul, 15, 94, 95, 227n50, 238n20
capitalism: expansion in, 69, 236n28; finance
capitalism, 2–3, 58, 195; Polanyi on, 7;
precarity in, 28
Carnegie Report, 27, 63, 66, 128–29, 174, 214
case method, 113–14, 128
casualization of workforce, 158, 175–76,
202–3, 230n74, 242n11; upward casualization,
40–42, 55, 231n28
Catholic law schools, 31, 231n20
C curve, 48–49, 55, 103
cheating cases, 104
Chemerinsky, Erwin, 15, 212, 228n54, 238n20
Chicago bar, 95
common law, 210, 215
comprehensive law, 81
conformity, 60–61
contracts for faculty, 6, 24, 44, 121–22, 157–58,
164–75, 241n4

corporations: corporate culture, 58, 213; and emotional intelligence (EQ), 74–78; and organic
solidarity, 28
corporatization, 6, 7, 225n21
cost-benefit analysis, 13–14
credit default swaps, 195–96
culture: corporate culture, 58, 213; counterculture, 60, 79–81, 82, 83; defined, 57–58, 233n1;
management culture, 60, 73–79, 82; policy
as, 58–60, 73, 79, 82, 83, 92, 213–14. See also
Law Corp mission culture

Department of Education (ED), 9, 25, 102, 178,
179, 187, 203, 224n11, 226n31, 242n3, 246n63;
access policies of, 91; gainful employment
(GE) rules, 180, 184; relations with ABA
Council, 6, 20, 182, 206–7
Department of Justice, 31
DePaul, 95
deregulation, 6, 9, 182, 204, 206, 219; relationship
to differentiation, 5, 41, 95; relationship to
moral hazard, 195–97, 203
DeVry, 92
differentiation, 17, 179; by marketization, 25,
132, 180, 205–8, 218, 224n16; relationship to
deregulation, 5, 41, 95
disciplinary power, 204
diversity: of faculty at NDSL, 11, 80, 236n43;
professional diversity, 23, 25, 178, 205; racial
diversity, 207–9; of students at NDSL, 1–2, 8,
11, 16–17, 51, 65–66, 177, 214
divided subject matter in legal education,
128, 130
DLA Piper, 85
doctrinal law teaching, 39–40, 41, 43, 66, 89, 114,
214; vs. lawyering practice (LP) teaching, 32,
43, 44–45, 55, 115, 122–23, 125, 135, 150
DOE. See Department of Education
Donskis, Leonidas, 58
Durkheim, Emile: on organic solidarity, 28

ED. See Department of Education
Eliot, Charles, 128
elitism, 15, 223n6, 228n54
Elsevier, 42
emotional intelligence (EQ), 74–78, 82, 92
employment in legal services, 3, 4, 5, 13, 15, 63,
69, 85–87, 94, 177–78, 181, 192, 206, 211; vs.
student loan debt, 30, 82, 86, 90–91, 199, 212,
213, 214, 215, 228n50

Engels, Friedrich: on ideology, 59, 60
entrepreneurial citizenship, 7–8
EQ (emotional intelligence), 74–78, 82, 92
ethnoracial minorities, 68, 80, 95–97, 195, 208,
    209, 214, 231n20, 242n2; marketing to, 1, 9,
    205, 206; at NDSL, 1, 19, 105, 170, 200, 203,
    206, 215

Facebook, 50, 170; sense of self at, 28
faculty at NDSL, 8, 11, 12, 14, 53–55, 58–59, 66–68,
    77–78, 79, 213–14; attitudes regarding
    student transfer requests, 101–2; as caring
    for students, 200–201, 239n34, 246n64;
    and charter review, 60, 69–73; compensa-
    tion of, 43, 94, 122–23, 125, 126–27, 132, 135,
    138–39, 144, 165, 174, 246n64; contracts, 6,
    24, 44, 121–22, 157–58, 164–75, 241n4; dissent
    among, 80, 81, 101, 107–8, 127, 130, 133, 135,
    136–39, 140–42, 145–50, 151, 152, 154–55, 158,
    163, 164, 165–67, 174–75, 176, 177, 186–87;
    diversity of, 1, 11, 80, 236n43; doctrinal law
    faculty, 43, 44–45, 55, 66, 89, 115, 122–23,
    124, 125, 126, 129, 132, 150; and Faculty 2.0,
    45, 121–27, 132, 135–36, 140; as informants,
    23, 37, 38–39, 60–61, 69–70, 71–72, 73, 77, 78,
    92, 93, 104, 111, 117–18, 120, 121, 124–26, 132,
    133–34, 137, 139, 142, 143–44, 146–48, 154–55,
    158–59, 160–61, 162, 172–73, 181, 185, 186, 197,
    198–99, 200–201; lawyering process (LP)
    faculty, 42–43, 44–45, 55, 89, 115, 122–23, 124,
    125–26, 129, 132, 135, 140, 142, 150; as mentors,
    164, 215; posttenure reviews, 122, 123, 166,
    241n5; promotion of, 62–63, 79, 122, 159;
    recruitment of, 3, 23, 27, 28, 31, 32–45, 49,
    55, 75, 80, 81, 89–90, 98, 109, 116, 122, 129, 150,
    158–59, 213, 233n56; reduction in force (RIF),
    3, 110, 224n8; relations with administra-
    tion, 24–25, 33, 38, 42, 45, 53–54, 57, 58,
    60, 64–65, 69–71, 77, 79, 80, 102, 107–8, 116,
    120–21, 126–27, 130–31, 132, 133, 135–36, 138,
    139–41, 142, 144–45, 146, 149, 151–52, 154–55,
    157, 159, 160–61, 162, 166–67, 172–74, 175, 176,
    198–99, 202, 241n6; termination of, 25, 74,
    127, 145–50, 154, 155, 157–58, 166–75, 176, 177,
    183, 186–87, 201–2, 213, 241n8; titles changed
    for, 39, 42, 124, 125, 165, 173–74, 213; voting on
    Legal Ed 2.0, 120, 121, 125, 126, 127, 132–33, 135,
    136, 137, 138–44, 151–52, 154, 174, 198, 241n7.
    See also faculty governance; faculty scholar-
    ship; faculty tenure

faculty governance, 17, 41, 42, 155; ABA Council
    standards, 70, 137, 167–68, 186; at NDSL, 42,
    75, 107, 110, 115, 120–21, 125–27, 130–31, 132,
    135–46, 174

faculty scholarship, 83, 94; ABA Council stan-
    dards, 5, 95, 179, 242n7

faculty tenure, 5, 40, 55, 62, 79, 89, 114, 116, 159;
    ABA Council standards, 29, 41–42, 95, 122,
    123–24, 179, 182–83, 242n7, 243n8; vs. faculty
    contracts, 44, 121–22, 127, 132, 157–58, 174–75;
    and neoliberalism, 123; termination of
    tenured faculty, 25, 74, 127, 145–50, 166–75,
    176, 177, 183, 213

Fassin, Didier: on moral anthropology, 19
federal financial regulations, 195–96
finance capitalism, 2–3, 58, 195
financial aid: federal student loans, 15, 30, 47,
    52, 55–56, 91–92, 177, 180, 182, 184, 185, 187,
    189, 199, 218, 224n11, 238n15, 242n3; as sales
    strategy, 46–49
financialization, 17–18, 30, 181, 225n21; defined,
    6–7
flipped classroom technique, 54, 233n53
focus groups, 136, 240n1
for-profit institutions: ABA accreditation of, 2,
    4–5, 8, 29, 31, 32–33, 41–42, 66, 80, 89, 111–12,
    178, 179, 199–200, 218, 246n63; vs. nonprofit
    institutions, 3, 4, 10–11, 13, 16–17, 29, 31, 55,
    68, 101, 105–6, 133, 139, 155–56, 159, 163, 168,
    179, 200–201, 207–8, 210, 211–12, 213, 216,
    224n10, 224n16, 233n55, 244n27, 245n37,
    248n27. See also Law Corp; New Delta
    School of Law; University of Phoenix
Foucault, Michel, 204
Fraser, Nancy, 7–8

gainful employment (GE), 179, 180, 184, 188,
    192–95, 199, 242n6
Garth, Bryant, 15, 95, 96, 97, 180, 238n20, 239n31;
    on faculty scholarship, 235n22; on for-profit
    legal education, 4
GE. See gainful employment
Geertz, Clifford: on culture, 234n1
General Electric (GE), 78, 79, 236n42
Georgetown Law Center, 216
GI Bill, 92, 187
Gilman-Opalsky, Richard, 225n19; on precarity, 28
globalization, 6, 8, 12, 14–15, 17–18, 28
Goleman, Daniel: Emotional Intelligence, 74;
    "What Makes a Leader?," 74

Goodman, Leonard H., 235n15

Good to Great, 38

Google: sense of self at, 28

governmentality, 194, 196, 204

GPA. *See* undergraduate grade point average (UGPA)

graduate income rates, 87, 181

Gramsci, Antonio: on hegemony, 228n55

Great Recession of 2009, 24, 45, 58, 63, 82, 112, 195–96; impact on legal services, 3, 69, 85–90

Greenhouse, Carol, 18

group work, 65

Habermas, Jürgen, 88, 237n9

Harvard Law School, 128, 199, 209

health insurance coverage, 9

hegemony, 16, 18, 52, 96–97, 204, 228n55

Heinz, John P., 95

hemispheric approach to legal education, 95–97

Henderson, William, 15, 227n50

Hewitt-White, Caitlin: on managed precarity, 230n74

Higher Education Act (HEA): 90/10 rule, 160, 161, 162, 163, 184, 187–88, 189, 241n2, 245n37; Title IV, 4–5, 8, 10, 11, 41, 49, 89, 107, 111, 159, 160, 180, 184, 185, 186, 187, 189, 194, 199–200, 218, 224n11, 226n40

Hippocratic Oath, 214–15

Ho, Karen, 3, 18, 181–82

Holland and Knight, 85

home mortgage lending, 9, 18

Huffman, James, 123

identity formation, 28–29

ideology: of access, 8, 24; as combined with business model at NDSL, 10–12, 24, 59–60, 71–73, 83, 92–94, 104, 109, 213–14; and ethnography, 83; Lukacs on, 60; Marx on, 59, 60, 63; policy as culture as form of, 58–60, 83, 92, 213–14; Weber on, 59, 83. *See also* neoliberalism

India, 14

informant interviews, 22–23, 25, 98, 109, 205, 223n1, 229n73, 236n31; with faculty, 23, 37, 38–39, 60–61, 69–70, 71–72, 73, 77, 78, 92, 93, 104, 111, 117–18, 120, 121, 124–26, 132, 133–34, 137, 139, 142, 143–44, 146–48, 154–55, 158–59, 160–61, 162, 172–73, 181, 185, 186, 197, 198–99,

200–201; with staff, 76, 90, 98, 106–7, 169–70, 189; with students, 1, 23, 46–47, 48–49, 66, 88, 92, 93, 99–100, 101, 104–5, 149, 150, 153–54, 170–72, 177–78, 189, 191–92, 198, 201, 202–3, 218

informational transparency, 15, 212–13, 243n13

Inside the Law School Scam, 170

International Law Society, 215

International Law Students Association, 159

interpretive anthropology, 229n70

interpretivism, 14

IRAC writing method, 50, 233n45

ITT Tech, 92, 238n19

JD degree, 14, 15, 16, 29, 32, 43, 93, 231n24, 240n7, 246n65; vs. LLB degree, 114, 231n22

John Marshall, 95

Jordhus-Lier, David, 231n28

justice: access to, 1–2, 8, 9, 15, 31, 69, 203, 205, 206, 208; adversarial system of, 215; and hegemony, 16; relationship to finance capitalism, 2; relationship to legal expertise, 18, 69, 235n24

Kaplan, 188–89

Kent, James, 128

Khan Academy, 54

Kilpatrick Stockton, 85

Klukohn, Clyde: on culture, 234n1

Kroeber, A. L.: on culture, 234n1

Langdell, Christopher, 113–14, 128

Laumann, Edward O., 95

Law and Economics thinking, 10

Law Corp, 29, 30, 33, 81–82, 86, 106, 123, 139, 155–56, 181, 182, 186–87, 195, 229n73, 238n15, 239n35; and casualization, 158; charter of, 60, 61–73, 77, 78, 162; consultants used by, 112, 114–21, 131–32, 152, 185, 240n10; and continuous improvement, 78–79; course in a box concept, 44; and emotional intelligence (EQ), 74–78, 82; individual strategic objectives (ISOs) at, 241n7; and international program development, 159–60; and Law Corp Futures (LCF), 53–54, 56; and lawyering process (LP) instruction, 42, 44–45; and Legal Education 2.0, 24, 112–31, 132, 135, 136, 138, 140, 141, 142, 146, 147; management culture at, 73–79; marketing by, 80, 90, 178; Nobi hired by, 118–20; policy as culture at,

58–60, 73, 79, 82, 83, 92, 213–14; relationship
to VPG, 30, 111–12, 161, 197–98, 203; Six Sigma
at, 78–79, 82; and Talent Plus, 37–39, 45, 74,
118, 213

Law Corp mission culture, 2–3, 49, 60–73, 77, 92,
110, 180; practice-ready training, 2, 44, 45, 61,
62, 63–67, 70, 114–15, 129, 150, 201, 206, 214;
serving the underserved, 2, 8, 11, 19, 32, 62,
68–69, 81, 82, 104, 200, 203, 214; student-
outcome centered learning, 2, 11, 31–32, 62,
67–68, 70, 104, 159, 162, 206, 214

law of defamation, 241n8

law of torts, 10, 102, 129–30

Law School Admissions Council (LSAC), 46, 105,
106, 107

Law School Admissions Test (LSAT), 1, 29, 47,
98, 105, 110, 218, 219, 232n38; score of NDSL
incoming students, 12, 45, 46, 50, 51, 68, 90,
99, 107, 108, 109, 133, 139, 183, 213–14

law school language, 18, 19, 181

Law School Transparency, 192

lawyering process (LP) teaching, 42–45, 89, 124,
125–26, 128–29, 132, 135, 142; vs. doctrinal
law teaching, 32, 43, 44–45, 55, 115, 122–23,
125, 135, 150

lawyers: as agents of the state, 9–10; fiduciary duties of, 18; and morality, 9, 10; and neoliberalism, 10; from nonelite law schools, 12–13. *See
also* legal services

leadership, 74–75

legal brief writing, 43, 130

Legal Education 2.0: course integration in,
128–31, 133–34, 135, 137, 138, 140, 142, 143,
150, 151, 155, 176, 177, 198, 214; Faculty 2.0, 45,
121–27, 132, 135–36, 140; and Law Corp, 24,
112–31, 132, 135, 136, 138, 140, 141, 142, 146, 147;
NDSL faculty voting on, 120, 121, 125, 126,
127, 132–33, 135, 136, 137, 138–44, 151–52, 154,
174, 198, 241n7; Program 2.0/Curriculum 2.0,
121, 123, 124, 125, 127–31, 132–34, 135, 136–44,
150–53, 171, 172, 174, 175, 176, 213, 241n7

legal education reformers, 15, 66, 123, 174, 179–81,
182, 192, 227n50, 232n40, 235n15

legal memo writing, 43, 130

legal positivism, 248n17

legal research and writing (LRW). *See* lawyering
process (LP) teaching

legal services: access to, 1–2, 19, 30, 31, 68, 200;
bubble in, 18; changes in, 14–15, 16–17,
227n49; employment in, 3, 4, 5, 13, 15, 63,

69, 85–87, 94, 177–78, 181, 192, 206, 211; and
globalization, 14–15, 17–18; during Great
Recession, 3, 69, 85–90; low-level legal tasks,
2, 30; and morality, 10, 18–19, 209–10, 215, 217,
226n34; structural change in law industry,
13, 14–17, 86–90

LegalZoom, 14

Lexis-Nexis, 42

LLB degree, 114, 231n22

LLM degree, 35, 231n24

LSAC. *See* Law School Admissions Council

LSAT. *See* Law SchoolAdmissions Test

Lukacs, Georg: on ideology, 60

Luxemburg, Rosa: on capitalist expansion,
236n28

marginal communities, 1–2, 3, 8, 19, 30, 68, 95,
206, 215

market fundamentalism, 6, 16, 225n19

marketization, 4–6, 11, 13, 21, 163, 196; attitudes
regarding, 15–16, 23, 25, 83, 181–82, 199–200,
204, 205, 206, 212–13, 218; defined, 6; differentiation by, 25, 132, 180, 205–8, 218, 224n16

Marx, Karl: on ideology, 59, 60, 83

Massachusetts School of Law at Andover (MSL):
ABA accreditation of, 30–31, 224n16; adjunct
faculty at, 31; faculty model at, 224n16

Maurer, Bill, 18

McEntee, Kyle, 192

McKinsey & Company, 115–18, 132, 152

Mertz, Elizabeth, 217; on law school language,
18, 19, 181

midterm exams, 55, 64

Mills, C. Wright: *White Collar*, 17

Millstein, Marianne, 231n28

Model Rules of Professional Conduct, 217

moral anthropology, 19, 229n70

moral hazard: in banking practices, 195–96;
defined, 195; in legal education, 5–6, 9, 19,
23, 25, 60, 82, 83, 123, 155, 197–203, 212, 213,
214–15, 216–17; relationship to deregulation,
195–97, 203; relationship to neoliberalism,
196–97; relationship to policy cascade, 199;
and social welfare, 196, 204; transmissibility
of, 199–202

morality: ethical judgment, 180–81; and legal
services, 10, 18–19, 209–10, 215, 217, 226n34;
and markets, 212–13, 218, 219, 229n70; moral
separation, 18–19, 209–10, 216–17; and open
access, 9

Motorola, 78, 79, 236n42

MSL. *See* Massachusetts School of Law at Andover

Nader, Laura, 194; on studying up, 229n72

National Jurist, 169

National Law Journal, 169

Native American Law Student Association, 35

NDSL. *See* New Delta School of Law

Neilly, Clark, 95

neoliberalism: access in, 7, 8, 9, 11, 204, 205–6, 208; best practices in, 233n54; defined, 6, 7; and emancipation, 7–8; and K-12 education, 215; and law, 209–11; and legal bubble, 18; among legal educators, 16; and market fundamentalism, 6, 16, 225n19; and morality, 218; and NDSL, 6, 7, 23, 24–25, 158, 210; as normative, 6; origin of, 225n18; relationship to moral hazard, 196–97; and social relations, 7, 225n22; and tenure, 123; workforce casualization in, 40–41. *See also* ideology

New Deal, 7

New Delta School of Law (NDSL): AAMPLE program, 50–52, 55, 98, 107, 110, 183–84, 244n26; ABA accreditation, 2, 32–33, 66, 80, 89, 91, 107, 110, 111–12, 120, 149, 154, 156, 159, 167–68, 177, 185–87, 194, 197, 199–200, 201, 224n16, 238n15; academic calendaring, 3, 11, 46, 141, 176, 201, 246n65; academic success counseling (ASC) at, 39, 42, 52, 103, 108–9, 124–25, 150, 173, 193, 214; administration-faculty relations, 24–25, 33, 38, 42, 45, 53–54, 57, 58, 60, 64–65, 69–71, 77, 79, 80, 102, 107–8, 116, 120–21, 126–27, 130–31, 132, 133, 135–36, 138, 139–41, 142, 144–45, 146, 149, 151–52, 154–55, 157, 159, 160–61, 162, 166–67, 172–74, 175, 176, 198–99, 202, 241n6; admissions standards, 1, 8, 12, 45–46, 50–52, 65, 81–82, 93, 103, 106, 107–8, 109, 110, 133, 135, 140, 177, 183, 190, 198, 200; bar passage rate, 12, 67, 82, 90, 101, 103, 108, 109, 118, 135, 137–38, 142, 149, 176, 177, 183–84, 190–92, 193, 199, 241n4; budget cuts at, 11, 12, 66, 159; C curve at, 48–49, 55, 103; clinics at, 66; combination of business model and ideology at, 10–12, 24, 59–60, 71–73, 83, 92–94, 104, 109, 213–14; curriculum design, 3, 11, 24, 31, 50, 54, 65, 70, 102, 115, 121, 123, 124, 125, 127–31, 132–34, 135, 136–44, 149, 151–55, 171, 174, 175, 176, 198–99, 201, 213, 214; deans of, 16, 31–32, 33, 57, 70–71, 93, 100, 103,

107–8, 119, 120–21, 126, 132, 135, 138, 139–41, 142, 144–45, 146, 149, 150, 151–52, 157, 159, 160–61, 162, 166–67, 168, 171, 172, 173, 178, 202, 241nn7,10; executive board, 185; financial aid officers, 46–49, 55; as for-profit institution, 2–3, 5–6, 11, 41, 48, 61, 68–69, 92–94, 97–98, 106, 150, 155–56, 162–63, 164, 168, 172, 181, 182, 204, 210; as fourth-tier law school, 12–13, 64, 80, 210, 213–14, 236n24; growth of, 24, 69, 81, 86, 89–90, 98–99, 105, 109, 115–16, 139, 183; innovation at, 44, 52–55, 56, 64, 65, 80, 129, 136, 139–40, 152–53, 233n50; international program development (IPD), 159–63, 165; investor obligations, 2–4, 5, 10–11, 13, 17, 19, 23, 24, 28–29, 30, 31, 45, 49, 59, 63, 68–69, 81, 83, 87, 89, 90, 98–99, 106, 107, 111–12, 127, 133–34, 135, 136, 138, 152, 153, 172, 174, 182, 197, 198, 211, 213, 219, 243n20; managed precarity at, 23, 28, 29, 54, 55, 230n74; marketing by, 1–2, 8, 46, 52, 62, 83, 89, 98, 109, 114–15, 120, 124, 131, 133–34, 135, 139, 149, 152, 200; midterm exams at, 55, 64; minimum GPA at, 102–4; myBAR program, 188–90, 191, 193; and neoliberalism, 6, 7, 23, 24–25, 158, 210; orientations at, 49–52; peer evaluations at, 58–59; as pseudonym, 21–22; public relations of, 92, 97–98, 169–70; recent graduates hired by, 193; recruitment from local bar, 39–40, 42, 43, 44, 66; reductions in force, 3, 110, 224n8; relations with Botswana, 24–25, 160–63, 245n38; tuition rates, 3, 41, 48–49, 68–69, 180, 199, 215, 246n60; UP program, 191, 193–94; visiting assistant professors (VAPs) at, 42. *See also* faculty at NDSL; Law Corp; Law Corp mission culture; Legal Education 2.0; students at NDSL

New England Association of Schools and Colleges (NEASC), 224n16

Nobi, 118–20

Northwestern Law School, 95, 158

optimism bias, 48, 49

Outside the Law School Scam, 13

outsourcing of legal expertise, 14

Papa, Mihaela, 14

Parsons, Talcott: "Law as an Intellectual Stepchild," 17

participant observation, 20, 22, 36–37, 205

Polanyi, Karl: on capitalism, 7

policy as culture, 73, 79, 82; as form of ideology, 58–60, 83, 92, 213–14

policy cascade: defined, 20–21, 185–87, 194–95; directionality of, 20–21, 185, 203–4; vs. governmentality, 194; as heuristic for studying through, 194–95; vs. individual interpretive work, 194

Polsby, Daniel, 123

Posner, Richard, 212–13

posttenure reviews, 122, 123, 166, 241n5

precarity, 27–28, 40, 55–56, 175; managed precarity, 23, 28, 29, 54, 55, 230n74

predatory formations, 27, 230n2

private equity investors: NDSL obligations to, 2–4, 5, 10–11, 13, 17, 19, 23, 24, 28–29, 30, 31, 45, 49, 59, 63, 68–69, 81, 83, 87, 89, 90, 98–99, 106, 107, 111–12, 127, 133–34, 135, 136, 138, 152, 153, 172, 174, 182, 197, 198, 211, 213, 219, 243n20; role in governance, 11, 197; short commitments of capital, 11, 83, 90, 197, 243n20

professionalism, 50

Prometheus Group, 161–62

Public Counsel, 30

public policy makers, 9

public policy studies, 229n72

public scrutiny of law schools, 90–91, 92, 93, 94, 97–98, 105, 168–71, 177–78

Rabinowitz, Richard W., 235n15

racial diversity, 207–9

racial inequality, 207

Rajah, Jothie, 225n20

ranking of law schools, 3, 30, 83, 95–97, 109–10, 152; NDSL as fourth-tier law school, 12–13, 64, 80, 210, 213–14, 236n24; and prestige, 80, 95, 100–101, 176; by *U.S. News & World Report*, 29, 80, 86, 95, 96, 98, 106, 112, 114, 138, 192, 193, 223n7, 235n19

rational-choice theory, 13–14

reasonable care, 10

Reinhold, Susan: on studying through, 194–95

responsibilization, 206, 210

Riles, Annelise, 17–18, 210

risk-utility balancing, 199, 218, 219, 246n61

Roosevelt, Franklin, 225n22

Sarbanes-Oxley Act, 243n20

Sassen, Saskia: on predatory formations, 230n2

security of position, 5, 42, 123, 163, 167, 173, 177, 182–83, 186; contractual vs. customary, 6, 24,

44, 121–22, 157–58, 174–75. *See also* faculty governance; faculty tenure

Segal, David: "Is Law School a Losing Game?," 90–91, 93, 94

shareholders, 7, 28, 181, 243n20

Shore, Cris, 10, 20, 229n72; on studying through, 194–95

Six Sigma, 78–79, 82

skill-based learning, 17, 114, 115

social abandonment, 11, 104

social capital, 7

social inclusion, 7

social media, 25, 28, 50, 169, 170

social protectionism, 6, 7, 28

socioeconomic minorities, 19, 95, 205, 206, 208, 242n2

Southern Poverty Law Center, 30

Stanford University, 240n7

structural change in law industry, 13, 14–17, 86–90

student-faculty ratio, 5, 31, 41, 89, 224n15, 237n12

student loan debt, 8, 19, 22, 47, 48, 68, 69, 81, 96–97, 98, 171, 189, 192, 217; vs. employment prospects, 30, 82, 86, 90–91, 199, 212, 213, 214, 215, 228n50; income-based repayment, 226n30; loan discharge, 9, 217, 226n30; as subprime, 18, 24, 59, 234n7. *See also* students at NDSL; tuition costs

students at NDSL: admissions standards, 1, 8, 12, 45–46, 50–52, 65, 81–82, 93, 103, 106, 107–8, 109, 110, 133, 135, 140, 177, 183, 190, 198, 200; diversity among, 1–2, 8, 11, 16–17, 51, 65–66, 177, 214; enrollment, 3, 8, 11, 12, 14, 23, 24, 28, 45, 49, 80, 88–89, 90, 98–99, 103, 105, 108, 109–10, 115, 129, 135, 153, 159, 198, 199, 206, 214, 239n35; as ethnoracial minorities, 1, 19, 105, 170, 200, 203, 206, 215; as informants, 1, 23, 46–47, 48–49, 66, 88, 92, 93, 99–100, 101, 104–5, 149, 150, 153–54, 170–72, 177–78, 189, 191–92, 198, 201, 202–3, 218; motivation of, 1, 2, 14, 63, 64, 81, 88, 99–100, 119, 133–34, 149, 159, 218; nontransfer attrition among, 102–5, 108, 109; orientations for, 49–52; recruitment of, 1, 2, 45–52, 55, 69, 71, 81–82, 83, 90, 98, 99, 110, 133–34, 149, 150, 187, 200; stigmatization of graduates, 25, 177–78, 206, 208; transfer attrition among, 13, 55, 65, 82, 90, 97–102, 109–10, 119, 129, 135, 137, 139, 149, 168, 170, 171, 176. *See also* student loan debt; tuition costs

studying through, 194–95, 219

subprime housing debt, 58, 195–96
summative vs. formative assessment, 64

Talent Plus psychometric evaluation, 37–39, 45, 74, 118, 213
Tamanaha, Brian, 15, 97, 227n50, 238n20; *Failing Law Schools*, 94–95, 238n21; on law school regulation, 94–95, 179–80, 238n25; on Massachusetts School of Law (MSL), 224n16; on "Ritz-Carlton" model, 179–80; on tuition rates and employment, 211–12
Taylor, Aaron: on diversity, 247n15
therapeutic jurisprudence, 81
Third Tier Reality, 13
Thomas, Clarence, 242n2
Thompson Reuters, 42
Title IV. *See* Higher Education Act
Top-Law-Schools.com, 51
tuition costs, 5, 15, 211–12; at NDSL, 3, 41, 48–49, 68–69, 180, 199, 215, 246n60. *See also* student loan debt
Twitter, 50
Tylor, E. B., 233n1

undergraduate grade point average (UGPA), 12, 45, 46, 48–49, 50, 68, 213–14, 218, 232n38
University of Baltimore School of Law, 211
University of California Berkeley, 207, 209, 240n7

University of California Irvine, 15, 105–6
University of Chicago, 95, 240n7
University of Illinois, 199
University of Michigan, 207
University of Phoenix, 29, 30, 92, 93
University of San Diego, 199
University of Southern California Gould School of Law, 39, 216
University of Texas, 207
University of Washington, 207
upward casualization, 40–42, 55, 231n28

Venture Partners Group (VPG), 30, 111–12, 161, 197–98, 203, 229n73

Wachovia, 195
Wall Street culture, 3, 18, 181–82
wealth maximization, 6
Weber, Max: on ideology as rationalization, 59, 83
Welch, Jack, 78
Wells Fargo, 195
Westlaw, 42
Wilkins, David, 14
William and Mary College, 113
Wright, Susan, 10, 20, 229n72; on studying through, 194–95

Zigon, Jarrett, 8

Anthropology of Policy

Cris Shore and Susan Wright, editors

SERIES DESCRIPTION:

The Anthropology of Policy series promotes innovative methodological and theoretical approaches to the study of policy. The series challenges the assumption that policy is a top-down, linear, and rational process and a field of study primarily for policy professionals. Books in the series analyze the contradictory nature and effects of policy, including the intricate ways in which people engage with policy; the meanings it holds for different local, regional, national, and internationally-based actors; and the complex relationships and social worlds that it produces.

One Blue Child: Asthma, Responsibility, and the Politics of Global Health
Susanna Trnka

2017

The Orderly Entrepreneur: Youth, Education, and Governance in Rwanda
Catherine A. Honeyman

2016

Coercive Concern: Nationalism, Liberalism, and the Schooling of Muslim Youth
Reva Jaffe-Walter

2016

Fragile Elite: The Dilemmas of China's Top University Students
Susanne Bregnbaek

2016

Navigating Austerity: Currents of Debt along a South Asian River
Laura Bear

2015

Drugs, Thugs, and Diplomats: U.S. Policymaking in Colombia
Winifred Tate

2015